4-5

D0733089

Landscaping with
NATIVE PLANTS
of Texas and the Southwest

Butterfly Weed

George O. Miller
Foreword by
David Northington

VOYAGEUR PRESS

Copyright © 1991 by George O. Miller

All rights reserved. No part of this work may be reproduced or used in any form by any means—graphic, electronic, or mechanical, including photocopying, recording, taping, or any information storage and retrieval system—without written permission of the publisher.

Printed in Hong Kong through Bookbuilders Ltd.
93 94 95 5 4 3 2

Library of Congress Cataloging-in-Publication Data

Miller, George O., 1943-
  Landscaping with native plants of Texas and the Southwest / George Miller ; foreword by David Northington.
      p. cm.
    Includes bibliographical references and index.
    ISBN 0-89658-138-1
    1. Native plant gardening—Texas. 2. Native plant gardening—Southwest, New. 3. Land scape gardening—Texas. 4. Landscape
    gardening—Southwest, New. 5. Native plants for cultivation—Texas. 6. Native plants for cultivation—Southwest, New. I.
    Title.
    SB439.24.T4M55 1990
    712'.6'09764—dc20   90-44298
                                                                        CIP

Published by Voyageur Press, Inc.
P.O. Box 338
123 North Second Street
Stillwater, MN 55082 U.S.A.
In Minn 612-430-2210
Toll-free 800-888-9653

Voyageur Press books are also available at discounts for quantities for educational, fund-raising, premium, or sales-promotion use. For details contact the marketing manager. Please write or call for our free catalog of natural history publications.

*This book is dedicated to
Ralph Griffing who owned Griffing Nurseries,
Beaumont, Texas, where I grew up and
learned to appreciate plants*

ACKNOWLEDGMENTS

A book such as this is necessarily a composite of many people's knowledge, opinions, and experience. Professors, students, landscapers, gardeners, horti-culturists, nursery owners, and native-plant lovers all influenced this book to a greater or lesser extent. Unfortunately, there have been too many people through the years to name them all here, but I do appreciate the cumulative help and encouragement I received.

A special thanks is due to my wife, Delena Tull, for proofreading the various drafts of the manuscript and for her helpful suggestions. Also, Martha Latta, past president of the National Xeriscape Council, Inc. and owner of Garden Ville of San Marcos, Texas, provided invaluable help with both her editorial comments and her beautiful drawings that illustrate the opening chapters.

CONTENTS

O Friend!
In the garden of thy heart plant naught but the rose of love . . . .
—Bahá'u'lláh

Palmer Penstemon

This passage from Bahá'u'lláh, which appears on page 23 of *The Hidden Words of Bahá'u'lláh*, copyright 1939, is reprinted with permission from the National Spiritual Assembly of the Baha'is of the United States.

FOREWORD

For several distinct and overlapping reasons, the desire and the need to use native plants in our planned landscapes is rapidly increasing. Nationally, our dependence on the same twenty to thirty traditional ornamental plant species has created an often boring homogeneous home and business landscape. Combine that with the "front-yard mentality" of mowed monoculture roadsides and public open spaces, and we have relinquished this country's regional uniqueness and floral diversity.

Beyond aesthetic considerations, the cost of maintaining a formal landscape is no longer defensible or even economically possible for many of us. And it is not only the financial cost of fertilizers, pesticides, gasoline, and equipment; it is the cost in free time for labor. Most importantly, however, the cost of watering these exotic landscapes can no longer be justified. Rapidly lowering water tables and seasonal drought have intensified the need to drastically cut back on the use of this most precious natural resource, fresh water.

The ecological need to reverse the removal of our native flora and their replacement with exotics is increasingly critical. Ecosystem balances, soil and water conservation, wildlife habitat, and maintained genetic biodiversity for potential human uses dictate that we must reestablish our indigenous native plant species and communities whenever possible.

Individually and collectively, these aesthetic, economic, and ecological factors have caught the attention of homeowners and business and public land managers across the nation. However, while the interest in using native plants in our planned landscapes is growing rapidly, the necessary "how-to" information progresses more slowly. What and when to plant, how to design a landscape using natives, how to maintain and manage such plantings, and where to find propagated plants for these landscapes are all questions that are slowly being answered by books such as *Landscaping with Native Plants of Texas and the Southwest* by George O. Miller.

A welcome new addition to the small list of excellent references, *Landscaping with Native Plants of Texas and the Southwest* combines the "why-to" understanding with the "what- and how-to" advice so desperately needed when entering the relatively pioneer world of landscaping with natives. Especially useful is Miller's coverage of microclimate and habitat specificity that can dictate the use of natives over nonnatives and the correct selection of the native species indigenous to a specific area.

Miller also presents an honest view to the reader, not overselling with the sometimes overstated "low maintenance" and always inaccurate "no maintenance" tags that some have attached to the use of native plants in planned landscapes. We still have much to learn about using native plants, and they are sometimes in short supply; however, the end result is more than worth the knowledge and effort required.

The fun of choosing from the 350 species so beautifully and thoroughly presented in this guide is a large part of the almost addictive nature of learning to landscape with native plants. Add to that the satisfaction of knowing that as one person, one plant at a time, we can all help with the repair of our environment, and the use of this reference for landscaping with natives has added depth.

David K. Northington
Executive Director
National Wildflower Research Center

MAP OF LANDSCAPE ZONES

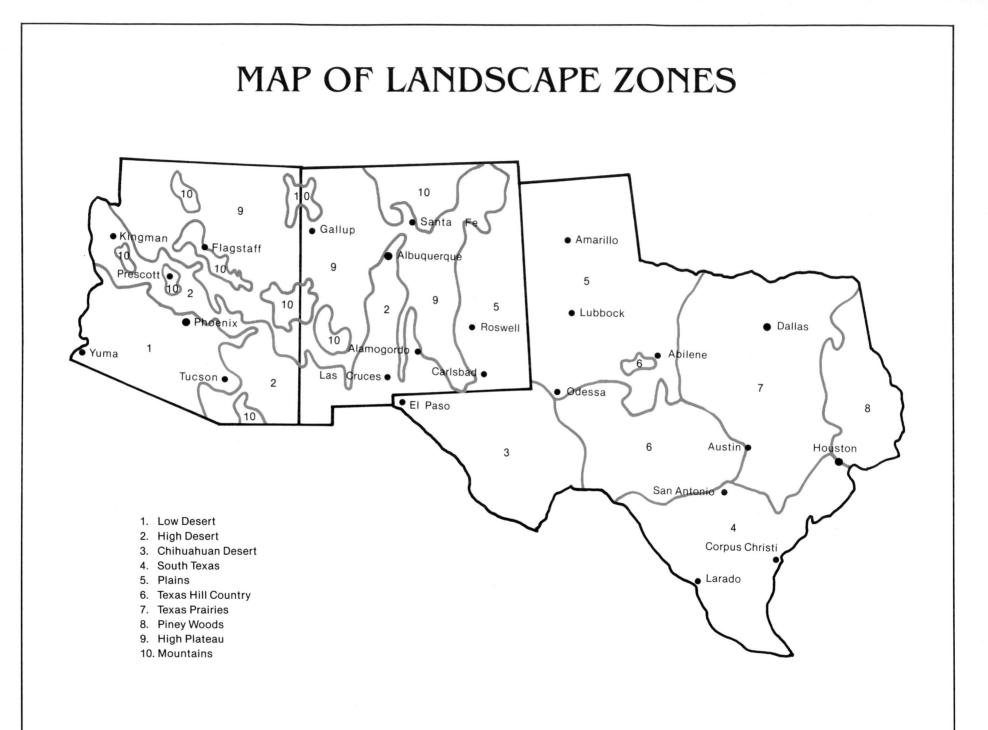

1. Low Desert
2. High Desert
3. Chihuahuan Desert
4. South Texas
5. Plains
6. Texas Hill Country
7. Texas Prairies
8. Piney Woods
9. High Plateau
10. Mountains

MAP OF ANNUAL PRECIPITATION

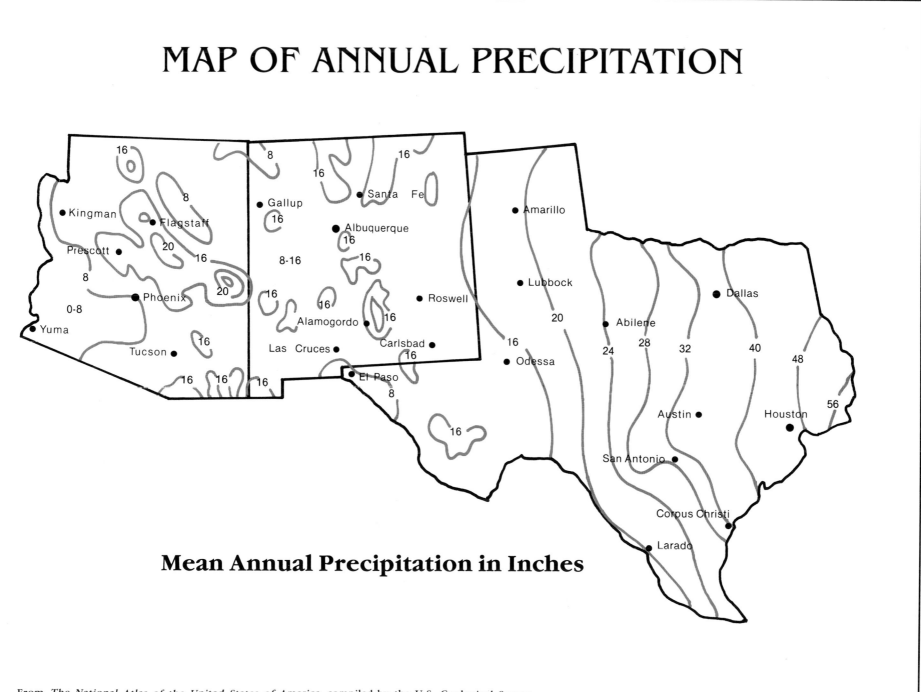

Mean Annual Precipitation in Inches

From *The National Atlas of the United States of America*, compiled by the U.S. Geological Survey, Washington, D.C.

MAP OF HARDINESS ZONES

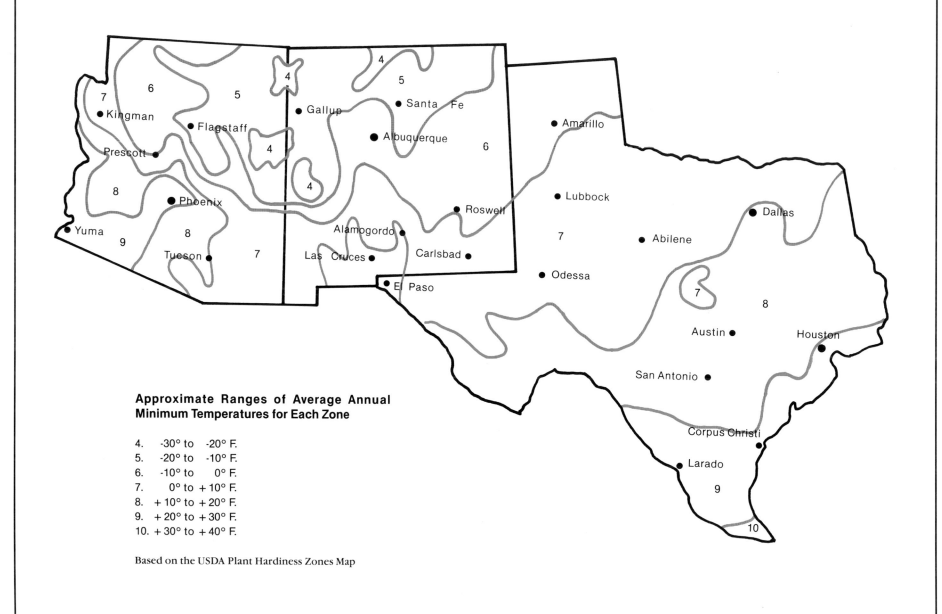

Approximate Ranges of Average Annual Minimum Temperatures for Each Zone

4. -30° to -20° F.
5. -20° to -10° F.
6. -10° to 0° F.
7. 0° to +10° F.
8. +10° to +20° F.
9. +20° to +30° F.
10. +30° to +40° F.

Based on the USDA Plant Hardiness Zones Map

HOW TO USE THIS BOOK

This book describes about 350 species of trees, shrubs, vines, wildflowers, ground-covers, and cacti with exceptional landscape merit. The species selected will enhance your landscape with attractive foliage, flowers, and fruit. I favored plants with a wide landscape range over those with very specific or demanding habitat requirements, though some exceptional specialties are included. This book gives a verbal description and, often more importantly, a photograph of the selected species to help homeowners, nursery workers, and landscapers decide which plants can best suit their needs.

A landscape plant must provide attractive foliage, flowers, fruit, or bark (preferably a combination) during a major portion of the year. Many of the thousands of native plants growing in our area have characteristics suitable for landscape use. This book describes each species and variety in detail, including the range; specific soil, moisture, and shade requirements; temperature tolerance; size, shape, and suitable landscaping uses; and flower, foliage, and fruit characteristics. The maps will help you identify the rainfall and temperature variation within your landscape zone, and ten chapters provide how-to information to help you devise a master plan to meet both your and the plants' specific needs.

This book assumes three premises. First, landscaping increases property values and aesthetic appeal and can decrease monthly utility expenses. Second, indigenous plants are superior to most imported species for landscaping because natives are naturally adapted to the region's climate and soil. Third, and to me most important, landscaping with plants from your area helps repair the environment. Human development can be expected to alter the countryside from its natural state, but it doesn't have to eradicate our native plants and animals. We can all do our part by replacing some of the plants removed to build our houses, streets, and businesses.

The botanical diversity of the Southwest stretches from scorching desert basins to dense boreal forests, delicate alpine meadows, and coastal prairies. Because a plant is native certainly does not imply that it can be planted anywhere within the region. Each of the major vegetative provinces has a unique community of plants adapted to its specific soil and climatic conditions. For the purposes of this book, the Southwest is divided into ten landscaping regions, depending on the temperature, moisture, and altitude gradients. This book will help you analyze your yard and decide which plants match your specific habitat.

The appendices in this book are invaluable for helping you decide which plants to choose for your landscape needs. Separate listings itemize evergreen plants and tell you how to colorscape for year-round beauty with flowering trees and shrubs. Individual chapters address the issues of landscape maintenance, landscaping to attract wildlife, and landscaping for energy and water conservation, including xeriscaping with drought-tolerant species. The chapters include listings of appropriate plants for each situation. When used together, the chapters, plant descriptions, and appendices answer the majority of questions that a landscaper will have about landscaping with native plants.

TERMS USED

Tree: a woody plant that usually has a single trunk and a mature height of more than fifteen feet tall.

Shrub: a woody plant that usually has multiple trunks or stems and a mature height of less than fifteen feet tall.

Drought tolerant: requires no supplemental water to survive extended periods of drought, but may need periodic deep waterings to maintain maximum flowering, foliage, and growth.

Cold hardy: can survive winter freezes.

Full sun: at least six hours of direct or reflected sun per day.

Partial shade: less than six hours of full or filtered sun per day.

Full shade: no direct sun; heavily filtered sun okay.

Scarifying seed: mechanically pricking, filing, or wearing down tough seed coat so it will absorb water and germinate.

Stratification: placing seeds in moist sand or other medium, sealing in polyethylene bags, and storing in the refrigerator for a designated time, typically three months at 40 degrees F.

Hardwood cuttings: from current season's growth, taken after wood matures in the fall or dormant season. Take a section from just above a leaf node, about twelve to sixteen inches long and up to one-half inch in diameter. Store the cuttings in moist sand until spring. To root, dust with a rooting powder and place in moist sand, vermiculite, or peat. Cover with polyethylene, which is permeable to oxygen but holds in water vapor.

Semihardwood cuttings: taken soon after seasonal growth stops but before the wood hardens, usually in the summer.

Softwood cuttings: taken from actively growing wood, usually in the spring.

USEFUL ORGANIZATIONS AND DEMONSTRATION GARDENS

National Wildflower Research Center
2600 FM 973
Austin, TX 78725

The NWRC is a clearinghouse and information source for all aspects of native plants. The center offers information sheets on growing different species of plants, recommended species for each state, how-to plant guides, guidelines for collecting seeds, a data file of regional organizations offering information and activities about native plants, and lists of nurseries and seed sources for each state. To order information, send a stamped, self-addressed, business-sized envelope and two dollars. Membership is $25 yearly and includes activities and a newsletter.

Texas, New Mexico, and Arizona all have active native plant societies and various special-interest clubs and groups that offer information on landscaping and conserving native plants. To find more about local organizations, contact your garden center or the National Wildflower Research Center. Also, visit one of the arboretums, nature and botanical centers, or public gardens in your area to see examples of how beautiful native-plant landscaping can be. Other sources for information are your county Agricultural Extension Service and the department of agriculture at major state universities; they offer printed material on landscaping with native plants.

Texas

San Antonio Botanical Center
555 Funston Place
San Antonio, TX 78209

Houston Aboretum
4501 Woodway
Houston, TX 77024

Armand Bayou Nature Center
8600 Bay Area Boulevard
Box 58828
Houston, TX 77258

Native Plant Society of Texas
Box 891
Georgetown, TX 78627

Dallas Nature Center
7575 Wheatland Road
Dallas, TX 75249

Robert A. Vines Environmental
  Science Center
8856 Westview
Houston, TX

Dallas Arboretum
8617 Garland Road
Dallas, TX 75218

Mercer Arboretum
22306 Aldine-Westfield Road
Humble, TX 77338

Chihuahuan Desert Research Institute
Box 1334
Alpine, TX 79831

Texas Agricultural Extension Service
Texas A&M University
College Station, TX 77843

Arizona

Arizona Native Plant Society
Box 41206 Sun Station
Tucson, AZ 85717

Arizona-Sonora Desert Museum
Route 9, Box 900
Tucson, AZ 85704

Boyce Thompson Southwest Arboretum
P. O. Box AB
Superior, AZ 85273

Desert Botanical Garden
1201 N. Galvin Parkway
Phoenix, AZ 85008
*has seed, plant, and source lists

Tucson Botanical Gardens
2150 N. Alverson Way
Tucson, AZ 85712

Tohono Chul Park
7366 Paseo del Northe
Tucson, AZ

Cooperative Extension Service
University of Arizona
College of Agriculture
Tucson, AZ 85721

New Mexico

Native Plant Society of New
  Mexico
Box 5917
Santa Fe, NM 87502

WHY USE NATIVE PLANTS?

Landscaping with native plants is the focus of considerable interest these days. From state agriculture departments to local garden clubs, native plants are popular topics. Texas has pledged to use 60 percent natives in its landscape projects. Water-conscious cities, including Phoenix, Austin, and San Antonio, have initiated xeriscape programs to encourage planting drought-tolerant species, and county extension agents carry the message to local groups and organizations.

More than five thousand species and subspecies of flowering plants grow within the borders of Texas, and Arizona has twenty-five hundred species just within the Sonoran Desert. Approximately one thousand of these are trees and shrubs, about half of which could be used as ornamental plants. Our rich botanical heritage is a treasure chest for landscapers. But beyond the diversity of plants available, there exist compelling reasons why our homes, businesses, and public properties should be landscaped predominantly with native plants.

ENVIRONMENTAL REPAIR

Most of us are uninformed about and isolated from our natural environment. Instead of placing an inherent value on nature, the source of all life and the root of our material and technological success, modern society relates to fast foods, high-tech toys, and single-digit inflation. Even the plants in our neighborhoods reflect the loss of our identity with our natural environment. The trees, hedges, and shrubs planted around our houses typically come from some distant country.

Today, as agriculture, ranching, and urban sprawl eliminate much of the natural plant communities, a growing number of people are concerned about preserving what remains of our environment. Community colleges, nature centers, and universities offer classes on nature-oriented topics. Many people visit state and city parks and greenbelts looking for natural areas representative of the native flora. In most metropolitan areas the natural associations of indigenous plants remain only in preserved sanctuaries.

Why can't our neighborhoods represent the natural plant diversity that is found in nature or that existed before our houses were built? A stroll down our own street could be a lesson in native plant ecology. Our children could grow up familiar with the same plants that provided food and fiber for the Indians who lived in the Southwest for thousands of years. We could live among the same plants that mystified the botanists who accompanied the first European explorers.

Trumpet Creeper

Plants are a part of our great natural heritage. The plants that have sunk their roots in Southwest soil since the last Ice Age can help us understand that our psyches and society are equally rooted to the earth.

Wildlife also benefits from the native plants in our yards. Few of the plants that provide forage and shelter for wildlife are left in the wake of urban and agricultural development. As subdivision developers destroy native plants and replant with imported species, our songbirds are replaced by starlings and house sparrows, themselves immigrants from Europe. We can encourage the return of our native birds and other wildlife by landscaping with plants that provide food and shelter. As the plants mature and begin to flower and fruit, we will once again be rewarded by the sight of butterflies dancing from flower to flower and by the melodies of birds singing in our trees.

LOW MAINTENANCE

Why choose native species over the readily available, inexpensive imported plants? Low maintenance – that means dollars saved. By selecting plants from your area, you have a landscape naturally adapted to whatever weather extremes may occur. After tens of thousands of years of climatic vicissitudes, only those species that could adapt have survived. When a landscape plant is firmly established, it will require little supplemental water, even in the driest years. Unusually frigid winters may nip tender twigs, but the plant will survive and fully recover with the next spring growth. Fewer plants will die and require costly replacement. Other than normal landscape maintenance such as pruning, a native plant requires little attention.

I'm not dismissing imported plants in toto. Some, such as crepe myrtle, santolina, and desert bird of paradise, have excellent landscape merit – beautiful foliage, flowers, and hardiness. A number of imported plants have become naturalized in the Southwest and are useful in low-maintenance, xeriscaped landscapes.

While the low-maintenance feature of our native plants is attractive for homeowners, it is an essential consideration for commercial landscapers. Large businesses allocate sizable budgets for landscaping office buildings and commercial developments. States and municipalities are concerned with plantings for buildings, parks, and thousands of miles of streets and highways. In 1984, the State of Texas spent $4.3 million on landscaping. Plants that minimize water use and labor costs mean sizable savings to you as a homeowner, a businessperson, and a taxpayer.

VARIETY

Southwestern plants come in all sizes, shapes, and colors. Why not use a variety of plants that provides visual interest throughout the year? You can plant a mixed assortment of natives for spring, summer, and fall flowers and colorful fruit. You can choose evergreen species with green, gray, or whitish foliage, or deciduous plants with spectacular fall colors.

The plants native to Southwest soil have so much variety that you can use them in an almost endless combination of landscape designs. And native plants provide a unique and regionally distinct beauty to our neighborhoods, parks, and commercial districts. As former First Lady Lady Bird Johnson said, "I want places to look like where they are. I want Alabama to look like Alabama, and Texas to look like Texas."

LANDSCAPE ZONES

This book divides the Southwest into ten different landscape zones. With this classification scheme, you easily can determine which plants are candidates for landscaping in your particular area. I based the landscape zone divisions on three of the most important factors that determine whether a plant can survive: moisture, temperature variation, and natural plant communities in each area.

Selecting plants for your yard involves more than simply determining your landscape zone. A plant has specific habitat requirements and rarely has a continuous distribution throughout its native range. Plants have adapted to certain environmental factors — moisture, exposure, soil chemistry, drainage, humidity, and temperature, to name a few. A plant thrives in habitats where it finds these parameters in the optimum combinations and grows in limited numbers in more marginal areas. A plant may not be suitable for your yard, even though it is listed as belonging to your zone. Each species description describes in greater detail what the plant requires to thrive and be healthy and attractive. By choosing those plants most suitable for the environmental conditions of your yard, you can have a beautiful landscape for years, even generations, with relatively little maintenance.

LANDSCAPE ZONE VS. NATIVE RANGE
In some cases, the landscape zones where a plant will grow may differ significantly from its natural range. The landscape zone includes those parts of the Southwest with similar soil type, moisture, and temperatures as the native range. For instance, if you live in South or Central Texas, you probably have sandy or rocky fast-draining soil. Many of the trees and shrubs from West Texas will grow well in your yard. If you live on the Gulf Coast, many of the plants from East Texas will be suitable if you have acidic, clay, or clay loam soil. A plant such as cenizo, or Texas ranger, *Leucophyllum frutescens*, is native to the Chihuahuan Desert of Texas, but will thrive in landscape settings in the Sonoran Desert in Arizona.

A plant always has the same basic habitat needs regardless of the landscape setting, but we can control or eliminate other limiting factors, primarily competition and predation. In the wild, a plant competes with other plants for light, moisture, and soil nutrients. By choosing the proper exposure and soil and isolating the plant from competitors, we give the plant an ecological advantage that it might never have in the wild. Besides competition, we try to eliminate

predation of herbivores and insects on our landscape plants. Trimming dead limbs helps prevent insect and fungal enemies from entering the plant. Watering and fertilizing until the plant is established improve its chances of success far above those of plants in the wild.

In some areas, the difference in plant communities between bordering landscape zones is dramatic. Near Austin the blackland prairies butt up against the Balcones Escarpment on the eastern edge of the Edwards Plateau. Rolling grasslands (now farmlands) abruptly give way to chalky hills covered with plateau live oaks and Ashe junipers. Conversely, in many places, the transition from one vegetation type to another is gradual and hardly recognizable. A seemingly endless stretch of limestone hills and open expanse separates the plains of the Texas Panhandle and eastern New Mexico from the high plateaus and mesas of northern New Mexico and Arizona. In determining plants suitable for your landscape zone, consider the specific conditions of your yard. In addition to the overall climatic factors, look at features that determine the specific habitat, or microhabitat, of your yard, such as the soil, slope, sun exposure, and the drying or chilling effects of wind.

Zone 1 – The Sonoran Desert
This area includes Phoenix and Tucson. The basin and range topography varies in elevation from one hundred to four thousand feet with broad valleys and low mountain ranges. Annual precipitation averages three to twelve inches, with a temperature range from summer highs above 100 to a winter low of about 20 degrees F. The temperature drops below freezing from six to twenty-two nights annually. The major vegetation types are creosote bush, Joshua tree, mesquite-saltbush, and palo verde–bursage–saguaro. Plants selected for this area should be adapted to extreme heat and drought and able to withstand occasional freezing.

Zone 2 – High Desert
Stretching through Arizona and New Mexico, this area includes Albuquerque, Douglas, and Kingman. It varies in elevation from three thousand to forty-five hundred feet, although isolated mountains within the zone exceed ten thousand feet. It averages eight to twelve inches of precipitation annually, with winter lows of 16 to 20 degrees F. More that one hundred nights have below-freezing temperatures. The major vegetation associations include chaparral, creosote

bush–tarbush–white thorn, and desert grassland. Plants selected for this area should be drought tolerant, adapted to well-draining soil, and able to withstand hard freezes.

Zone 3 – Chihuahuan Desert

The area west of the Pecos River in Texas includes diverse habitats ranging from eighty-five-hundred-foot mountains with Rocky Mountain species to scorching deserts with the most drought-resistant plants in the state. Rainfall over most of the area averages less than twelve inches annually, but varies from sixteen inches in the highest mountains to eight inches at El Paso. Winter lows average 10 to 20 degrees F., with 230 to 245 frost-free days annually. Dominant vegetation types in the desert area include creosote-tarbush, gramma grassland, and yucca-juniper savannahs. Landscaping plants should be adapted to extreme heat and drought, well-draining alkaline soil, and occasional hard freezes.

Zone 4 – South Texas

The Rio Grande plains and brushland of South Texas vary from sea level to one thousand feet in elevation, with open prairies and thickets of small trees and thorny shrubs. This landscape zone also includes much of the coastal bend prairies and marshes. San Antonio and Victoria are in this zone. The southern tip of Texas enjoys a subtropical climate with 320 frost-free days. The northern section of the zone has mild winters, with a 275-day growing season. Annual rainfall ranges from thirty-six inches near Corpus Christi to sixteen in Del Rio. Plants selected for this zone should be adapted to heat and occasional droughts, well-draining soil, and winter temperature lows of 20 to 30 degrees F.

Zone 5 – The Plains Region

The high plains of eastern New Mexico and the Texas Panhandle and the rolling plains of Northwest Texas vary in elevation from eight hundred to forty-five hundred feet. Rainfall averages twenty-two inches in the east and twelve in the west, with periodic droughts. Winter temperatures may drop to -10 degrees F. Amarillo, Abilene, and Lubbock are in this zone. The area has an average of 179 to 225 frost-free days per year. Plants selected for this zone should be adapted to well-draining alkaline soil, drought, and extremely hard winters. Grasses are the dominant vegetation type, with mesquite invading.

Zone 6 – The Texas Hill Country

The scenic Hill Country west of Austin varies from one thousand to three thousand feet in elevation and is known for its rugged terrain and sheltered canyons. Rainfall varies from thirty-five inches in the east to less than fifteen on the west, with prolonged droughts and raging flash floods common. Winter temperature lows average from 10 to 20 degrees F. Dominant plants include Ashe juniper, plateau live oak, mesquite, and grasses. Plants selected for this zone should be adapted to well-draining alkaline soil, prolonged periods of drought, hot dry summers, and occasional hard freezes.

Zone 7 – Texas Prairies

This zone includes both blackland prairies with calcareous clays and acid sandy loams and post oak savannas with slightly acid sandy and clay loam soils. Dallas, Fort Worth, and Waco are in this zone. Rainfall ranges from forty inches in the east to twenty-five to thirty inches in the west. The growing season averages 230 to 275 frost-free days annually. Plants selected for this broad area should be adapted to moderate rainfall, periods of drought, well-draining neutral to acid soil, and winter temperatures that may drop as low as 0 degrees F.

Zone 8 – Piney Woods

The timber belt of East Texas has a gently rolling terrain and averages from forty-four to fifty-six inches of rain annually. The soils are deep sand and sandy loam and are usually acid. The winters are mild, with brief periods of freezing temperatures occurring throughout the winter. The southern end of this zone includes Houston and portions of the coastal prairie and marshes. Dominant plants include pines, oaks, and other hardwoods. Plants selected for this area should be adapted to acid soil, heat, humidity, mild freezes, and ample moisture.

Zone 9 – High Plateaus

The high plateaus and mesas of Arizona and New Mexico vary in elevation from forty-five hundred to seven thousand feet and receive from six to twenty inches of annual precipitation. The area includes Santa Fe, Taos, and Flagstaff. Winter lows range from -3 to -34 degrees F, with a growing season of 150 to 200 frost-free days. The major vegetation types include pinyon-juniper, sagebrush, salt-desert shrub, and shortgrass. Plants selected for this zone should be drought tolerant and extremely cold hardy.

Zone 10 – Mountains

The mountainous landscape zone includes elevations above seven thousand feet and can exceed twelve thousand feet. Santa Fe and Flagstaff border this zone. It has snowy winters, with frost possible on any day of the year at the higher elevations. Precipitation averages twenty to forty inches annually, and snow remains on the ground for extended periods. Dominant plants include ponderosa pine, spruce, and fir. Plants selected for this zone should be adapted to high elevations and hard winters.

THE ABCs OF NATIVE PLANT LANDSCAPING

At least two schools of thought have developed concerning landscaping with indigenous plants. The traditional approach substitutes native plants for the commonly used imported species. Native plants can be used for foundation hedges around buildings, border hedges along walks and drives, and sheared hedges, as accent shrubs planted alone, or as container plants. They can be used in any formal or informal landscape design.

At the other end of the spectrum is the attempt to duplicate the natural plant associations found in the wild, whether prairie, desert, or woodlands. A yard would in effect be a microcosm of nature. There would be no hedges, shaped shrubs, or species not from the immediate area.

Of course these extremes can be modified considerably. Many intermediate designs lie between the formal and wild landscapes. One approach that combines the concepts of maintaining natural plant associations and using plants to visually accent open areas is to design with landscape islands. Instead of delineating an area by hedges and a few accent shrubs or trees, use a mass planting, or island, of mixed species. A landscape island can be completely contained in an open area or curve out from a building. It can include one side of a drive or accent a corner.

Mass plantings combine compatible species to make your landscape visually dramatic. Compatible species have the same habitat requirements and have leaves of a similar size and shape. A group planting can have a different accent for every season. You can provide year-round color, as well as food and shelter for birds and butterflies. Species with gray foliage provide a picturesque contrast to green-leafed species. Use deciduous plants to provide shades of bright green with new spring leaves and spectacular autumn hues. Use evergreens to add foliage color during the barren winter months. Hedges, borders, and backgrounds do not have to consist of a single evergreen species, but can combine the best nature has to offer. The flexibility of the landscape island concept provides a multitude of design possibilities for an attractive yard throughout each season.

FOUR STEPS FOR DEVELOPING A MASTER PLAN
Step 1: The Dreaming Stage
Landscaping your yard is an investment of money and a commitment to the time a plant takes to mature. You want plants that will be healthy and vigorous and at the same time fulfill your landscaping needs. The first step is to decide what you need and expect from a plant. Do you want a large tree with an expansive canopy, or a small tree to shade an entrance way? Do you want an evergreen or a deciduous tree, a loosely growing shrub or a dense one that can be shaped? Don't worry about selecting particular species at this point.

If you are just starting to landscape your yard, develop a master plan for your entire lot. Pay special attention to the chapter "Landscaping for Energy and Water Conservation." You can save money on utilities throughout the year by proper planting of deciduous and evergreen trees and shrubs. The section on xeriscaping tells you how to reduce your summer water bill by as much as 44 percent in an arid climate by using drought-tolerant species.

If you want to attract birds and other animals, the chapter "Landscapes That Attract Wildlife" will be of particular interest. It lists species that provide year-round flowers, fruits, and berries for our feathered friends. The chapter "Landscaping with Vines" describes numerous vines that will enhance any landscape. Vines are fast growing and most tolerate either sun or shade, making them adaptable to almost any landscape design.

The chapter "Using Native Plants as Groundcovers" explains alternative uses for many of the plants described in this book. Native groundcovers can reduce yard maintenance, prevent erosion, and add an extra touch of beauty. If you don't like spending your weekends cutting and trimming your lawn, the chapter "Lawns: Buffalograss and Turf Alternatives" is for you.

The photographs and landscape drawings in this book will give you many ideas on landscaping your yard. Besides the utilitarian benefits (shade, windbreaks, etc.), plants provide a visual accent for an area. Plants add beauty to driveways, sidewalks, patios, pools, porches, corners, and courtyards. Use border plantings to enhance a building's foundation, wall, and fences. A distinctive plant at the corner of the house or entryway adds special visual appeal. Mass plantings of shrubs or vines beautify slopes, medians, open areas.

Decide where you want hedges, border plants, large and small shade trees, vines, and groundcovers. Choose evergreens where you want year-round shade, deciduous species for winter sun, and spring- and fall-flowering species for color throughout the year. Use tall evergreen hedges for visual privacy, and densely branching species

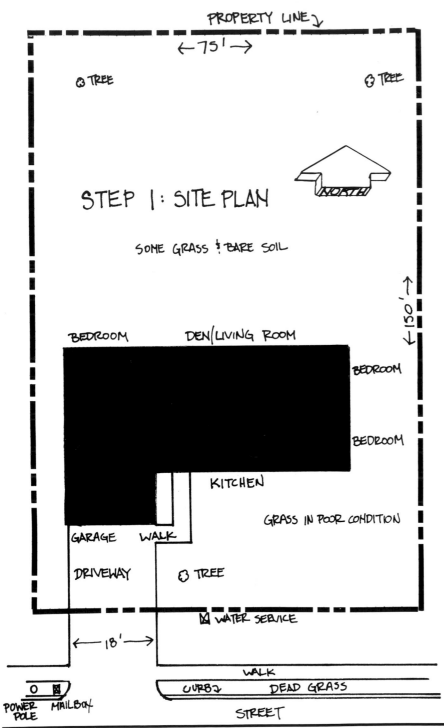

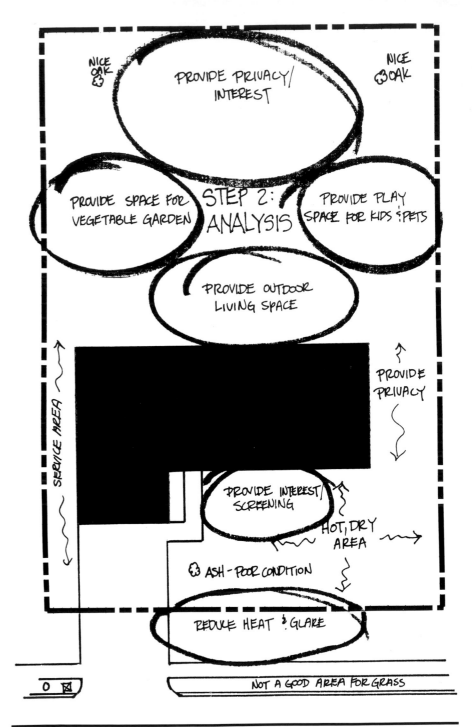

The four steps for developing a master plan. Step 1: The Dreaming Stage.

The four steps for developing a master plan. Step 2: Site Analysis.

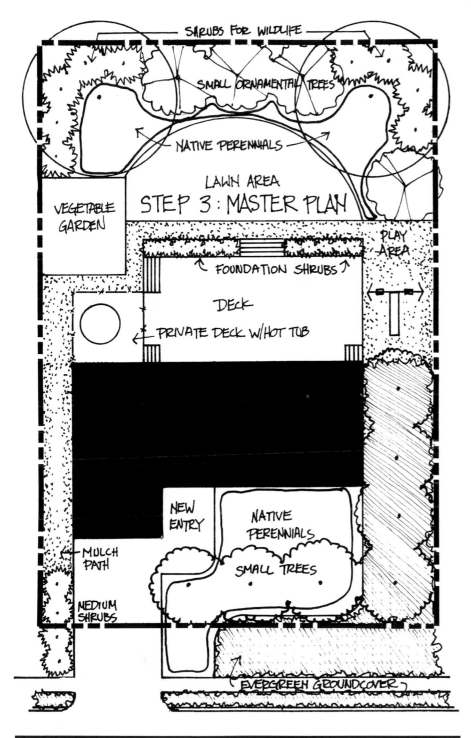

SHRUBS FOR WILDLIFE

SMALL ORNAMENTAL TREES

NATIVE PERENNIALS

LAWN AREA

STEP 3: MASTER PLAN

VEGETABLE GARDEN

PLAY AREA

FOUNDATION SHRUBS

DECK

PRIVATE DECK W/HOT TUB

NEW ENTRY

NATIVE PERENNIALS

SMALL TREES

MULCH PATH

MEDIUM SHRUBS

EVERGREEN GROUNDCOVER

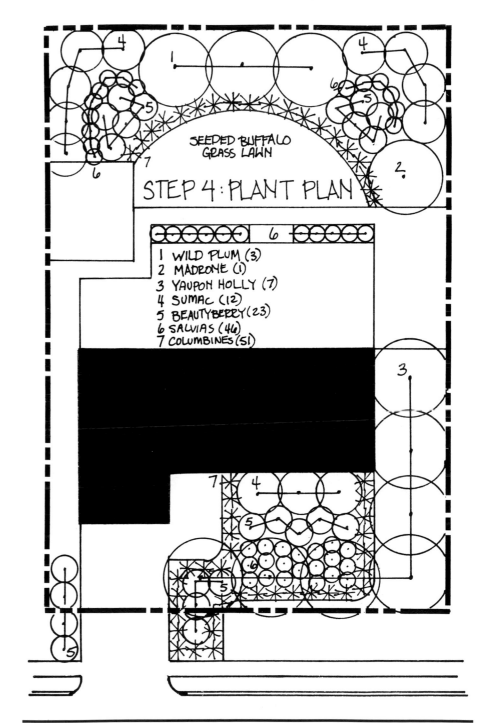

SEEDED BUFFALO GRASS LAWN

STEP 4: PLANT PLAN

1 WILD PLUM (3)
2 MADRONE (1)
3 YAUPON HOLLY (7)
4 SUMAC (12)
5 BEAUTYBERRY (23)
6 SALVIAS (46)
7 COLUMBINES (51)

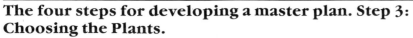

The four steps for developing a master plan. Step 3: Choosing the Plants.

The four steps for developing a master plan. Step 4: Planting.

for physical barrier hedges. You can add the plants year by year as budget and time allow.

Step 2: Site Analysis

One of the most important factors determining the success of a landscape plant is where it is planted. In the wild, a plant casts its seeds to the wind, trusting that a few will find an optimum habitat and survive. We can't afford this trial-and-error method. We want our plants not just to survive, but to grow vigorously and be attractive. A species that requires full sunlight will look spindly and stunted if planted in partial shade. Before you turn a spade of soil, carefully analyze the environmental conditions of your yard and choose plants naturally adapted to the existing growth conditions. This is the most important step for low-maintenance landscaping.

For optimum performance, the plant must be adapted to four major habitat parameters: the soil, moisture, drainage, and exposure of your yard. Just because a plant grows in your landscape zone, or even in your area, does not mean that it will grow well in your yard. Many plants have very exacting requirements. Look at your soil, and not just the fill the developer may have spread over your lot. Is it sandy loam, blackland clay, or rocky soil? How fast does it drain after a heavy rain? If your yard stays muddy for a day or so after a rain, don't plant species that require fast-draining soil.

Even a small yard has subtle differences in exposure and drainage that can make big differences in the survivability and healthy appearance of a plant. Plants on the north side of the house receive much less sun and heat than those planted on the south. Shade-tolerant species and those more cold hardy should be used for northern exposures. A southern exposure receives sunlight most of the day, making it hotter and drier in the summer and warmer in the winter. Select sun-loving, drought-tolerant species for southern exposures. Plants along a concrete drive or patio or in a rock garden receive an extra dose of radiated heat that may create a desert habitat. Shaded entryways provide the shade and coolness of a dense woodland.

The way you prepare the soil for planting also can create significantly different growth conditions. A layer of mulch several inches thick will protect a plant's roots from drying out and excessive heating, thus simulating a cooler habitat.

The microhabitats in your yard can change as your landscape matures. In nature, plants modify their environment enough to allow a succession of different plant associations through time. This can also occur in your yard. Years of mulching, or years of a hot dry exposure, can change the soil conditions significantly. As saplings develop into large trees, their shade changes the habitat around them. Sun-loving species may die out and shade-loving ones thrive under the new conditions. When designing your master plan, consider the mature sizes of the species you choose and what they will look like in five or ten years. Choose plants that will remain compatible as your landscape matures. For instance, you might rather plant one large canopy tree and several small understory trees instead of three large trees that would completely shade your whole yard.

Step 3: Choosing the Plants

After you have determined the growth characteristics of the plants desired and the exposure, soil, and drainage, you are ready to compile a list of tree and shrub species. The plants most adapted to the local growing conditions are those that grew in your area before it was developed. However, you are not limited to just those plants common to your region. The Southwest has an abundance of trees and shrubs with striking flowers, fruit, and seeds that make them excellent ornamental landscape plants.

First, look at the map of landscape zones in the front of this book and identify your zone. The appendices list evergreen plants and flowering trees and shrubs. Also refer to the suggested plants in the sections on attracting wildlife and on energy and water conservation. Make a list of plants you would like to plant in your yard. Then refer to the species descriptions of each plant to determine which are compatible with your particular growing conditions. The species are listed in alphabetical order by scientific name. Armed with a list of the trees, shrubs, wildflowers, vines, and groundcovers having the same habitat requirements as your yard, you are ready to begin shopping for plants.

Step 4: Planting

Most plants should be transplanted in the dormant season, December through February, or before the last frost in the spring. A freshly dug plant can survive the shock of having most of its roots removed in the winter because its leaves are not demanding a constant supply of water. Container plants will have time to grow an expanded root system before the stress of summer.

You can give your plant a head start by proper soil preparation. Preparing the soil helps the plant to begin growing immediately and to establish a healthy root system. Dig a hole about twice as wide as the root ball or container. Large trees should have one-foot clearance around the root ball. This allows for loose, well-prepared soil to surround the root system and stimulate growth. Dig the hole deep enough for six inches of loose soil on the bottom. Very importantly, the plant should not be planted too deeply. Maintain the original juncture of the trunk with the soil.

The most important roots of a plant are the surface feeder roots. These tiny rootlets absorb the moisture and nutrients essential for a plant's growth. Soil compaction physically impedes the growth and spread of the rootlets, which directly limits the development of the entire plant, and water-logged soil will drown the roots. Before you set your plant, loosen the soil six to twelve inches deep for several yards around the hole, depending on the size of the plant. Once a plant is established, never disturb the surface roots by tilling or covering with over an inch of fill dirt.

After placing the plant and filling the hole, prepare a slight mound of soil

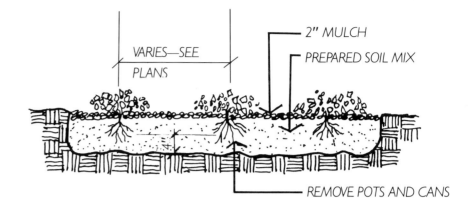

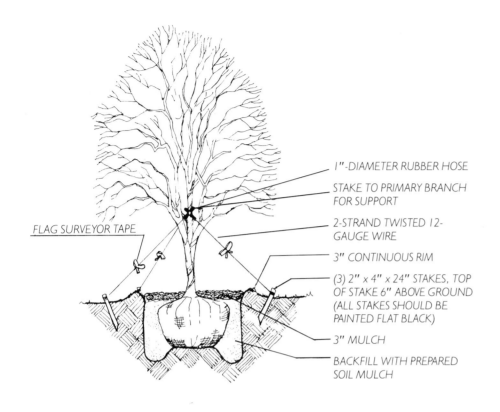

FLAG SURVEYOR TAPE

1"-DIAMETER RUBBER HOSE

STAKE TO PRIMARY BRANCH FOR SUPPORT

2-STRAND TWISTED 12-GAUGE WIRE

3" CONTINUOUS RIM

(3) 2" x 4" x 24" STAKES, TOP OF STAKE 6" ABOVE GROUND (ALL STAKES SHOULD BE PAINTED FLAT BLACK)

3" MULCH

BACKFILL WITH PREPARED SOIL MULCH

TREE PLANTING & STAKING DETAIL

NOT TO SCALE

2" MULCH

PREPARED SOIL MIX

VARIES—SEE PLANS

REMOVE POTS AND CANS

GROUNDCOVER PLANTING DETAIL

NOT TO SCALE

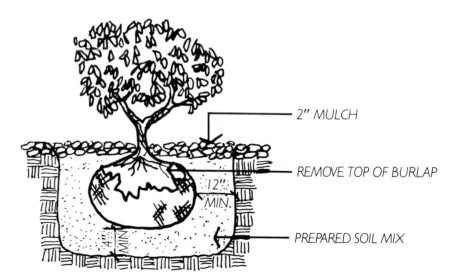

2" MULCH

REMOVE TOP OF BURLAP

12" MIN.

4" MIN.

PREPARED SOIL MIX

SHRUB PLANTING DETAIL

NOT TO SCALE

around the circumference of the hole to help hold in water. Saturate the soil immediately after planting. Weekly watering, particularly of small plants, may be necessary through the first summer, especially if it is extreme. Mulching around the base of the plant reduces water loss and heat buildup in the soil. It also keeps grass from growing around the plant and competing for water. Grasses can reduce the growth of a plant by as much as 50 percent, so keep the area around the transplant cleared.

Adding fertilizer granules or time-released pellets to the fill around the plant will stimulate plant growth and sometimes double or even triple the growth rate normal in a wild setting. Some nurseries achieve six to eight feet of growth the first year from seedling oaks with a regular fertilizing and watering schedule. Remember, until a plant grows a network of surface feeder roots, it will need tender loving care and water during dry periods.

For the first year, the plant is in a susceptible condition and should be protected against climatic extremes. Water as frequently as necessary during the first summer. Observe the plant and water when signs of stress appear. A slight leaf wilt or curl, loss of vibrant green color, and browning around the leaf margins are sure signs of insufficient water. If the surface feeder roots die, recovery is slow and growth inhibited. For plants whose major growing season is spring and summer, watering during the first summer after transplanting is even more important. By the second summer, the plant has gone through two spring growing seasons and should be hardy enough to survive on its own without irrigation unless the summer is abnormally dry.

By not allowing lack of water to inhibit a plant's growth for the first season, you ensure that a new plant will grow rapidly and become well established. But be careful to avoid overwatering. Most natives dislike wet feet. Overwatering quickly kills species adapted to well-draining soil, a lesson hard learned by those of us accustomed to thirsty plants imported from wet climates.

So Where Can I Find Those Wonderful Natives?

Many nurseries are well stocked with native trees, shrubs, wildflowers, and seeds, and some sell indigenous plants exclusively. Wholesale growers now propagate natives in large quantities to meet the growing demand for home and commercial landscaping. Container or nursery-conditioned stock is much preferred to plants straight from the fields because the former have better developed root systems. In the wild, a tree's roots spread out over a large area to gather water and nutrients. When transplanted, such a tree loses many of its roots and is more susceptible to losing important branches or dying. After a tree transplanted from a natural habitat has been nursery conditioned (watered, pruned, and fertilized), it has more roots in its ball and is more likely to grow rapidly when planted in your yard. Ask about the history and age of trees and shrubs before buying them. If you can find a retailer knowledgeable in natives, he or she will probably be willing and eager to advise you on plants suitable for your landscaping situations.

Digging of trees and shrubs by home landscapers almost always results in the death of the plant. The job is best done by professionals who have the experience, equipment, and knowledge for proper transplanting. Without expensive mechanized equipment, digging a large root ball is a labor-intensive operation, and no shortcuts make the job easier. Besides the slim chance of success, digging plants from the wild impoverishes the countryside. Once a plant is economically valuable, it easily can be removed from nature much faster than it can naturally replenish itself. Over 30 percent of the cacti in the United States are endangered or threatened with extinction because of overcollecting from the wild. Stripping plants from nature contradicts the major philosophy of the native-plant movement: repairing our damaged environment. Demand nursery-propagated plants. It is more ecologically sound and economically wise.

A landscaping plan for a small yard

MAINTAINING YOUR LANDSCAPE

No home or commercial landscape is totally maintenance free. Hardy native plants come close to that ideal, but any landscape design needs some maintenance to keep the integrity of its appearance. Indigenous plants require far less care than many imported exotics, so a landscape design that incorporates the natural shape and size of natives will require much less periodic attention and seasonal expense than one using exotics.

Regardless of which plants you use in your landscape, some basic knowledge and skills in plant husbandry will help you keep your plants healthy and attractive. The following information will help you develop the landscape skills required to keep your yard beautiful.

PERIODIC MAINTENANCE

A firmly established, vigorously growing plant that has adjusted to its exposure and survived several growing seasons needs little attention. If properly chosen, it will not outgrow its setting and will survive whatever extremes nature has to offer.

In the wild, a plant often reacts to extremes of drought and temperature by leaf loss, twig damage, die-back, or a generally scrubby appearance. In our landscape, however, we want to avoid these responses and maintain the optimum — or at least average — growing conditions, regardless of how stressful the weather may be. For example, even though the plants might easily survive periods of drought, we may want to provide supplemental watering for the sake of appearance.

Fertilizing

Fertilizing with a complete fertilizer in the spring stimulates foliage, flower, and fruit production, primary characteristics we desire in our landscape plants. Fertilizing ensures that the plant will develop its maximum genetic potential, just as it would in an optimum habitat in nature. If the plant is well adapted to its new location, fertilizing after the first year or two is usually unnecessary and unwanted.

Complete fertilizers supply the three main nutrients required for a plant's growth: nitrogen, phosphorus, and potassium. In general, nitrogen stimulates foliage growth; phosphorous, root growth. The three-number rating of a fertilizer expresses the percentage of these compounds. A 10-6-4 fertilizer contains 10 percent nitrogen, 6 percent phosphorus, and 4 percent potash, or potassium. Fertilize early in the year — January or February — before initiation of spring growth. Fertilizing can be time consuming and expensive, so don't waste money buying unnecessary fertilizers. Before applying fertilizers, have your soil analyzed to determine if nutrients are lacking. The county agricultural extension agent provides this useful and inexpensive service.

Pruning

Almost every tree and shrub in your landscape will at one time or another require pruning. Pruning can make a plant tall or short, open branching or densely foliated, or can even convert a tree into a hedge. Pruning encourages compactness if the shrub is naturally an intricately branching plant. Some species, like yaupon holly and little-leaf sumac, make densely foliated shaped or sheared hedges. Others, such as bee brush and false indigo, are open branching and suitable for informal hedges. Know the growth habit of your plant before you assault it with pruning shears. The plant descriptions in this book indicate the growth habits and pruning requirements of most species. Swear allegiance to the following cardinal rules of pruning before grasping your shears or saw.

1. Know the natural growth habit (shape and size) of the plant. Pruning should train the plant toward its natural form, unless you are developing a shaped hedge. Pruning against the natural growth pattern is fighting the plant instead of training it and will require regular maintenance.

2. Make cuts that will heal rapidly — every branch has a collar of growing cells that reinforces the limb and seals it off from the trunk if it dies. If you trim limbs flush with the trunk, you remove this protective collar and expose the conductive tissues to possible invasion by fungi. Branch collars vary greatly between species; some are prominent, while others are less distinct. Look for a bulge or series of ridges in the bark around the base of the limb. Make your cut flush with the branch collar, and it will heal rapidly.

Remove large limbs in sections, or at least with three cuts. First cut into the limb on the underside six inches from the collar. Remove the limb with a second cut four inches farther out; and finally, cut the stub, leaving the branch

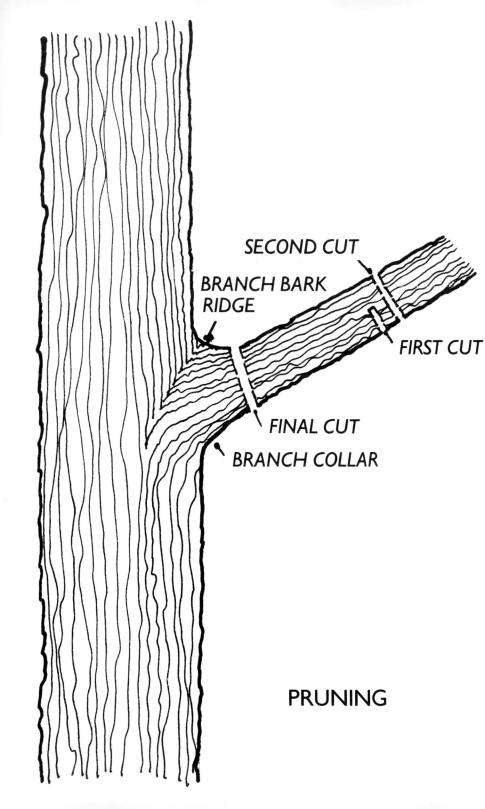

SECOND CUT

BRANCH BARK
RIDGE

FIRST CUT

FINAL CUT

BRANCH COLLAR

PRUNING

collar bulging from the trunk. This procedure prevents a partially severed limb from falling and peeling a strip of bark down the trunk. Always use sharp tools suited for the size of the job.

3. Avoid topping a tree — removing the terminal growing section of a tree destroys its natural shape and appearance, stunts its growth, and weakens it. You probably will want to remove limbs that compete with the terminal leader.

4. Prune in the right season — prune evergreens and most deciduous trees and shrubs in the dormant season, December through February. This is particularly important for oaks in Texas, which are susceptible to oak wilt. Refer to the section on oaks for important guidelines.

Wait until after the first freeze so pruning will not stimulate new growth. Plants that bloom in the late spring and fall usually produce flowers on the current season's new growth. Dormant-season pruning allows them to produce new wood in the spring before blooming. Early-spring-flowering species, such as redbuds, produce blooms on the previous year's new growth. Prune them immediately after flowering, before new growth starts.

Observe two exceptions to the seasonal guidelines. Remove broken or otherwise damaged limbs immediately, and trim back foliage if you transplant a tree. The diminished root system cannot supply water to the full canopy of foliage, and the plant will die unless the foliage is reduced in proportion to the root loss. Trim back the branch tips, or remove most of the leaves.

5. Prune for a reason. Carefully consider the four primary objectives of pruning: improving appearance, directing growth, encouraging fruit or flowers, and maintaining health. Remove a limb only for a very specific purpose; don't vent your frustration from a stalled lawn mower on a nearby shrub.

IMPROVING APPEARANCE

Even though you've chosen a plant because its natural growth habit complements your landscape, trees and shrubs often display little regard for our wishes. A shrub may grow scattered branches or a tree produce wayward limbs. Even in the best designed landscape, some degree of control by pruning is usually required. Just as water and fertilizer maximize growth, intelligent and timely pruning helps the plant to rapidly develop a full size and attractive shape.

Perhaps one reason native plants have been ignored so long by plant growers and landscapers is their often unsightly appearance in nature. A shrub may have dead limbs, spreading branches, an irregular profile, and other characteristics undesirable for a landscape setting. The unkempt appearance of wild plants results from lack of care. Pruning can transform many native plants into premier landscape specimens.

DIRECTING GROWTH

Thinning

Thinning maintains the symmetrical shape and desired size of a tree or shrub by removing excessive or unsightly branches. Removing wayward limbs channels the plant's growth into the desirable limbs. A developing young tree or shrub, especially if it is rapid growing, produces numerous branches, some of which compete with each other for light. The ones that win the race for the sun shade the others, which eventually die. Removing these from the beginning prevents the tree from wasting growth on limbs destined to die.

After a hard freeze or severe pruning, a tree often produces water sprouts — straight, rapid-growing, vertical limbs that branch from the trunk or older interior limbs. These can destroy the natural shape and should be removed. Thinning keeps lower limbs of trees from obstructing vision or blocking access beneath the tree. When thinning small branches, make a smooth cut where the branch connects with the main stem. You can change the direction a branch is growing by pruning it one-fourth to one-half inch beyond a twig growing in the desired direction. The twig will assume the primary growth of the branch. Light pruning of the branch tips of many shrubs stimulates new growth and gives the plant a fuller appearance.

Rejuvenation

As some plants, such as desert willow and cenizo, age they develop unproductive wood that produces few leaves or flowers. Cutting back the old limbs, or even the entire plant nearly to the ground, will stimulate growth of vigorous new branches. You may need to remove the old branches over a two- or three-year interval and thin the new branches as they appear.

Encouraging Flowers and Fruit

Many flowering shrubs benefit from light pruning in the dormant season. Pruning the branch tips of salvias, yaupon holly, and lantana produces denser foliage and more flowers. Thinning interior limbs allows light to penetrate into a flowering or fruiting plant and stimulate more blooms. Some plants, such as turk's cap, desert willow, and white honeysuckle, must be severely pruned every few years to maintain an attractive, full-flowering condition. The species descriptions indicate which plants benefit from heavy pruning.

Maintaining Health

A plant will not only be more attractive, it will be healthier if damaged, dead, or diseased limbs are removed. Limbs broken by winds, freezes, or careless handling are open doors for invasions of fungi and parasites. Remove them immediately.

Evergreen Sumac

LANDSCAPING FOR ENERGY & WATER CONSERVATION

IT PAYS TO LANDSCAPE

The Southwest sizzles in the summer, and bone-chilling blue northers sweep down from the mountains in the winter. Summer lingers far into September with 90-degree temperatures, and winter is as unpredictable as the north wind. We insulate ourselves from the extremes of nature by adjusting the thermostats in our climate-controlled houses and offices. But we pay the price for this independence from nature. Our creature comforts cost us every thirty days when we receive our utility bills. A judicious choice of landscape plants and a well-thought-out landscape design plan can reduce your bills, make your house more comfortable throughout the year, and make your yard a more enjoyable recreational space.

The walls of your house provide a buffer between the outdoors and the interior environment, and the landscape plants can be an effective extension of that protection. Trees, shrubs, vines, and groundcovers reduce direct sunlight and reflected heat, provide cooling shade, increase humidity, and block the chilling breezes of winter. Landscaping yields tangible utilitarian benefits, as well as beautifies your home.

THE DECIDUOUS SOLUTION

Nature has its own energy conservation program: deciduous plants. The purpose of a leaf is to capture solar energy and convert it into food, and this is most efficiently accomplished in the spring and summer. Many plants have adopted the strategy of losing their leaves in the winter. This prevents water loss through the leaves at a time when food production is at a minimum. Thanks to nature's ingenious scheme, we have plants that provide cooling shade in the summer, yet allow the sun's warming rays to penetrate in the winter.

In the summer, the southern and western walls of a structure receive direct radiation from the sun from dawn to dusk. Regardless of how well insulated, a house absorbs a tremendous heat load that the air-conditioning system must dissipate. Anything that reduces that heat load reduces utility bills. A deciduous tree provides the perfect solution. A tree large enough to shade the roof can reduce the interior temperature of a house by eight to ten degrees.

For optimum shading, a deciduous tree should be planted fifteen to twenty feet away from a building. Choose a tree that grows large enough so that the lower limbs will not block air circulation around the house. Elms, ashes, maples, and oaks are traditional favorites and have superior landscaping qualities, though other indigenous trees, such as walnut, pecan, huisache, sweet gum, and sycamore, will suffice beautifully. Avoid the temptation to plant fast-growing species that are short-lived and prone to wind damage, a prime consideration for trees with limbs near the roof.

You probably will want to shade the east side of your house without completely blocking the cheerful morning rays of sun. Low shrubs and trees, such as desert willow, mesquite, and retama, let morning light filter in while blocking heat buildup. Cactus gardens and groundcovers help by reducing heat reflected from the ground.

Another way to obtain summer shading is by planting vines, either climbing on a trellis or arbor or clinging directly on a masonry wall. (Vines on a wooden exterior tend to hasten decomposition and must be removed when your house needs painting.) The layer of vegetation against the side of your house will block the sun's rays and provide an insulating dead-air space. An arbor both shades the side of the house and provides a shady outdoor area for recreation. Arbors enhance pools, porches, and patios.

The air-conditioning compressors of many houses are placed without regard to exposure. A unit on the south side of a house is in the sun continually and labors much harder than one in the shade. You can increase the efficiency and life of the compressor by planting a tree or shrub to provide shade without blocking airflow. For the same amount of energy, the compressor may keep the interior temperature as much as three degrees cooler.

Broad circle drives leading to your front door, paved patios, and rock gardens may be attractive, but they absorb and radiate heat just like a shopping mall parking lot. The air temperature above grass and groundcovers may be as much as fifteen degrees cooler than above concrete or rock aggregate. You can reduce the heat radiated onto your house and make your patio or pool more bearable in the summer by planting around walks and drives.

WINTER ROLE REVERSALS

In the summer, we resent the villainous sun and welcome the gentle breezes, but in the winter the roles reverse and we praise the warming sun and curse

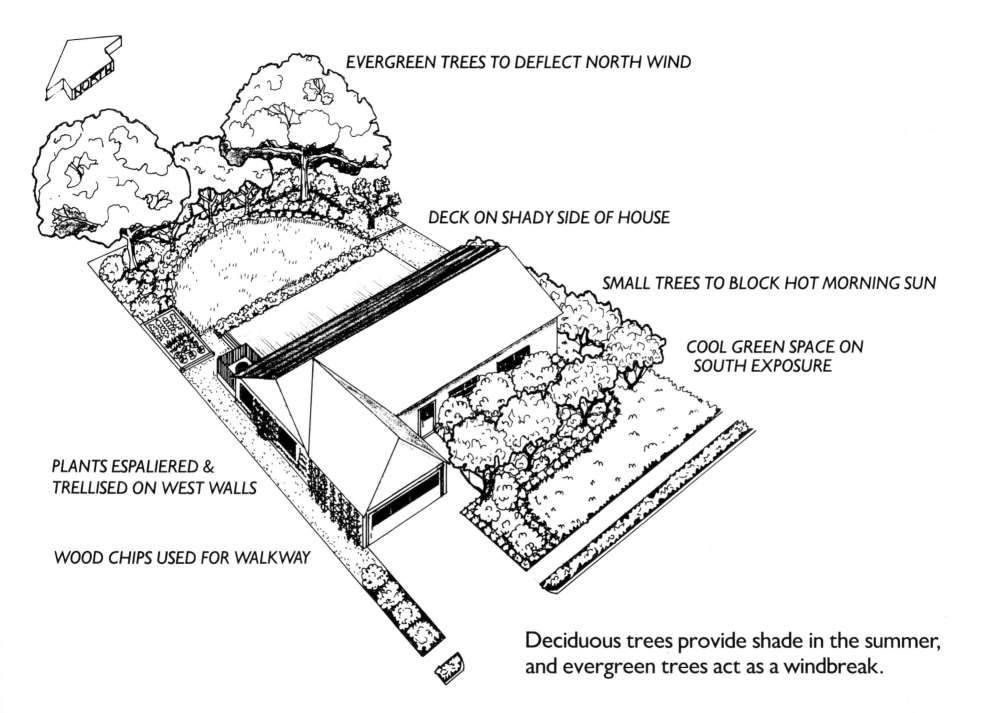

EVERGREEN TREES TO DEFLECT NORTH WIND

DECK ON SHADY SIDE OF HOUSE

SMALL TREES TO BLOCK HOT MORNING SUN

COOL GREEN SPACE ON SOUTH EXPOSURE

PLANTS ESPALIERED & TRELLISED ON WEST WALLS

WOOD CHIPS USED FOR WALKWAY

NORTH

Deciduous trees provide shade in the summer, and evergreen trees act as a windbreak.

the wind. Deciduous shade trees cooperate by dropping their leaf cover and allowing the sun's heat to warm our houses. Trees and shrubs also can alter the airflow around your house and buffer the chilling winter breezes. A row of evergreen trees or large shrubs planted on the northwest side of your house will deflect the arctic north winds without blocking the cooling summer southern breezes. An evergreen hedge five feet from the house will reduce the wind velocity striking the structure and create an insulating dead-air space. This decreases the airflow, and resulting heat loss, through the outside walls. Tests showed that a thirty-foot-tall planting reduced the wind velocity by 55 percent as far as 320 feet downwind.

With the rising cost of utilities, homeowners cannot afford to pass up the bargain that landscaping represents. A beautifully landscaped yard can add thousands of dollars to the value of your house, makes it easier to sell, makes your living space more attractive and enjoyable, and reduces monthly utility expenses.

XERISCAPING

Anyone contemplating landscaping a home or business is concerned with the time and expense of plant maintenance. Expensive summer watering bills can offset some of the savings in air-conditioning costs. If you use plants not adapted to your yard, fertilizing, soil conditioning, spraying, pruning, and replacing dead plants represent a continual expense. Native plants go a long way toward avoiding these common problems. Once established, natives require a fraction of the maintenance of many imported species. One of the primary expenses of maintaining a landscape is water. As much as 60 percent of residential water consumption goes to watering yards. The choice of plants can greatly reduce the moisture required to keep your landscape attractive and healthy. Of the thousands of plants native to the Southwest, some are water spendthrifts, and some are as frugal as a Depression loan officer.

A plant grows by capturing solar energy and, through the process of photosynthesis, converting raw elements into useful nutrients. The roots absorb water and dissolved minerals, which are channeled through the plant's vascular system to the food factories in the leaves. The leaves transpire, or lose, a major portion of the water supplied by the roots. Some plants have developed ingenious methods to reduce water loss from the leaves, and many of these species have exceptional landscape value. Plants combat water loss through the leaf surface by small leaves or leaves covered with a waxy or woolly coating and by internal cellular and structural adaptations. These xerophytic, or drought-tolerant, plants thrive under conditions that kill or severely stress plants native to more moist areas. From Central Texas westward, drought-tolerant species should be the dominant plants in any landscape design.

Many cities in the Southwest have initiated xeriscape programs to actively encourage landscaping with plants that have a low water consumption. *Xeriscape* was coined by combining the Greek word *xero*, meaning "dry," with "landscape." Most Southwest metropolises must find ways to conserve water, or their reservoirs and wells will run dry in the near future. Former Texas Governor Mark White termed water the state's most precious resource. By conscientious landscaping, each of us can help relieve the demand for this critical resource and reduce our personal utility expenses.

SEVEN PRINCIPLES

Xeriscaping does not mean just using yuccas and rock gardens. It is a philosophy that incorporates good gardening principles and can be practiced anywhere. The following principles are recommended by the National Xeriscape Council, Inc.

1. Start with a good design. A master plan incorporates existing and future plants, soil, slope, exposure, and your house and play areas into a design that meets your needs and conserves water.

2. Improve the soil. A plant needs a healthy root system to thrive and beautify your yard. Compacted, shallow, rocky, or sandy soil may not allow a plant to develop a root system that can sufficiently support luxuriant foliage growth. You can improve your soil by tilling in at least two inches of organic material, such as composted leaves, grass clippings, or rotted manure. If you have shallow soil, add two to four inches of loam topsoil. The proper soil is loose enough for the roots to penetrate, has the proper pH for the roots to absorb iron, and allows water to slowly percolate into the root zone.

3. Use mulch. A mulch covers the soil, prevents moisture loss, inhibits weed growth, and modifies extreme soil temperatures. Bark, wood chips, leaves, grass clippings, and colored gravel make good mulching materials. Use two to four inches of mulch around trees and shrubs, in flower beds, and in landscaped areas. The mulching itself can be an attractive design element in your overall landscape plan.

4. Reduce lawn areas. Turf grass is necessary for outdoor recreation areas, and it dissipates heat and provides a cool space around your house or patio. But in arid parts of the country, lawns guzzle water in the summer and require regular maintenance. To conserve water and save on utility bills, limit your lawn to small recreation and border areas around your house and choose the grass best adapted to your climate and yard. Consider using wildflowers, trees, shrubs, and mulch for the majority of your landscape. (See the chapter "Lawns: Buffalograss and Turf Alternatives.")

5. Water efficiently. Put the water where the plant needs it, when it needs it, and you can cut your water consumption, and bill, by as much as 30 percent. Learn to tell when a plant needs water. Grass curls and lies flat. Leaves may droop, drop, or lose their shine. Water often enough to avoid drought stress, without overwatering.

The way you water influences how much water a plant needs to thrive. Place the water in the root zone and water deeply. Shallow watering encourages a shallow root system, which requires more frequent watering since the upper portion of the soil dries out faster. Drip irrigation, soil basins around plants, early- or late-day watering, and mulch all conserve water. Sprinkler systems used improperly can lose considerable water to evaporation and runoff.

6. Practice good maintenance. Maintenance keeps your plants healthy and attractive. Weeds, injured or dead limbs, or sickly plants detract from your landscape, increase your water bill, and can require costly replacement of plants. (See the chapter "Maintaining Your Landscape.")

7. Choose low-water-use plants adapted to your area. Going west, the amount of rainfall decreases linearly from the Texas coast to the New Mexico border. Southeast Texas receives fifty-six inches annually, while El Paso receives less than eight inches. In New Mexico and Arizona, annual precipitation depends primarily on elevation. The mountains receive as much as sixteen inches annually and the low deserts as little as three inches. As can be expected, most southwestern plants must be drought tolerant to survive, but some are better adapted to drought than others. Some species grow only along streams and rivers or in cooler mountainous areas with greater precipitation. They would quickly perish in the hot, arid desert or in an arid landscape setting. The following list, though not inclusive, delineates many species of trees, shrubs, vines, and groundcovers that will tolerate periods of drought.

DROUGHT-TOLERANT PLANTS FOR XERISCAPING

Vines

Campsis radicans – Trumpet creeper
Clematis species – Clematis
Cocculus carolinus – Carolina snailseed
Lonicera species – Honeysuckle
Maurandya antirrhiniflora – Snapdragon vine
Parthenocissus inserta – Thicket creeper
Parthenocissus quinquefolia – Virginia creeper

Groundcovers

Acacia angustissima var. *hirta* – Fern acacia
Artemisia ludoviciana – Artemisia
Berberis repens – Creeping barberry
Dalea greggii – Gregg dalea
Muhlenbergia lindheimeri – Lindheimer muhly
Phyla species – Frogfruit
Sedum species – Stonecrop

Trees

Acacia greggii – Catclaw
Acacia smallii – Huisache
Acacia wrightii – Catclaw (Wright)
Arbutus texensis – Texas Madrone

Celtis species – Hackberry
Cercidium floridum – Blue palo verde
Cercis canadensis var. *texensis* – Texas redbud
Chilopsis linearis – Desert willow
Condalia hookeri – Brasil
Cordia boissieri – Wild olive
Cupressus arizonica – Arizona cypress

Diospyros texana – Texas persimmon

Fraxinus cuspidata – Fragrant ash
Fraxinus pensylvanica var. *texana* – Texas ash

Gleditsia triacanthos – Honey locust

Juglans macrocarpa – Little walnut
Juglans major – Arizona walnut
Juniperus species – Junipers

Leucaena retusa – Goldenball leadtree

Parkinsonia aculeata – Retama
Pinus cembroides – Mexican pinyon pine
Pinus edulis – Colorado pinyon pine
Pistacia texana – Texas pistache
Pithecellobium flexicaule – Texas ebony

Prosopis glandulosa – Mesquite
Prunus mexicana – Mexican plum
Prunus serotina var. *eximia* – Escarpment black cherry
Prunus serotina var. *virens* – Black cherry

Quercus arizonica – Arizona oak
Quercus buckleyi – Texas oak
Quercus emoryi – Emory oak
Quercus fusiformis – Plateau live oak
Quercus gambelii – Gambel oak
Quercus glaucoides – Lacey oak
Quercus gravesii – Chisos red oak
Quercus grisea – Gray oak
Quercus hypoleucoides – Silverleaf oak
Quercus marilandica – Blackjack oak
Quercus oblongifolia – Mexican blue oak
Quercus pungens var. *vaseyana* – Vasey oak
Quercus stellata – Post oak
Quercus turbinella – Shrub live oak
Quercus virginiana – Coastal live oak

Rhus lanceolata – Prairie flame leaf sumac
Robinia neomexicana – Rose locust

Sambucus mexicana – Mexican elderberry
Sapindus saponaria – Soapberry
Sophora affinis – Eve's necklace

Ulmus crassifolia – Cedar elm
Ungnadia speciosa – Mexican buckeye

Shrubs

Acacia rigidula – Black brush
Agave species – Century plants
Aloysia gratissima – Bee brush
Amorpha fruticosa – False indigo
Anisacanthus thurberi – Desert honeysuckle
Anisacanthus quadrifidus var. *wrightii* – Flame anisacanthus
Artemisia filifolia – Sand sagebrush
Artemisia tridentata – Big leaf sagebrush

Baccharis sarothroides – Desert broom
Bauhinia congesta – Anacacho orchid tree
Berberis species – Barberries
Bouvardia ternifolia – Scarlet bouvardia
Buddleja marrubiifolia – Woolly butterfly bush

Ceratoides lanata – Winterfat
Cercocarpus montanus – Mountain mahogany
Chamaebatiaria millefolium – Fernbush
Choisya dumosa – Starleaf Mexican orange
Chrysactinia mexicana – Damianita
Chrysothamnus nauseosus – Rabbitbrush
Cowania mexicana – Cliffrose

Dalea formosa – Feather dalea
Dalea frutescens – Black dalea
Dalea scoparia – Broom dalea
Dasylirion species – Sotol

Ephedra species – Joint fir
Ericameria laricifolia – Larchleaf goldenweed
Eupatorium havanense – Shrubby boneset
Eupatorium wrightii – Wright boneset
Eysenhardtia texana – Kidneywood

Fallugia paradoxa – Apache plume
Fouquieria splendens – Ocotillo
Fraxinus greggii – Gregg ash

Garrya ovata – Silktassel
Guaiacum angustifolium – Guayacan

Hesperaloe parviflora – Red yucca

Ilex decidua – Possum haw
Ilex vomitoria – Yaupon

Lantana horrida – Texas lantana
Larrea tridentata – Creosote bush
Leucophyllum candidum – Cenizo
Leucophyllum frutescens – Cenizo
Lonicera albiflora – White honeysuckle
Lycium pallidum – Wolfberry

Malvaviscus drummondii – Turk's cap
Mimosa borealis – Fragrant mimosa

Nolina species – Beargrass

Parthenium argentatum – Guayule
Parthenium incanum – Mariola
Pavonia lasiopetala – Rose pavonia

Rhus microphylla – Little-leaf sumac
Rhus trilobata – Three-leaf sumac
Rhus virens – Evergreen sumac

Salvia greggii – Autumn sage
Salvia regla – Mountain sage
Schaefferia cuneifolia – Desert yaupon
Senna wislizenii – Shrubby senna
Shepherdia argentia – Silver buffaloberry
Simmondsia chinensis – Jojoba
Sophora secundiflora – Texas mountain laurel

Tecoma stans – Yellow trumpet flower

Vauquelinia angustifolia – Chisos rosewood
Vauquelinia californica – Arizona rosewood
Viguiera stenoloba – Skeleton leaf goldeneye

Yucca species – Yucca

A landscaping plan including a redbud tree

LANDSCAPES THAT ATTRACT WILDLIFE

To me, the most compelling reason for landscaping with plants native to my area is to repair some of the environmental damage caused by urban growth. Habitat alteration is inevitable, but we can lessen the impact by preserving as much of the indigenous plant community as possible. If we maintain a diverse association of plants, our neighborhoods will attract and support a variety of birds, butterflies, squirrels, and other small wildlife.

Wildlife and urban development can be compatible. Many species of animals can coexist with humans if certain requirements are met. Like us, wildlife need food, shelter, water, and space to carry on daily, or nightly, activities. The animals most successful in cohabiting with humans are birds, butterflies, reptiles, and small nocturnal mammals. These share our urban environment without getting in our way too much.

PUT OUT A YEAR-ROUND WELCOME MAT

Many people go to extreme measures and great expense to attract birds to their yards. You can easily spend hundreds of dollars on birdhouses for purple martins, wrens, chickadees, and other hole-nesting species. Maintaining feeders with varieties of seeds and suet can be a time-consuming daily task. For those who love wildlife, having a yard full of birds is worth the trouble and expense. But with the proper selection of landscaping plants, you can let nature furnish most of the room and board, while you relax and enjoy the company.

As you design your landscape, consider the two primary requirements for attracting birds and other wildlife — food and shelter. Select plants that provide a year-round supply of seeds, nuts, and fruit. Plants with tube-shaped flowers (particularly red) attract hummingbirds; acacias are famous nectar plants for honey bees; milkweeds, members of the sunflower and verbena families, and most other showy flowers attract butterflies. Trees and brushy shrubs provide nesting locations for birds that build open nests, such as mockingbirds, cardinals, doves, vireos, and jays. With a diversity of plants in your yard that meet the habitat requirements of a variety of species, you can enjoy a year-round population of resident and migratory birds.

A creek, a wooded park, or even a vacant lot can be the home of an opossum, raccoon, ringtail cat, or skunk. At night they emerge and unobtrusively forage for food, often dining on rodents and reptiles, as well as gleaning spilled trash and uneaten dog food. For five years, we have had an opossum, skunk, and cat living under our house in perfect harmony with each other and us. Wild mammals are usually considered vermin and reservoirs of disease for our domestic animals and eradicated when possible. However, in most instances they are as harmless as the squirrels we enjoy in our trees. Snakes suffer a similar, only worse, reputation. The few poisonous species have instilled such fear in humans that most people consider all snakes public enemies. The harmless snakes eat rodents, lizards, frogs, and toads and should be welcomed neighbors. The following lists of plants are particularly suitable for supplying the food and shelter requirements of birds. All are described in this book. Choose ones that fit into your landscape design and that are adapted to your landscape zone.

SEED AND FRUIT PLANTS FOR BIRDS
Spring and Summer

Trees
Acer species — Maples
Cordia boissieri — Wild olive
Ehretia anacua — Anacua
Fraxinus species — Ashes
Pinus species — Pines
Pistacia texana — Texas pistache
Populus tremuloides — Aspen
Prunus caroliniana — Laurel cherry
Prunus mexicana — Mexican plum
Prunus serotina — Black cherry
Prunus virginiana — Chokecherry
Rhamnus caroliniana — Carolina buckthorn
Sabal mexicana — Sabal palm
Ulmus americana — American elm

Shrubs
Agave species — Century plants
Berberis species — Barberries
Condalia hookeri — Brasil
Lycium species — Wolfberry
Ribes aureum — Golden current
Sambucus species — Elderberries
Schaefferia cuneifolia — Desert yaupon
Shepherdia argentia — Buffaloberry
Symphoricarpos species — Snowberry
Yucca species — Yucca

Vines
Parthenocissus quinquefolia — Virginia creeper
Parthenocissus inserta — Thicket creeper
Passiflora incarnata — Passion flower

Fall and Winter

Trees

Arbutus texensis – Texas Madrone
Carya illinoinensis – Pecan
Celtis species – Hackberries
Cercis canadensis – Redbud
Chilopsis linearis – Desert willow
Condalia hookeri – Brasil
Cornus florida – Flowering dogwood
Diospyros texana – Texas persimmon
Ilex opaca – American holly
Juglans species – Walnuts
Juniperus species – Junipers
Liquidambar styraciflua – Sweetgum
Magnolia grandiflora – Magnolia
Persea borbonia – Red bay
Picea pungens glauca – Blue spruce
Pinus species – Pines
Pistacia texana – Texas pistache
Platanus occidentalis – Sycamore
Prosopis glandulosa – Mesquite
Quercus species – Oaks
Rhamnus caroliniana – Carolina buckthorn
Rhus species – Sumacs
Sambucus mexicana – Mexican elderberry
Taxodium distinctum – Bald cypress
Ulmus crassifolia – Cedar elm
Vaccinium arboreum – Farkleberry
Viburnum rifidulum – Rusty blackhaw

Shrubs

Amorpha fruticosa – False indigo
Bauhinia congesta – Anacacho orchid tree
Callicarpa americana – American beautyberry
Cephalanthus occidentalis – Button bush
Cornus drummondii – Roughleaf dogwood
Dasylirion species – Sotols
Ilex decidua – Possum haw
Ilex vomitoria – Yaupon holly
Lonicera albiflora – White honeysuckle

Malvaviscus drummondii – Turk's cap
Myrica cerifera – Wax myrtle
Nolina species – Beargrass
Rhus species – Sumacs
Symphoricarpos orbiculatus – Coralberry

Vines

Cocculus caroliniana – Carolina snailseed
Ibervillea lindheimeri – Balsam gourd
Lonicera species – Honeysuckles

FLOWERING PLANTS THAT ATTRACT HUMMINGBIRDS

Spring

Flowers

Aquilegia canadensis – Columbine
Castilleja species – Paintbrushes
Delphinium species – Larkspurs
Echinocereus triglochidiatus – Claret cup cactus
Hibiscus cardiophyllus – Heartleaf hibiscus
Lupinus species – Lupines
Monarda species – Lemon mints
Salvia coccinea – Red sage

Trees, Shrubs, Vines

Bouvardia glaberrima – Smooth bouvardia
Bouvardia ternifolia – Scarlet bouvardia
Cercis canadensis – Redbud
Lonicera sempervirens – Coral honeysuckle
Lycium species – Wolfberries
Pithecellobium flexicaule – Texas ebony
Sophora secundiflora – Texas mountain laurel
Ungnadia speciosa – Mexican buckeye
Yucca species – Yuccas

Summer–Fall

Wildflowers

Castilleja species – Paintbrushes
Hibiscus species – Hibiscus

Ipomoea leptophylla – Bush morning glory
Ipomopsis aggregata – Skyrocket
Ipomopsis rubra – Standing cypress
Lobelia cardinalis – Cardinal flower
Malvaviscus drummondii – Turk's cap
Mirabilis multiflora – Giant four-o'clock
Monarda species – Lemon mints
Penstemon barbatus – Scarlet bugler
Penstemon species – Beard tongues
Salvia species – Sage

Trees, Shrubs, Vines

Agave species – Century plants
Anisacanthus species

Bouvardia glaberrima – Smooth bouvardia
Bouvardia ternifolia – Scarlet bouvardia
Campsis radicans – Trumpet creeper vine
Chilopsis linearis – Desert willow
Fouquieria splendens – Ocotillo
Hesperaloe parviflora – Red yucca
Lonicera species – Honeysuckle
Pavonia lasiopetala – Rose mallow
Robinia neomexicana – Rose locust
Salvia greggii – Autumn sage
Salvia regla – Mountain sage

LAWNS: BUFFALOGRASS & TURF ALTERNATIVES

Lawn maintenance can be more than a weekend chore; it can be a pain in the pocketbook when you pay your summer water bills. Watering lawns accounts for 40 to 60 percent of residential water consumption. The broadleaf turf grasses so prevalent today wither and die without regular watering during the hot Southwest summers. With water rationing common in many cities, people find they must postpone weekend outings so they won't miss their scheduled day for watering. Some spend considerable sums on programmable computerized sprinkling systems so they can go on vacation without worrying about their yard dying. Naturally, we all want healthy, attractive yards, but you don't have to be a slave to your lawn.

How would you like to forget mowing and to water only once a month through the summer and still have a luxuriant stand of grass? If withering Saint Augustine has you buffaloed, consider the advantages of buffalograss, the only native turf grass available that can beat the heat. Once established, buffalograss thrives in dry weather and alkaline soil. It keeps its rich green color through the hot months and survives even the coldest winters.

This attractive turf grass does have limitations and some specific requirements. First, it is not shade tolerant. It requires full or only slightly filtered sunlight. It grows well in loams and clays, but not sandy soils. Second, it cannot stand heavy foot traffic. Plant it only in areas that receive minimal or infrequent use. Third, it does not compete well with weeds or other grasses. Buffalograss is native to and does best in Landscape Zones 4 to 7, where it receives twelve to twenty-four inches of rain annually. Zoysia and Burmuda grasses are more drought tolerant than the popular Saint Augustine, which survives well in the higher rainfall and humidity east of Austin and along the Texas coast.

ESTABLISHING A LAWN

Since buffalograss is a poor competitor, establishing a lawn is most successful if all grasses and weeds are removed initially. The following planting procedure is recommended by the National Wildflower Research Center in Austin.

After removing all weeds, till two inches deep and rake and roll lightly to firm up the seedbed. Sow pretreated seeds and cover with a thin layer of top soil, less than one-half inch. Firm down the soil and keep it moist for about four days while the seeds germinate. Planting in one-foot rows allows easy removal of weeds with a hoe. Water lightly every day for one to two weeks to establish the seedlings, then once a month. Best germination occurs with 80 to 95 degree F. day temperatures and a night temperature above 65 degrees F. Plant after the last frost date in the spring or early summer. Recommendations vary from two to four pounds of seeds per one thousand square feet of lawn. You should have complete coverage in three months to a year, depending on growing conditions.

Buffalograss forms tufts and spreads by runners, as well as seeding itself. The fastest way to establish it is to plant plugs about one foot apart and water until established. The grass will cover the bare spots in one season. Buffalograss grows to eight inches in height and spreads best when mowed to about three inches. Many homeowners find that a single mowing per year, in August, is sufficient. Like most grasses, it goes dormant and turns brown in the winter. Improved cultivars are now available that make this excellent turf grass even better.

ALTERNATIVES TO GRASS

You can reduce the amount of lawn you have to maintain by designing areas that combine groundcovers and mulch. Many vines, low shrubs, and wildflowers provide a dense cover and are shade tolerant. (Refer to the chapters on ground-covers and wildflowers for suitable species.) If an area will not support a thick growth, fill in with a mulch of bark or leaves. Use groundcovers of rock aggregate with care. Rocks tend to increase the ground temperature and reflect heat. By designing to minimize the amount of turf in your yard, you can include plants with attractive flowers and foliage and add visual variety to your yard.

USING NATIVE PLANTS AS GROUNDCOVERS

Almost every landscape, whether small or large, private or commercial, has areas that receive no foot traffic but are unsuitable for trees, shrubs, or turf grass. A groundcover can turn a visually empty space into an eye-catching attraction. Groundcovers serve two general purposes, one utilitarian, the other aesthetic: they prevent erosion and cover unsightly bare spots; and they add an active or unifying element to a landscape design, a dimension of visual interest beyond a cover of turf grass or crushed stone.

A grassy lawn is necessary for play and entertaining, but many areas of turf serve no function other than contributing a tailored appearance to the yard. On the other hand, a border filled with sprawling or prostrate plants provides visual relief to a building front, wall, drive, or sidewalk. Decorative plants can colorfully accent the area beneath open-branching shrubs and trees. A planting within a large paved area breaks the monotony and imparts a soft, cool feeling to the overall landscape. In some cases, a tall plant would block the view in front of a window or store front. A vine or low-growing shrub can enhance the scene without obscuring the view.

Groundcovers also come to the rescue for areas that are difficult to maintain or have marginal growing conditions. Shady sites or rocky, dry slopes need some type of vegetative cover. When used as an integral feature of a landscape design, groundcovers provide low-maintenance cover, as well as an extra touch of beauty.

GROUNDCOVER QUALITIES

For a plant to be both an effective and an attractive groundcover, it must exhibit special growth characteristics. In searching for native groundcovers, landscapers and propagators look for plants that have a low growth habit and dense foliage and that can adapt to a wide variety of habitats. The plant must be able to survive and thrive in harsh environmental conditions, such as shade, heat, drought, and infertile soil. In addition, the ideal groundcover grows and spreads rapidly and has evergreen foliage.

Nature has endowed many plants with some of these basic characteristics, but precious few have them all. Unfortunately, plants adapted to habitats severely limited in soil nutrients, moisture, or light seldom grow rapidly or develop dense foliage. The task of the propagators is to find those plants that have most of the basic requirements.

Fortunately, many naturally low-growing shrubs, mat-forming wildflowers,

and weakly climbing vines are suitable for use as groundcovers. Some species adapt to almost any situation, while others require a particular habitat. The best have evergreen leaves, attractive flowers, or decorative fruit.

PLANTING AND MAINTAINING GROUNDCOVERS

Don't expect to set out a few recommended plants on an arid and rocky or compacted and shady site and get a dense cover of vegetation the next growing season. That a plant has the potential for thick growth doesn't mean it can achieve that growth under marginal conditions. You want the plant to thrive, not just survive. A plant can cope with less than the best if it has a robust root system. In many cases, soil preparation is the key to establishing a successful groundcover planting.

If you want a complete cover, you must first remove all the competing vegetation, especially grasses. Do it in the beginning, and you won't have to spend hours later removing unsightly weeds. You also may need to work some organic matter, such as peat, compost, or manure, into the upper eight to twelve inches of soil to give the roots a healthy growing medium. Third, mulch between the new settings to hold in soil moisture and to reduce weed invasion. In one or two growing seasons, the plants should reach their potential.

Once established, a dense groundcover is not totally maintenance free. Many plants begin to loose their vigor in two to four years, and bare spots develop. You may need to periodically replace plants to keep the cover complete. Other plants grow so vigorously that they need regular pruning to maintain a tailored appearance. A dense groundcover requires less attention than a lawn, but don't expect it to be maintenance-free.

Maybe you're not enamored of a groundcover that requires regular attention. Remember that a groundcover doesn't have to provide complete foliage cover. Many low-growing deciduous shrubs have decorative foliage, flowers, or fruit through most of the year, and perennial wildflowers can provide a seasonal accent. A mixture of ornamental native shrubs and perennial wildflowers can give your landscape seasonal variety and an elegance far exceeding that of a solid planting of turf grass or dwarf junipers.

Many native plants particularly suited for use as groundcovers are listed below. Also, most wildflowers can be used as seasonal groundcovers. For a full description of the shrubs, wildflowers, and vines, refer to those sections in the book.

GROUNDCOVERS

Low-Growing Shrubs Suitable for Groundcovers

Choisya dumosa – Starleaf Mexican orange
Chrysactinia mexicana – Damianita
Dasylirion species – Sotol
Ilex vomitoria nana – Dwarf yaupon
Lantana horrida – Texas lantana
Myrica pusilla – Dwarf wax myrtle
Nolina species – Beargrass
Rhus microphylla – Little-leaf sumac
Rhus tridentata – Prostrate three-leaf sumac
Salvia greggii – Autumn sage
Symphoricarpos orbiculatus – Coral berry

Perennial Wildflowers Suitable for Groundcovers

Datura wrightii – Sacred datura
Dyssodia pentachaeta – Dogweed
Ipomoea leptophylla – Bush morning glory
Linanthastrum nuttallii – Nuttall gilia
Melampodium leucanthum – Blackfoot daisy
Mirabilis multiflora – Giant four-o'clock
Oenothera speciosa – Prairie primrose
Penstemon species – Penstemons
Psilostrophe tagetina – Paperflower
Salvia coccinea – Red sage
Verbena bipinnatifida – Prairie verbena
Zinnia grandiflora – Desert zinnia

Vines Suitable for Groundcovers

Clematis ligusticifolia – Western virgin's bower
Gelsemium sempervirens – Carolina jessamine
Lonicera sempervirens – Coral honeysuckle
Lonicera arizonica – Arizona honeysuckle
Parthenocissus quinquefolia – Virginia creeper
Parthenocissus inserta – Thicket creeper

Fern Acacia

Fern Acacia, *Acacia angustissima* var. *hirta* (A. hirta)

NATIVE DISTRIBUTION: grasslands, hillsides, mesas, oak woodlands at 3000–6000-foot elevations in southern Arizona and New Mexico; widespread in Texas; Mexico.

LANDSCAPE ZONE: 2–7, 9.

SIZE: 1–3 feet tall.

LEAVES: deciduous.

FLOWER: summer–fall, ½ inch, white, round head; fruit 2–3-inch pods.

SOIL: adaptable, well draining.

EXPOSURE: full sun, partial shade.

TEMPERATURE TOLERANCE: cold hardy.

WATER: drought tolerant.

PROPAGATION: scarified seed, softwood cuttings.

This thornless acacia has fine-textured, fernlike leaves and a low growth pattern, and it spreads by rhizomes – three ideal characteristics for a groundcover. It's also mowable and has dainty little flowers well into the fall. It grows equally well on rocky, sunny slopes or in mottled shade under an open shrub or tree. Fern acacia forms thick colonies on calcareous roadsides in Texas, so it should survive well in most Southwest yards. Still, an occasional watering will keep it lush.

Artemisia

Artemisia or White Sagebrush *Artemisia ludoviciana*

NATIVE DISTRIBUTION: throughout the Southwest to 8500-foot elevations.

LANDSCAPE ZONE: 1–10.

GROWTH: 1–3 feet tall.

LEAVES: evergreen.

FLOWER: summer–fall, insignificant, releases allergenic pollen.

SOIL: adaptable, well draining.

EXPOSURE: full sun, partial shade.

TEMPERATURE TOLERANCE: heat tolerant, cold hardy.

WATER: drought tolerant.

PROPAGATION: root division.

The silver evergreen foliage, low stance, and colony-forming habit make this plant an ideal groundcover. In addition, it thrives from scorching desert to mountain forest environments. Plant white sage as a border along a hot wall, walk, curb, or foundation. You can use it to surround a tree or upright shrub, or as an accent patch in a rock garden, but be careful about planting it in rich garden soil; it might get out of hand. Mowing or cutting it back in the summer keeps it thick and densely foliated.

Creeping Barberry

Creeping Barberry, *Berberis repens*

NATIVE DISTRIBUTION: shaded mountain slopes at 4500–10,000-foot elevations, West Texas to California, north to Canada.

LANDSCAPE ZONE: 5, 9, 10.

SIZE: 4–12 inches.

LEAVES: evergreen turning red in winter.

FLOWER/FRUIT: spring, clusters of small yellow blooms; black berries.

SOIL: adaptable, well draining.

EXPOSURE: shade, partial shade.

TEMPERATURE TOLERANCE: cold hardy but not heat tolerant.

WATER: moderately drought tolerant.

PROPAGATION: fresh, triple-stratified, or scarified seeds, semisoftwood cuttings, suckers.

With hollylike evergreen leaves, colorful flowers, ornate fruit, and a naturally low growth habit, this is almost the perfect groundcover. Almost, because it just can't tolerate much heat. It likes the cool summers of higher elevations. If you live in an arid climate, try mulching around this beautiful groundcover to keep the soil cool and moist, and plant it in the shade. These plants grow moderately slowly and sprout from underground stolons, making a dense mat. Plant them 10 to 12 inches apart for immediate cover.

Gregg Dalea

Water Clover

Lindheimer Muhly

Gregg Dalea, *Dalea greggii*

NATIVE DISTRIBUTION: limestone mountains of the Trans-Pecos in Texas; Southeast Arizona at 2000–4500-foot elevations; Mexico.

LANDSCAPE ZONE: 1–7.

SIZE: 4–9 inches tall, 3 feet across.

LEAVES: deciduous.

FLOWER: spring–fall, cluster of tiny purple flowers.

SOIL: sand, loam, limestone, well draining.

EXPOSURE: full sun.

TEMPERATURE TOLERANCE: heat tolerant, freezes to ground.

WATER: drought tolerant, 12 inches/year.

PROPAGATION: fresh seeds, semihardwood cuttings.

You'll find this low-branching shrub with trailing limbs a perfect groundcover for dry, sunny exposures. The branches root at the nodes, forming densely foliated clumps up to 3 feet in diameter. Plant them 1½ to 2 feet apart for complete cover. From spring through fall, clusters of purple pealike flowers with yellow throats accent the woolly grayish green foliage. The ¼-inch flowers have the distinct keel common in members of the legume family. The gray leaves and delicate flowers provide dramatic contrast when combined with lustrous green plants, such as damianita, starleaf Mexican orange, and salvias. You'll have to prune it back if it freezes in hard winters, but it recovers rapidly in the spring. Occasional deep watering speeds growth. Just be sure the soil drains fast enough to keep the roots from getting waterlogged. Another mountain species, silver dalea, *Dalea argyraea*, grows to 3 feet tall and makes an equally attractive groundcover.

* * *

Water Clover, *Marsilea macropoda*

NATIVE DISTRIBUTION: marshes, streambanks, southern Texas, north to Austin.

LANDSCAPE ZONE: 4.

SIZE: 6–10 inches tall.

Perennial.

SOIL: adaptable, well to poor draining.

EXPOSURE: shade, partial shade, full sun.

TEMPERATURE TOLERANCE: not cold tolerant.

WATER: requires regular moisture.

PROPAGATION: root division.

You would never guess this little plant were a fern by its name, or its looks, unless you looked closely and saw the delicate little fiddleheads. With cloverlike leaves, it forms dense colonies, perfect for borders along walks, patios, or a poolside garden. You don't have to create a bog to enjoy its lush growth. It survives well in a garden setting.

* * *

Lindheimer Muhly, *Muhlenbergia lindheimeri*

NATIVE DISTRIBUTION: limestone soils of South, Central, and North Texas; Mexico.

LANDSCAPE ZONE: 4–7.

SIZE: 2–5-foot-tall bunches.

LEAVES: dormant in winter.

FLOWER: September–December.

SOIL: alkaline, well draining.

EXPOSURE: full sun, partial shade.

TEMPERATURE TOLERANCE: cold hardy.

WATER: drought tolerant.

PROPAGATION: clump division, seeds.

You'll love the picturesque effect of this tall bunch grass either as an accent in a mixed planting or as a groundcover. You can use it to surround the bare trunk of a tree or tall shrub or as a focal plant to balance a corner garden. It's a perfect match for limestone rockwork or accent boulders. The graceful, arching seed heads decorate the plant in the fall, and the pale green blades contribute color until the plant goes dormant in late winter. Even then its artistic shape and grayish brown hues continue to complement your yard.

Frogfruit

Frogfruit, *Phyla* species

NATIVE DISTRIBUTION: moist soils, throughout most of Texas, New Mexico, and Arizona; California to Florida, north to Pennsylvania.

LANDSCAPE ZONE: 1–9.

SIZE: 3–8 inches tall.

Perennial.

FLOWER: May–October, cluster of tiny white flowers on 4-inch stem.

SOIL: adaptable, well to poor draining.

EXPOSURE: shade, partial shade, full sun.

TEMPERATURE TOLERANCE: cold hardy.

WATER: moderately drought tolerant.

PROPAGATION: plant division.

Frogfruit may have an unglamorous name, but it forms an attractive matlike groundcover. The sprawling stems root at the leaf nodes to form thick colonies. The tiny verbenalike flowers contribute a little, but not much, to the plant's appearance. You'll need to give it extra water to keep it lush, especially during the hottest parts of the year. It goes dormant in hard winters. Numerous species of frogfruit grow throughout the Southwest. *Phyla incisa* and *P. nodiflora* are probably the most widespread, growing from Yuma to Houston.

Bracken Fern

Bracken Fern, *Pteridium aquilinum*

NATIVE DISTRIBUTION: dry woodlands, eastern half of Texas; open slopes in pine forests and stream banks at 5000–8500-foot elevations in mountains of New Mexico and Arizona; throughout North America.

LANDSCAPE ZONE: 6–10.

SIZE: 1–3 feet tall.

LEAVES: deciduous.

SOIL: adaptable, well draining.

EXPOSURE: shade, partial shade.

TEMPERATURE TOLERANCE: root hardy, freezes to ground.

WATER: moderately drought tolerant.

PROPAGATION: dormant root division.

Nothing creates that idyllic forest atmosphere like a stand of bracken fern underneath a canopy of trees. If you don't have your own private woods, use ferns to surround a mature pine or other tree with a tall trunk and shade-producing crown. This fern needs loose, rich soil to allow its rhizomes to spread to develop a thick colony. Keep it moist until the rhizomes become established. The eastern variety *pseudocaudatum* grows in Texas, while the variety *pubescens* grows at high elevations in the western United States. Other native ferns are also available from nurseries. The species with luxuriant foliage generally require con-

Stonecrop

stantly moist soil, semishade, and moderately humid conditions.

❋ ❋ ❋

Stonecrop, *Sedum* species

NATIVE DISTRIBUTION: throughout Texas and in mountains of New Mexico and Arizona.

LANDSCAPE ZONE: 1–10.

GROWTH: 2–12 inches tall.

Perennial.

FLOWER: spring–fall, tiny, pink, white, or yellow.

SOIL: adaptable, well draining.

EXPOSURE: full sun, partial shade, shade.

TEMPERATURE TOLERANCE: cold hardy.

WATER: drought tolerant

PROPAGATION: cuttings.

These sprawling little succulents make the perfect accent for your rock garden. Sedums thrive in dry locations, complement small cacti, and spread to cover bare ground. You can root them in a porous rock for a picturesque interest, or let them dangle out of a rock crevice. They have delicate stems, which break easily if you're trying to remove weeds or leaves from your garden. But that's not so bad. Just stick the pieces in loose soil, and they're guaranteed to root. Some imported species become rather aggressive in a rich garden setting.

LANDSCAPING WITH VINES

UPRIGHT FLOWER BEDS AND HANGING GARDENS

How would you like to turn that nondescript fence in your yard into an upright flower bed covered with fragrant blossoms? Why not transform your mailbox, gaslight, or porch column into a hanging garden of colorful flowers? Nature has supplied the perfect plants for such a conversion: vines. These versatile plants add natural beauty to your home landscape and require little maintenance.

Nature adapts each plant to a particular habitat and niche. Trees reach their arching limbs toward the sky, shrubs fill the spaces beneath the trees, and grasses and herbs cover the ground. In between twine the vines. Many vines cling to their support with tendrils; some twist and twine around other objects; others cling with holdfasts.

Vines have other natural features that make them extraordinary landscaping plants. Adapted to growing in the dappled shadows beneath tree limbs, most vines can tolerate both partial shade and full sun. They grow vigorously and are hardy, and many have ornamental foliage, flowers, and fruit. Wherever vines grow, they add natural beauty and visual interest.

Before buying a plant or turning a shovel of soil, you should determine how a vine will best fit into your yard. Do you want a dominant feature, a dense groundcover, or a graceful accent? Low-growing vines with slender stems provide a delicate touch, while high-climbing or thickly branching species rapidly become a major landscape element. Let's see how these special plants can beautify your landscape.

VINES AS DOMINANT FEATURES

Wire fences and rock or masonry walls can support vigorously growing, densely foliated vines such as Carolina jessamine and cross vine. The thick evergreen foliage turns an ordinary wire fence into an extraordinary privacy hedge covered with flamboyant yellow flowers in the spring. If you want scarlet spring and summer flowers, plant coral honeysuckle, or try a mixture of the three for variety. You can enjoy brilliant shades of red and orange in the autumn by planting a Virginia creeper along your fence or on an arbor. A slender stemmed vine with dense foliage can turn a gaslight, a mailbox, or even an unsightly old stump into a prominent landscape feature in your yard. However, most vines will overrun their supports if not pruned periodically.

VINES AS ACCENT PLANTS

An accent vine should complement but not obscure the object supporting it. Low-climbing vines with thin foliage are good for this. They bring visual interest and gracefully accent a wire fence without obscuring the view. A rock, rail, or lath fence forms the perfect backdrop for slender climbers, such as the unusual passion flower. The small, delicate features of scarlet clematis complement mailboxes without overpowering them. A gaslight draped with the scarlet fruit of a Carolina snailseed becomes an eye-catching center of interest.

Don't forget that vines can work their magic on porch railings and columns, too. Vines quickly cover chicken wire or a guide wire wrapped around a post. Some of my earliest memories are of playing on our front porch, shaded by a screen of jasmine growing on chicken wire stretched from the ground to the porch roof.

CUSTOMIZE YOUR LANDSCAPE

The next step after determining whether you need a dominant or accent planting is to choose the type of vine. Do you want a woody or herbaceous species, one with evergreen or deciduous leaves, or one with colorful flowers or fruit? For privacy and screen plantings, you'll want evergreens. In most other applications, deciduous and evergreen vines work equally well. Woody vines will densely cover a fence, porch column, or trellis. The high-climbing species, such as trumpet creepers, develop thick, heavy branches and should be used only on fences or posts that provide adequate support. Most low climbers have slender twining branches that will not damage lath fences or trellises and that are easier to contain. Herbaceous perennial vines grow rapidly during the spring and summer and die back to the ground with the first freeze. The root stock survives the winter and sprouts in the spring.

PLANTING

Like any landscape addition, vines require careful planning and selection. For a dense cover along a fence, plant a high-climbing vine with thick foliage every eight to twelve feet and low-climbing vines with slender stems every three to four feet. For variety, plant one section of your fence with a spring-blooming species and another with a summer or fall bloomer. Twining vines and those with tendrils quickly climb on fences, trellises, and guide wires around posts, while those with holdfasts climb well on rock and masonry. Avoid letting vines cover wooden buildings. They hasten decay and must be removed or destroyed when the surface requires painting.

Nurseries offer a wide selection of woody vines, and you can choose herbaceous varieties from seed stores and catalogs, or gather your own seeds. Each vine listed in this book has flamboyant flowers, ornamental foliage, or colorful fruit and will provide generations of beauty in your yard. So, plant a vine and watch it twine!

Cross Vine

Cross Vine, *Bignonia capreolata*

NATIVE DISTRIBUTION: moist woods, East Texas to Florida, Illinois to Virginia

LANDSCAPE ZONE: 2, 4–10.

GROWTH: climbing to 60 feet; tendrils, holdfasts.

Woody perennial.

LEAVES: evergreen.

FLOWER: March–May, 2 inches, funnelshaped, yellow to red.

SOIL: adaptable, poor to well draining.

EXPOSURE: partial shade, full sun.

TEMPERATURE TOLERANCE: cold hardy.

WATER: moderately drought tolerant.

PROPAGATION: seeds, softwood cuttings, root suckers.

Unlike some high-climbing natives, cross vine has slender, pencil-sized stems and is easy to control. Its small stems make it perfect for trellises and fences. Holdfasts allow it to climb posts and masonry without support wiring. For a thick cover along a fence, set plants about 5 feet apart. With evergreen leaves and clusters of red and yellow multicolored flowers, it will provide year-round color for your landscape. This forest vine does well in shade, though it needs some sun to bloom. Though it spreads by root suckers, cross vine is well mannered and not particularly aggressive.

Trumpet Creeper

Blue Jasmine

Western Virgin's Bower

Trumpet Creeper, *Campsis radicans*

NATIVE DISTRIBUTION: forests and edges of woods, eastern half of Texas to Florida, north to Canada.

LANDSCAPE ZONE: 2, 4–10.

GROWTH: climbing to 40 feet; holdfasts, tendrils.

Woody perennial.

LEAVES: deciduous.

FLOWER: May–October, 3 inches, trumpet shaped, orange; fruit a 6-inch cylindrical capsule.

SOIL: adaptable, well draining.

EXPOSURE: full sun, partial shade.

TEMPERATURE TOLERANCE: cold hardy.

WATER: moderately drought tolerant.

PROPAGATION: seeds, root suckers.

This vine does everything vines are supposed to, and better than you might wish for your yard. It grows fast, climbs high on every conceivable object, develops a dense cover of heavy, stout stems and foliage, and spreads by suckering. But you have to agree with the hummingbirds that its profuse clusters of flaming orangeish red flowers are attractive. If you have a back fence or neglected area that needs some enhancement, plant this robust, hardy vine, but keep it off buildings.

It freezes to the ground in hard winters and appreciates extra summer water west of its native range. Several horticultural varieties are available, some smaller and some with different shades of flowers.

* * *

Blue Jasmine or Curly Clematis, *Clematis crispa*

NATIVE DISTRIBUTION: wet soils, stream banks, East Texas to Austin, east to Florida, Missouri to Virginia.

LANDSCAPE ZONE: 7, 8.

GROWTH: climbing to 10 feet; twining leaf stalk.

Herbaceous perennial.

FLOWER: April–August, 1–2 inches, rose to violet.

SOIL: sand, clay, loam, poor draining.

EXPOSURE: partial shade.

TEMPERATURE TOLERANCE: cold hardy, freezes back.

WATER: requires regular moisture.

PROPAGATION: fresh seeds, softwood cuttings.

Use this slender vine where you need a delicate accent. Its foliage won't attract much attention, but the purple bell-shaped blooms will. The edges of the unusual flowers curl back, revealing scalloped edges. This low climber needs a wire or trellis for its twining leaves to cling to, and it won't climb very high above your head. It dies back to the ground in the winter, but recovers and blooms quickly in the spring.

* * *

Western Virgin's Bower, *Clematis ligusticifolia*

NATIVE DISTRIBUTION: moist soils, roadsides, thickets, woods, 3000–8500 feet, New Mexico to California, north to Canada.

LANDSCAPE ZONE: 2, 9, 10.

GROWTH: climbing to 20 feet; twining leaf stalk.

Herbaceous perennial.

FLOWER: May–September, clusters of ½-inch white flowers; feathery seed heads on female plants.

SOIL: adaptable, well draining.

EXPOSURE: full sun, partial shade.

TEMPERATURE TOLERANCE: cold hardy, freezes back.

WATER: drought tolerant.

PROPAGATION: fresh seeds, semisoftwood cuttings.

This vigorously growing vine will quickly cover a lattice shading your porch or patio or sprawl across an open slope. Plant it on a fence or trellis to shade your windows or air-conditioning unit in the summer. The dense flower clusters attract an abundance of bees and other insects, and the female plants have showy, feathery seed heads. Though it dies back in the winter, it's hard to eradicate once established. It prefers moist soil, but at the Grand Canyon I saw one with luxuriant foliage covering at least 30 square feet when it hadn't rained in six months. A similar species, old man's beard, *Clematis drummondii*, also has feathery seeds, but has nondescript flowers and is nearly impossible to eliminate.

Scarlet Clematis

Scarlet Clematis, *Clematis texensis*

NATIVE DISTRIBUTION: bottomland soils, Central and South Texas.

LANDSCAPE ZONE: 2, 4, 6, 7.

GROWTH: climbing to 10 feet; twining leaf stalks.

Herbaceous perennial.

FLOWER: March–July, 1 inch, pitcher shaped, red.

SOIL: adaptable, well draining.

EXPOSURE: partial shade, full shade.

TEMPERATURE TOLERANCE: cold hardy, freezes back.

WATER: moderately drought tolerant.

PROPAGATION: fresh seeds, softwood cuttings.

Native to Texas, but listed in ornamental plant journals since the 1920s, this delicate vine has brilliant red flowers. The leathery blooms dangle like ornaments from the slender vine and will gaily decorate a fence or trellis. It's a shade lover, so don't plant it in a parched location. Mulching will help keep the roots cool in hot climates. Like all clematis, it needs a support for the leaf stalks to twist around. It dies to the ground in the winter. A related species, *Clematis pitcheri*, has blue flowers. It grows from Central Texas to Nebraska and is cold hardy enough for Zones 5 and 9.

Carolina Snailseed

Carolina Snailseed or Moonseed, *Cocculus carolinus*

NATIVE DISTRIBUTION: rich soils, woods, eastern half of Texas to Florida, north to Kansas, Virginia.

LANDSCAPE ZONE: 4–8.

GROWTH: climbing to 10 feet; tendrils.

Herbaceous perennial.

FRUIT: fall, dangling cluster of scarlet drupes.

SOIL: adaptable, well draining.

TEMPERATURE TOLERANCE: cold hardy, freezes back.

EXPOSURE: full sun, partial shade.

WATER: moderately drought tolerant.

PROPAGATION: seeds.

Plant this low-climbing vine for brilliant fall color. By September, beautiful 6-inch clusters of shiny red fruit dangle artistically from the slender stems. From spring to winter, attractive heart-shaped leaves cover this delicate vine, giving it almost year-round color. The dark green leaves and conspicuous fruit make a picturesque accent for a mailbox or wooden fence. It looks best when the fruit can hang freely in space. The fruits are toxic to humans, but birds eat them readily. The vine dies to the ground in the winter.

Carolina Jessamine

Carolina Jessamine, *Gelsemium sempervirens*

NATIVE DISTRIBUTION: moist sandy soils, open woods, East Texas to Florida, north to Virginia; Mexico.

LANDSCAPE ZONE: 1–8.

GROWTH: high climbing to 20 feet; twining.

Woody perennial.

LEAVES: evergreen.

FLOWER: February–April, 1–1½ inch, funnel shaped, yellow.

SOIL: adaptable, poor to well draining.

EXPOSURE: full sun, partial shade.

TEMPERATURE TOLERANCE: cold hardy.

WATER: drought tolerant.

PROPAGATION: cuttings.

This vine has twisted its way around the hearts of landscapers throughout the South and West. It's evergreen, is robust but easy to contain, and has spectacular flowers; what more could you want? Give it a trellis or wire lattice to cover, and you'll get a stunning curtain of dark green foliage with masses of bright lemon yellow flowers. It will twine around lamp posts and fences or make a dense groundcover to 3 feet high. If necessary, you can trim it or even prune it back severely. You can grow it anywhere with a mild winter; but in arid climates, it will need supplemental water. The flowers and leaves are poisonous.

Balsam Gourd

Coral Honeysuckle

Snapdragon Vine

Balsam Gourd, *Ibervillea lindheimeri* (includes *I. tenuisecta*)

NATIVE DISTRIBUTION: rocky hills, dry woods, thickets, Central Texas west through southern New Mexico and southeastern Arizona; Oklahoma; Mexico.

LANDSCAPE ZONE: 1–7.

GROWTH: low climbing, tendrils.

Herbaceous perennial.

FLOWER: April–September, ½ inch, yellow; fruit showy 1–2-inch globe, bright orange to red.

SOIL: adaptable, well draining.

EXPOSURE: partial shade, full sun.

TEMPERATURE TOLERANCE: freezes back.

WATER: drought tolerant.

PROPAGATION: fresh seeds.

You will hardly give this delicate low climber a second glance until it begins to fruit. Then brilliant reddish orange balls dangle from the slender stems like Christmas ornaments. The tiny picturesque gourds colorfully accent a wire fence, patio lattice, or lamp post. The dark green lobed leaves are scattered along the branching stems, giving the vine a dainty appearance. You don't have to worry about it getting out of hand because it dies to the ground in the winter. The thin-skinned fleshy fruit is not edible.

Coral Honeysuckle, *Lonicera sempervirens*

NATIVE DISTRIBUTION: East Texas to Florida, north to Maine, Nebraska.

LANDSCAPE ZONE: 2, 4–10.

GROWTH: shrubby.

Woody perennial.

LEAVES: evergreen.

FLOWER: throughout year, mostly spring, summer; clusters of 1–2-inch-long trumpet-shaped red flowers.

SOIL: adaptable, well draining.

EXPOSURE: partial shade, full sun.

TEMPERATURE TOLERANCE: cold hardy.

WATER: moderately drought tolerant.

PROPAGATION: fresh seeds, softwood or semihardwood cuttings.

Unlike its Japanese relative, this native honeysuckle is well mannered and never trespasses. Give it some type of support and it will form a dense, low-climbing shrubby plant. Clusters of flamboyant scarlet flowers contrast the round evergreen leaves throughout most of the year, making this an eye-catching addition to your yard. You can plant it along a fence at about 4- to 6-foot intervals for a visual barrier, or let it sprawl over an open area as a groundcover. I used mine to surround a utility pole, and in two years it was a rounded mass about 5 feet high. In the West, try to find its close relative, Arizona honeysuckle, *Lonicera arizonica*, which grows at 6000- to 9000-foot elevations.

* * *

Snapdragon Vine, *Maurandya antirrhiniflora*

NATIVE DISTRIBUTION: sandy soils, limestone hills, South, Central, West Texas; central, southern New Mexico and most of Arizona at 1500–7000-foot elevations; California; Mexico.

LANDSCAPE ZONE: 1–10.

GROWTH: low climbing; twining.

Herbaceous perennial.

LEAVES: evergreen unless frozen.

FLOWER: February–October, 1 inch, purple to pink.

SOIL: adaptable, well draining.

EXPOSURE: partial shade, sun.

TEMPERATURE TOLERANCE: freezes back.

WATER: drought tolerant.

PROPAGATION: seeds.

This prostrate to low-climbing vine has a jumble of slender, tangled stems, small leaves, and a few flowers blooming all the time – nothing glamorous, but definitely interesting, especially the unusual flowers. Each petite bloom has two brightly colored "lips" and a creamy yellow "throat." To best show off the subtle beauty of this vine, let it dangle over a rock border, out of a crevice, or on a slope beneath a shrub. It reseeds itself readily, even in cold climates where it grows as an annual. Another western species, *Maurandya wislizenii*, has very similar flowers.

Virginia Creeper

Passion Flower

Virginia Creeper, *Parthenocissus quinquefolia*
Thicket Creeper or Woodbine, *Parthenocissus inserta (P. vitacea)*

NATIVE DISTRIBUTION: *P. quinquefolia*: woods, bottomlands, eastern half Texas to Florida, eastern United States. *P. inserta*: West Texas to California, 3000–8000 feet; north to Canada.

LANDSCAPE ZONE: 1–10.

GROWTH: high climbing; tendrils.

Woody perennial.

LEAVES: deciduous, brilliant fall reds, oranges.

FRUIT: fall, blue berries, poisonous.

SOIL: adaptable, well draining.

EXPOSURE: full sun, partial shade, shade.

TEMPERATURE TOLERANCE: cold hardy.

WATER: moderately drought tolerant.

PROPAGATION: fresh seeds, cuttings.

Plant a robust creeper vine where it can climb unchallenged. It has dense foliage with five leaflets and will rapidly cover masonry, a fence, or a trellis with a luxuriant growth. The thick layer of leaves provides an insulating dead-air space against a building and in the fall paints it with brilliant shades of red, orange, and burgundy. You also can use these vigorous growers as groundcovers, if you keep them trimmed off trees and shrubs. The main difference between the eastern and western species is that woodbine does not have invasive adhesive tips on its tendrils, needs more sun, and is less aggressive. Don't let either species become established on wooden structures that need periodic painting.

Passion Flower or Maypop, *Passiflora incarnata*

NATIVE DISTRIBUTION: fields, edges of woods, along streams, East Texas to Florida, north to Missouri; Bermuda.

LANDSCAPE ZONE: 1–10.

GROWTH: low climbing, tendrils.

Herbaceous perennial.

FLOWER: April–August, 2–3 inches in diameter, lavender; fruit 2 inches long, yellow to orange.

SOIL: adaptable, well draining.

TEMPERATURE TOLERANCE: freezes back.

EXPOSURE: partial shade, full sun.

WATER: drought tolerant.

PROPAGATION: fresh seeds.

The creative force of nature will amaze you when you see the intricate flowers of this vine. The branching stamen surrounded by delicate petals and a lacy threadlike crown look more like products of the plastic-flower section of a discount store than a native wildflower. But they're real — and a guaranteed attention grabber. And when the flowers fade, they produce an equally ornate, brightly colored fruit. Let your passion flower decorate a porch side, patio trellis, or wooden fence, or let it climb wantonly into a low shrub for a woodsy effect. The juicy flesh around the seeds is edible. This vine spreads by root runners, but dies back in the winter. *Passiflora foetida*, a similar species with a smaller flower, grows from South Texas to southern Arizona and will thrive in climates with mild winters. Numerous tropical passion vines are also sold in the nursery trade.

CACTUS GARDENING

As the first European botanists crisscrossed the Americas, they discovered a bizarre family of plants unknown in the Old World. Unsure of the classification, they applied the Greek word *kaktos*, meaning "thistle." Modern botanists still argue about the proper organization of these puzzling plants. But one thing is constant: from the fifteenth century until the present, plant enthusiasts have found these unique plants irresistible. The demand for cacti was immediate and has increased through the centuries. Today, collectors annually strip tons of cacti from our deserts to sell in souvenir shops and nurseries. With many species now either threatened or endangered, we literally are loving our native cacti to death. Fortunately, many cacti propagated from seeds and cuttings are available in the nursery trade. As a point of principle, be sure the cactus you buy wasn't collected from the countryside. Our native plants belong in nature, too.

HANDLE WITH CARE

Cacti look tough, feel tough, and grow in a harsh environment, but they need tender care to survive in rock gardens. You see, cacti are specialists. They have adapted to marginal conditions with extremes of heat, light, and drought. Though cacti grow from fourteen-thousand-foot mountain peaks to torrid desert basins, most suffer if moved far from home. Many species have become so specialized to local conditions that they exist only in a single desert valley or on a particular geological outcropping. If you want your cacti to thrive, you must know what makes them different from other landscape plants; otherwise, you may inadvertently kill them with kindness.

Cacti have drastically modified leaves, stems, and roots to catch, store, and conserve water in a desert environment. A netlike root system spreads out and rapidly soaks up moisture from fickle but usually torrential rains. To combat extended droughts, thick succulent stems store water for long periods. Instead of normal leaves, which lose considerable water, cactus leaves have evolved into rigid spines. This dense armament both shades and cools the plant and protects the succulent interior from thirsty desert creatures. With no leaves for photosynthesis, the green stems perform the task of food production. A thick, waxy epidermis covers cacti to further reduce water loss. Some cacti are so well adapted to their arid habitat that they transpire six thousand times less water than ordinary plants. As a result of this reduced transpiration, many cacti grow at an extremely slow rate.

OVERWATERING: THE KISS OF DEATH

Cacti roots soak up water as fast as possible, and the stems store and hold water as tenaciously as possible. In your garden, you want to find the magic line between watering enough to maximize growth and flowering, and overwatering, which can kill some cacti overnight. A root crown standing in water for twenty-four hours is susceptible to root rot and fungus invasion. A well-draining pot or garden is an absolute must. In the winter some cacti lose water to protect against frost and may appear shriveled. Don't water a wilted cactus unless you know the plant is stressed for water. The plant is probably just adapting to the overall environmental conditions. In Texas we have a saying, "Don't water your cactus until it rains in Presidio." Substitute Phoenix if you live in Arizona, and your cacti will feel right at home.

Having the right soil mix for potted cacti or in a rock garden is necessary for success. Potted cacti do well in a neutral soil, with an inch or so of granite gravel on the bottom for good drainage, then several inches of garden potting soil. Fill the remainder of the pot with coarse sand. For gardens, mix sand in with your garden soil if necessary to ensure proper drainage, and plant each cactus on a slightly elevated mound. Be sure your garden doesn't get regular runoff from lawn irrigation. Most of all, pay attention to the natural habitat of the cactus. Some species grow under desert shrubs and benefit from some added leaf mulch. Before transplanting a cactus or cutting, let it sit bare-rooted in a shady location for several days until the roots have thoroughly dried and calloused. Fungus easily invades fresh cuts or damaged roots.

LIGHT IS RIGHT

To bloom, cacti need heat and light. Many cacti do not begin photosynthesis until the temperature exceeds 75 degrees F. Your garden should receive more than a half-day of full sunlight to stimulate flowering and growth. The delicate flowers typically burst into bloom during the heat of the day, and many wither by nightfall. Both the spectacular flowers and the short blooming period represent adaptations that help the flower win a race against time. To ensure pollination, the flower must attract insects, thus the showy blossoms. Insects are active when the day is hottest, so the fragile flowers open in the afternoon. A bloom unpollinated during its first day may never get another chance. Many of the unprotected flowers become tidbits for the hungry critters active during the cool of the night. Night-blooming cacti, such as saguaro, usually have flowers on tall stems, out of reach of small herbivores.

When your cacti burst into bloom, you can feel a sense of satisfaction for two reasons. First, the ephemeral flowers add a flamboyant, yet delicate, beauty to your yard. Second, you know that your garden duplicates the plant's environmental requirements closely enough for it not just to survive, but to thrive and bloom.

Saguaro, *Carnegiea gigantea*

NATIVE DISTRIBUTION: rocky foothills, plains, and washes, 600–3500 feet, southwestern Arizona desert; Mexico.

LANDSCAPE ZONE: 1, 3.

SIZE: 20–50 feet.

FLOWER: spring, 3–4 inches, white; fruit red to purple, 2–4 inches long, edible.

SOIL: rocky, well draining.

EXPOSURE: full sun.

WATER: 8 inches/year.

PROPAGATION: seeds.

The saguaro is probably the best-known cactus in the United States. It's illustrated in practically every elementary science textbook. Though synonymous with the Southwest in the minds of many Americans, saguaros grow only in a limited portion of the Sonoran Desert. If you live in the desert, you can have one in your yard. But you'll have to grow it yourself unless you have a few thousand dollars to spend, with no guarantee of a successful transplant. Nurseries price them by the size and number of arms. A large specimen weighs tons and needs guy wires for support until the anchor roots become established. If the taproot is damaged, the plant will slowly die, though it may take years before you know it. Rigid laws control collecting of saguaros from the wild, but seedlings are readily available. Don't plant one in sandy soil, or it will topple over some day. As with most cacti, water is a saguaro's worst enemy, so avoid lawn or irrigated locations. In the right habitat, a saguaro can grow as much as a foot per year — or as little as an inch.

Saguaro

Strawberry Cactus

Rainbow Hedgehog

Claret Cup Cactus

Barrel Cactus

Strawberry Cactus or Hedgehog, *Echinocereus engelmannii* (*Echinocereus stramineus*)

NATIVE DISTRIBUTION: deserts, West Texas to Arizona; western United States; Mexico.

LANDSCAPE ZONE: 1–4, 6.

SIZE: 10-inch stems forming a mound 2–3-feet in diameter.

FLOWER: spring, 3–4 inches, red; fruit 1–2 inches long, red to purple, spiny, edible.

SOIL: sandy, rocky, well draining.

EXPOSURE: full sun.

PROPAGATION: seeds.

You'll run for your camera when the flamboyant red flowers of this cactus begin blooming. The spectacular blossoms will be the focal point of your rock garden, especially if you have a very large mound. And when the fruit matures, you'll know why they're called strawberry cacti, but you'll have to fight your way through the dense spines protecting the succulent fruit. When planting this cactus, be sure its roots will never be waterlogged, or it will rot. About seven species and numerous varieties of strawberry hedgehogs grow throughout the Southwest, all with gorgeous bright red flowers. For the best results, buy one propagated from a local species.

Rainbow Hedgehog or Pitaya, *Echinocereus pectinatus* (*E. dasyacanthus*)

NATIVE DISTRIBUTION: limestone hills and desert grasslands throughout the Southwest.

LANDSCAPE ZONE: 1–4, 6.

SIZE: 4–12-inch cylindrical stem.

FLOWER: spring–summer, 2–5 inches, magenta or yellow; fruit greenish, 1–2 inches long.

SOIL: sandy, rocky, well draining.

EXPOSURE: full sun.

PROPAGATION: seeds.

A dense lacelike mat of spines covers the stems of this cactus, making it a fine-textured accent for your rock garden. The stems often form small branches and grow in a loosely clumped cluster. The large, brilliantly colored flowers, which later develop into fruit, seem totally out of place on the spiny arms. The flamboyant flowers vary from pink to lavender, giving this cactus its common name, "rainbow cactus." Of the several varieties, *neomexicanus* has bright yellow flowers and is common in the Trans-Pecos of Texas and in southeastern New Mexico.

Claret Cup Cactus or Hedgehog, *Echinocereus triglochidiatus*

NATIVE DISTRIBUTION: hills and mountains from Central and West Texas through New Mexico and Arizona at 3000–8000 feet; western United States; Mexico.

LANDSCAPE ZONE: 1–6, 9.

SIZE: 1-foot stems forming a mound 1–4 feet in diameter.

FLOWER: spring, summer, 1–2 inch, scarlet; fruit spiny, red.

SOIL: sandy, igneous, rich in humus, well draining.

EXPOSURE: full sun.

WATER: drought tolerant.

PROPAGATION: seeds.

This wide-ranging and highly variable species has confused botanists since it was first named in 1848. Experts can't decide whether it's one species with numerous varieties or multiple species. But they do agree that the waxy, long-lasting flowers are spectacular. With age, this cactus forms rounded mounds, a picturesque addition to your rock garden, especially when covered with scarlet blooms. Since some varieties are adapted to desert chaparral while others thrive in montane forests, try to buy one propagated from a locally indigenous plant. They normally grow in humus-rich soil, so plant them in well-draining leaf mold.

Barrel Cactus, *Ferocactus* species

NATIVE DISTRIBUTION: about six species in the Southwest deserts.

LANDSCAPE ZONE: 1–4, 6.

SIZE: unbranched cylindrical stems to 10 feet tall.

FLOWER: spring, summer, yellow to orange, 1–3 inches; mature fruit yellow, 1–2 inches long.

SOIL: gravelly, sandy, well draining.

EXPOSURE: full sun.

PROPAGATION: seeds.

Barrel cactus provides a medium-height accent between the taller chollas and prickly pears and the smaller hedgehogs and pincushions. A half dozen or more of the red to tangerine to yellow flowers bloom at once in a circle around the tip of the stem, followed by yellow, barrel-shaped fruit. Heavy, sometimes hooked, spines cover the stem to protect its succulent flesh from the thirsty predators of the desert. The dense cover of spines of some species gives the cactus a yellow or reddish color. The golden barrel cactus from Mexico is popular in cactus nurseries.

Pincushion Cactus

Tree Cholla

Pincushion Cactus, *Mammillaria* species

NATIVE DISTRIBUTION: about fourteen species in Southwest deserts.

LANDSCAPE ZONE: 1–4, 6.

SIZE: 1–8 inches in diameter.

FLOWER: spring, summer, white, ¼–1 inches, in circle around top; fruit ¼–1 inch, fleshy, red.

SOIL: gravelly, sandy, limestone; well draining.

EXPOSURE: full sun.

PROPAGATION: seeds.

Mammillarias, many from Central and South America, are some of the most popular cacti available in the nursery trade. Numerous species grow throughout the Southwest. The creamy flowers blooming on the round, un-branched stems form a circle around the apex, with as many as a dozen opening at the same time. A layer of red fruit usually surrounds the new blooms, adding bright color to the arrangement. Some pincushion cacti are golf ball-sized, while others grow to almost a foot in diameter. The name *mammillaria* comes from the nipple-shaped tubercles covering the stem. If you like the idea of your rock garden representing native species, buy cactus propagated from pincushions indigenous to your area.

Tree Cholla, *Opuntia imbricata*

NATIVE DISTRIBUTION: desert grass-lands, plains, from Kansas and Colorado south through western half of Texas, New Mexico, and southern Arizona; Mexico.

LANDSCAPE ZONE: 1–6, 9.

SIZE: 3–8 feet tall.

FLOWER: spring–summer, 2–3 inches, red-dish purple; fruit, yellow, 1–2 inches long.

SOIL: sandy, gravelly, well draining.

EXPOSURE: full sun.

PROPAGATION: scarified seeds, stem division.

You'll probably never find a very large cholla in a nursery; they're just too thorny to handle. To grow one, simply stick a stem joint in the ground and stand back. The intricately branching stems look like braided ropes, with each section ready to break off and hang onto any unfortunate passerby; then it roots where it drops. In the spring, showy red flowers crown the tips of the canelike stems. The size of this cactus makes it a good focal plant for your rock garden. Teddy bear cholla, *Opuntia bigelovii*, common around Phoenix and Tucson, has a more ornate appearance due to its dense array of viciously barbed thorns. Its flowers are about half the size of tree cholla's. Other species of cholla with similar landscape applications are also available.

Violet Prickly Pear

Violet Prickly Pear, *Opuntia violacea (O. macrocentra)*

NATIVE DISTRIBUTION: desert grass-lands, 3000–5000 feet, West Texas through southern New Mexico and Arizona; Mexico.

LANDSCAPE ZONE: 1–4, 6.

SIZE: 3–7 feet tall.

FLOWER: spring–summer, 2–4 inches, yellow; summer, fall, fruit 1–2 inches long, purple to red, edible.

SOIL: sandy, gravelly, well draining.

EXPOSURE: full sun.

PROPAGATION: scarified seeds, stem division.

The red-tinged pads distinguish this cactus from the many other species of prickly pears common throughout the Southwest. During the winter or extreme droughts, the 4- to 8-inch roundish pads turn a maroon red, pro-viding a striking accent for your otherwise dormant cactus garden. In the spring, the cac-tus comes to life, with yellow roselike flowers lining the spiny pads. Not all varieties have the 4- to 7-inch-long spines of the Texas specimen illustrated. The others have 1½- to 2½-inch thorns. Prickly pear pads root easily and grow rapidly when placed in loose, well-draining soil. Englemann prickly pear, *Opuntia engelmannii*, is a widespread related species usually available.

LANDSCAPING WITH WILDFLOWERS

PAINT YOUR YARD WITH WILDFLOWERS

Nature seems to defy the logic of every conscientious gardener. Beautiful flower beds are the result of laborious hours of fertilizing, of fighting weeds, disease, and vermin, and of carefully mulching and watering the tender seedlings. Yet without a gardener's care, patches of undisturbed ground across the countryside abound with a luxurious growth of wildflowers from early spring into the fall.

The beauty radiating from nature's helter-skelter flower arrangements inspires every flower lover. Like magic, the stony hills, open prairies, and deep woodlands burst forth with flower displays that make the most expert gardener envious. What a treat if we could have those unspoiled scenes of nature duplicated in our own yards!

Though you use the same gardening techniques for growing both domestic and native flowers, cultivating wildflowers is a dimension removed from formal flower gardening. The standard green-thumb skills and intuition are needed, as well as the ability to recognize the unique growing conditions that enable each species of wildflower to thrive. Traditionally, growers boast of their flower "gardens," but the wildflower enthusiast will want to show you his or her newly created wildflower "habitat."

The first step in cultivating wildflowers is to analyze the growing conditions in your garden area. Carefully scrutinize soil, light, and moisture conditions. What was the habitat before houses modified the environment? Don't expect moist woodland species to thrive on a sand-filled lawn.

Each species of wildflower grows within a certain range of environmental conditions. These conditions — the soil pH, texture, and composition, the slope, exposure, and moisture — define the flower's optimum habitat. The gardener must duplicate the natural conditions as closely as possible if the favored plant is to grow successfully in the home plot.

The wildflower aficionado, before burying a seed or digging a plant, becomes well acquainted with the flower's needs. A little homework will avoid the oft-repeated mistake, and resulting disappointment, of planting a shade-loving plant in full sunlight, or one requiring moisture and humidity in a hot, dry exposure. Choosing the species of wildflowers for your yard should receive as much consideration as planning the most formal landscape.

Perhaps you can create several micro-habitats within your yard. An open lawn is ideal for sun-adapted plants, a tree-shaded corner for shade-tolerant species, or an enclosed entryway for moisture-loving flowers.

BEAUTY COMES IN SMALL PACKAGES

The quickest way of stocking your garden is by purchasing seeds, seedlings, or plants from a nursery. If this is your preferred course, beware of spectacular offers in almanacs and Sunday supplements. Avoid seed packs with general mixes of wildflowers. They usually contain incompatible shade- and sun-loving plants. Many native seed sources offer mixes specifically designed for the different regions in the Southwest. For instance, you can buy mixes for the low desert, high desert, shady mountain meadow, high plains, and for Texas.

Enticing offers of orchids, sundews, and Venus's-flytraps often offer plants dug from the wild, depleting the woodlands of nature's rarest treasures. They invariably die after one season since they are adapted only to the soil and climate of the moist eastern woodlands. If possible, purchase plants and seeds from a native-plant nursery in your area. Since they collect local seeds, you can be assured that their stock is adapted to your climate.

SEED COLLECTING

Many wildflower lovers are not content with buying prepackaged seeds. Obtaining seeds and plants for your carefully prepared garden can be a year-round hobby. Discovering a specimen flower, marking it, and returning to collect the seeds adds to the sense of accomplishment of a successful garden. The timing of seed harvesting is critical, or the collector may find an empty seed pod on the prized flower. Remember, collecting the plants themselves on public property, including roadsides, is illegal.

Many flowers have elaborate methods for dispersing their seeds. Numerous composites, members of the sunflower family, send their seeds floating in the breeze, while the dry pods of legumes split open, scattering their seeds on the ground. You can either pick the ripe pods and heads before they completely dry or place a muslin or paper sack over the flowers after the seeds have formed. Dry the seeds completely before storing them so they won't mold. Some seeds have succulent pulp that must be removed by rubbing on a screen. Sometimes you can clean small seeds in a blender at very low speed without damaging them.

Store the cleaned seeds in the refrigerator in jars, or in a cool, dry place safe from insects. Keep seeds in paper bags, not plastic, to prevent molding, and plant within one year for best results.

Plants adapt to winter freezes by producing seeds that go through a dormant period. This prevents premature germination on warm fall days. After several months of cold weather, the inherent dormancy is broken, allowing the seeds to germinate as the soil warms up to 40 degrees F. If you obtain seeds in the early spring, you can break the temperature dormancy by storing them in the refrigerator for two to eight weeks before planting.

WHEN TO PLANT
Wildflowers naturally reseed themselves several weeks after blooming, in the spring for early-blooming species and in summer or fall for late bloomers. Generally, you will want to plant your seeds from late August through November, depending on your elevation and the onset of hard winter. This allows the winter temperatures to break any seed dormancy. Other seeds need the fall rains to germinate, winter moisture to develop a root system, and spring rains to bloom.

SOWING THE SEED
First, prepare a seedbed. Indiscriminately scattering seed is just setting the table for seed-eating insects and birds. Remove all vegetation just as you would when planting a vegetable garden. Rake the soil to break up the surface no more than an inch deep. Since some wildflower seeds are so small, you might want to mix your seeds with damp sand to give a more even distribution. After evenly scattering the seeds, lightly rake them into the soil, no deeper than two to four times their diameter. Firm up the soil and lightly water.

WATERING AND WAITING
All seeds need water to germinate, so water lightly three to four times a week to ensure optimum germination. If there are no fall rains, water the seedlings and the seedbed weekly until the first freeze, then again in December and January. This will ensure that spring-germinating seeds get sufficient moisture. If you have a dry spring, supplemental watering will provide for optimum growth and blooming.

You may want to plant your seeds in a protected seedbed, cold frame, or peat pots and wait until the seedlings are well established before transplanting to your garden. You can start many species indoors from January to March, or four to six weeks before they are to be transplanted.

NATURAL RESEEDING
Though annuals live only one growing season, and many perennials only a few, you can have a beautiful wildflower garden year after year by letting the flowers reseed themselves. After the flowers fade and the plants die, be sure to wait until the seeds have fallen before mowing or removing the old plant. Give the plants a good shake to dislodge all the seeds. If you have a naturalized area, leave the mowed stubble to cover and protect the seeds.

If you want a more dependable display of wildflowers, plant perennials along with the annuals. Most perennial wildflowers are herbaceous and die to the ground in the winter, but sprout from the roots with the first warm weather. They add color and beauty and may even spread to form flamboyant blankets of color and mixed bouquets that get prettier as the years pass. As a bonus, many bloom until the first freeze.

PERENNIAL FLOWER GARDENS
Imagine a flower garden, bordering your walk, decorating the corner of your yard, or edging your pool, that greets each season with a profusion of different-colored blooms. As the seasons progress, you have a different combination of flowers, from early-spring bloomers to fall ones that don't fade until the first frost.

A perennial garden takes more forethought than just planting low flowers in the front and tall ones in the back. Half the fun is becoming the artist and arranging the blooming times and colors as though the garden were your canvas. Plant so you'll have a good balance of colors throughout the year. Use masses of each flower to create bold splashes, with adjacent colors complementing each other. Remember, your garden is a three-dimensional canvas. Mix naturally mounding plants with upright, sprawling, and cascading species so that one doesn't overrun another. Don't forget foliage color, either. You can combine various shades of grays and greens for a delightful variation of hues.

Place species with attractive foliage, like damianita, blackfoot daisy, and guayule, in the foreground, and for a year-round good appearance, use enough evergreens to cover the bare spots left when deciduous species die back. Planting a perennial wildflower isn't the same as planting a tree. Many perennials live only a few seasons, so your flower garden will need periodic maintenance. You'll need to thin and cut back vigorously growing flowers and occasionally replace some plants, but no major replanting will be necessary.

Amelia's Sand Verbena

Yarrow

Red Columbine

Golden Columbine

Amelia's Sand Verbena, *Abronia ameliae*

NATIVE DISTRIBUTION: sandy soils in Texas from the Panhandle to the Rio Grande, east to Houston.

LANDSCAPE ZONE: 1–8.

SIZE: 1–2 feet.

Perennial.

FLOWER: March–June, 3-inch round clusters of pink flowers.

SOIL: sand, well draining.

EXPOSURE: full sun.

WATER: drought tolerant.

PLANTING: fall, soak seeds overnight.

Give this flower plenty of room to sprawl, and it will cover a sandy area with brilliant balls of pink flowers. You can plant it in mass for a showy spring groundcover or in the foreground of a perennial garden. The fragrant flowers bloom on short stalks and vividly contrast the dark green heart-shaped to round leaves. Two other abronias are also available. Snowball, *Abronia fragrans*, has white blooms in late summer. In Phoenix and Tucson, plant sand verbena, *Abronia villosa*, a rose-colored annual that blooms from February to October if given ample water.

Yarrow or Milfoil, *Achillea millefolium*

NATIVE DISTRIBUTION: Eurasian native widely naturalized across United States.

LANDSCAPE ZONE: 1–10.

SIZE: 12–18 inches.

Perennial.

FLOWER: April–July, rounded cluster of white flowers.

SOIL: adaptable.

EXPOSURE: full sun, partial shade.

WATER: moderately drought tolerant.

PLANTING: fall-sown seed.

The rosette of delicate, fernlike leaves of yarrow looks like lace spread on the ground. In moist soil, it spreads by underground rhizomes and can form an attractive groundcover. From spring through the summer, a cluster of snowy flowers atop a slender stalk crowns the basal rosette. If you crush a leaf and smell the pungent volatile oils, you'll know why this is an historically important medicinal plant. You may want to add color to your flower garden by choosing a yellow- or rose-flowered variety. A related native, *Achillea lanulosa*, grows in the mountains of New Mexico and Arizona above 5000 feet. If you plant yarrows in full sun, they will need extra water.

Red Columbine, *Aquilegia canadensis*

NATIVE DISTRIBUTION: moist canyons and stream banks, Texas to Canada.

LANDSCAPE ZONE: 2–10.

SIZE: 1–3 feet.

Perennial.

FLOWER: March–May, red-tipped with yellow, 1½ inches with spur.

SOIL: moist, well draining.

EXPOSURE: shade, partial shade.

WATER: needs moisture.

PLANTING: fresh seed in fall, stratified seed in spring.

This moisture-loving plant is perfect for shady entryway gardens. Give it rich but well-draining soil, and enjoy the gorgeous flowers. In a flower bed in Austin, one was 3 feet high and wide, with scores of blooms. It's most dramatic when it cascades over an accent boulder, wall, or fountain similar to its natural habitat — porous boulders and seeping cliffs. The bell-shaped blooms, with long spurs, dangle from stalks above a rounded mound of light green foliage. The lacy leaves resemble maiden hair fern. The cliff columbine, *Aquilegia triternata*, closely resembles red columbine. Rocky Mountain columbine, *Aquilegia caerulea*, the state flower of Colorado, has beautiful blue and white flowers.

Golden Columbine, *Aquilegia chrysantha*

NATIVE DISTRIBUTION: moist soils in canyons and mountains above 3500 feet.

LANDSCAPE ZONE: 2–10.

SIZE: 1–3 feet.

Perennial.

FLOWER: April–September, yellow, 3–5 inches long with spur.

SOIL: sand, loam, well draining.

EXPOSURE: shade, partial shade.

WATER: needs moisture.

PLANTING: fresh seeds in fall, stratified seeds in spring.

Protect this delicate plant from full sun or arid locations, and you will marvel at the abundant golden flowers and fine-textured foliage. The flowers waving in the breeze seem to float on a cloud of light green leaves. Columbines make a colorful perennial border or accent plant tucked among rocks. At low elevations, be sure they get enough water in the summer or they will go dormant — or worse, die. However, high humidity and water-logged roots are just as deadly. Other native yellow columbines are sometimes available.

Butterfly Weed

Desert Marigold

Winecup

Butterfly Weed, *Asclepias tuberosa*

NATIVE DISTRIBUTION: prairies, open woods, mountains to 7000-foot elevations of the eastern half of the United States to New Mexico and Arizona.

LANDSCAPE ZONE: 1–10.

SIZE: 1–3 feet.

Perennial.

FLOWER: April–September, clusters of orange and red flowers.

SOIL: adaptable, well draining.

EXPOSURE: full sun, partial shade.

WATER: drought tolerant.

PLANTING: fall-sown seeds.

The brilliant clusters of multicolored flowers crowning the stout, waving stalks make butterfly weed an impressive background accent in your perennial garden. Or you can mass plant them in a corner plot or against a wall. I planted mine just outside my window so I could see the monarchs and other butterflies that flocked to the vivid blooms all summer. Mine bloomed the first year from seed, but others report that the plants spend several years developing their taproot before flowering. The deep taproot allows the plant to survive drought conditions, but it needs regular water to maintain flowers.

Desert Marigold, *Baileya multiradiata*

NATIVE DISTRIBUTION: sandy and gravelly desert soils, West Texas to California; Mexico.

LANDSCAPE ZONE: 1–6.

SIZE: 1½ feet.

Short-lived perennial.

FLOWER: anytime, 1–2-inch yellow daisy-like flower.

SOIL: adaptable, well draining.

EXPOSURE: full sun.

WATER: drought tolerant.

PLANTING: fall-sown seed.

This wildflower of the low deserts rivals the most pampered garden variety for beauty and showmanship. Its mound of lemon yellow flowers on 1- to 2-foot stems above the grayish green woolly leaves presents a striking color combination, especially in a cactus garden or mixed planting. The fall-sown seeds form a small basal rosette of leaves, with the bright bouquets of flowers appearing about three months after planting and continuing until frost. For profuse blooming, water weekly if rains fail. The flowers reseed themselves readily for year-round flowers in mild winters. In Texas they can be planted as far north and east as Abilene.

Winecup, *Callirhoe involucrata*

NATIVE DISTRIBUTION: sandy, gravelly soils, throughout Texas, north to North Dakota.

LANDSCAPE ZONE: 1–9.

Perennial.

SIZE: 1 foot high, 3-foot sprawling stems.

FLOWER: February–July, 2 inches, purple to red.

SOIL: adaptable, well draining.

EXPOSURE: full sun, partial shade.

WATER: drought tolerant.

PLANTING: fall-sown seed.

With water, this proficient bloomer will decorate your yard with bouquets of gorgeous flowers until the heat of summer burns it back. The dense array of sprawling stems makes a colorful groundcover or mass planting, or you can plant it to complement summer- and fall-blooming species such as dogweed, bluebell, gayfeather, penstemons, and blue flax. An accent patch will beautify your landscape island of shrubs, and it adds brilliant colors to a perennial border. Wherever you plant it, be sure to give it plenty of elbow room to spread. It overwinters as a small rosette of leaves.

Sego Lily

Blue Mist Flower

Sego Lily, *Calochortus nuttallii*
Mariposa Lily, *Calochortus kennedyi*

NATIVE DISTRIBUTION: *C. nuttallii*: open slopes, pine forests, 4500–8000 feet, New Mexico to California, north to Oregon, North Dakota, Nebraska. *C. kennedyi*: deserts and grasslands below 5000 feet, southern Arizona, California, Nevada; Mexico.

LANDSCAPE ZONE: *C. nuttallii*: 2, 9, 10; *C. kennedyi*: 1–3.

SIZE: 8–18 inches tall.

Perennial, bulb.

FLOWER: April–July, 2–3 inches wide, white, yellow, lavender, or orange.

SOIL: adaptable, well draining.

EXPOSURE: full sun.

WATER: drought tolerant.

PLANTING: fall-sown seeds; may take two years to bloom.

Numerous species of sego lilies grow throughout the Southwest, but these two are the most abundant. With such spectacular flowers, no wonder *Calochortus nuttallii* is the state flower of Utah. Its delicate blooms seem to burst from parched soils like jewels scattered across the countryside. The variety *aureus* has brilliant golden yellow flowers. The desert mariposa lily, *Calochortus kennedyi*, can cover the desert floor in April with rich orangish red blooms. Be sure you have perfect drainage, and then wait to be delighted when these treasures spring from the ground. For a gorgeous midspring display of colors, plant them with blackfoot daisy, paintbrush, blue flax, lupines, and spiderwort.

* * *

Indian Paintbrush, *Castilleja indivisa*

NATIVE DISTRIBUTION: sandy loam soils from the coastal and eastern half of Texas to Oklahoma.

LANDSCAPE ZONE: 1–4, 6–8.

SIZE: 6–12-inch-tall clumps.

Annual.

FLOWER: May–June, spike of showy red bracts enclosing small flowers.

SOIL: adaptable, well draining.

EXPOSURE: full sun.

WATER: drought tolerant.

PLANTING: fall-sown seeds.

Few sights in nature exceed the beauty of a hillside blanketed with paintbrushes and bluebonnets, each complementing and intensifying the vivid colors of the other. This annual paintbrush grows easily from seed in a mass planting or in your wildflower garden. The upright clump of blooming spikes make a colorful foreground or border plant for corner and courtyard gardens. Apparently, like some others of its genus, it is at least partially parasitic on grass roots, so it will feel right at home in a naturalized yard. Numerous species of paintbrushes grow across the Southwest, from the low deserts to mountain meadows, so try to find the species best adapted to your soil and climate. Most are perennial, difficult to establish from seed, and almost impossible to transplant from the wild. They are a major forage plant for many Southwestern hummingbirds.

* * *

Blue Mist Flower, *Conoclinium coelstinum (Eupatorium coelestinum)*

NATIVE DISTRIBUTION: moist woods, sandy streambanks, Central Texas to New Jersey, north to Kansas.

LANDSCAPE ZONE: 2, 4, 6–8.

SIZE: 1–3 feet tall.

Perennial.

FLOWER: July–November, purplish blue heads of ¼-inch flowers.

SOIL: adaptable, moist, well to poor draining.

EXPOSURE: partial shade, full sun.

WATER: requires regular moisture.

PLANTING: fall-sown seeds, spring-planted rhizomes.

This plant will feel right at home in a moist or poor-draining area in your yard. Its triangular light green leaves, dense upright to sprawling stems, and delicate flowers will accent foundation and entry gardens, borders, and the bases of shady trees and large shrubs. It spreads by underground roots, so you can divide the plant easily and establish new colonies. Don't let it get parched if you live in an arid climate.

Golden Wave

Sacred Datura

Golden Wave or Plains Coreopsis, *Coreopsis tinctoria*

NATIVE DISTRIBUTION: moist soils and roadsides, Louisiana to California, north to Canada.

LANDSCAPE ZONE: 1–10.

SIZE: 1–2 feet.

Annual.

FLOWER: February–December, 1-inch yellow head with reddish brown center.

SOIL: adaptable, well draining.

EXPOSURE: full sun.

WATER: drought tolerant.

PLANTING: early-spring-sown seed.

Mass plant this bright flower in a naturalized area and, as the name implies, you'll have waves of golden blooms dancing in the spring breezes. It flowers periodically after its spring burst of color, depending on the rains. It competes well with grasses and reseeds itself, making it a popular component of meadow mixes, along with bluebonnet, paintbrush, Indian blanket, lemon mint, black-eyed Susan, and Mexican hat. In dry areas, it might need supplemental water to sustain a long blooming season. Several varieties are available, including a dwarf, a red and yellow, and a double-flowered selection. If you want a long-lived perennial, plant lanceleaf coreopsis, *Coreopsis lanceolata.*

Sacred Datura or Jimsonweed, *Datura wrightii (Datura meteloides)*

NATIVE DISTRIBUTION: loose sand, bottomlands, East Texas to California; Mexico.

LANDSCAPE ZONE: 1-10.

SIZE: 2–4 feet.

Perennial.

FLOWER: May–November, 6–8 inches long, white, funnel shaped.

SOIL: adaptable, deep, well drained.

EXPOSURE: full sun, partial shade.

WATER: drought tolerant.

PLANTING: seed.

A dozen delicate white flowers may cover this large mounding, spreading plant in the morning before the midday sun causes them to fold. The snow-white flowers contrast vividly against the dark green foliage. As with many fragrant white-flowered plants, datura blooms open at night and are pollinated by moths. Plant this vigorous grower where it has plenty of room to expand, because each year it gets bigger and bushier. With its long blooming season, you'll see flowers accompanied by the unusual fruit, a 1- to 2-inch spine-covered capsule. All parts of this plant are poisonous.

Prairie Larkspur

Prairie Larkspur, *Delphinium carolinianum* (includes *D. virescens, D. vimineum*)

NATIVE DISTRIBUTION: Arizona to Tennessee, north to Canada.

LANDSCAPE ZONE: 1–10.

SIZE: 1–3 feet.

Perennial.

FLOWER: April–July, spikes of blue to white 1-inch flowers with spurs.

SOIL: adaptable, well draining.

EXPOSURE: full sun, partial shade.

WATER: drought tolerant.

PLANTING: fall- or spring-sown seeds.

Larkspurs are an old-time garden favorite. I can remember them in my grandmother's yard, waving in the breeze with hollyhocks. They're still a favorite, and our native species are just as attractive as the domestic garden varieties. The spurred flowers crowd the erect stalk of each plant. Since each plant has only one flowering stem, you'll need to plant them about 6 inches apart for a thick display. Sow the seeds and thin after germination. You can plant an accent patch or use them as a border. They go dormant in the summer, so for all-season color, plant them with summer and fall bloomers such as mealy blue sage, prairie verbena, Mexican hat, gayfeather, Texas bluebell, and Indian blanket. You'll find these perky flowers in most meadow mixes. The western species, *Delphinium scaposum*, has the same landscape qualities.

Dogweed

Purple Coneflower

Cutleaf Daisy

Dogweed, *Dyssodia pentachaeta*

NATIVE DISTRIBUTION: dry rocky soils, North, Central, South Texas; New Mexico and Arizona at 2500–4000-foot elevations; Mexico.

LANDSCAPE ZONE: 1–7.

SIZE: 4–10 inches tall, 1-foot diameter.

Short-lived perennial.

FLOWER: spring–fall, ½ inch in diameter, yellow.

SOIL: adaptable, alkaline, well draining.

EXPOSURE: full sun.

WATER: drought tolerant.

PLANTING: fall-sown seeds.

What a delightful little plant this is. Numerous dime-sized flowers on 1- to 4-inch stems cover mounds of dark green, fine-textured leaves. The petite clumps, which may range from the size of a dinner plate to 3 feet in diameter, make perfect border or accent plants for your cactus or patio garden — or plant one in a rocky crevice. As a groundcover, it makes a colorful bouquet with blackfoot daisy, zinnia, and damianita. You can count on a dogweed's delicate beauty year after year because it reseeds itself readily. Many species of *Dyssodia* grow throughout the Southwest, all dainty and strongly scented. But don't be choosy. Any one will look good in your yard.

Purple Coneflower, *Echinacea purpurea*

NATIVE DISTRIBUTION: prairies, open woods, Northeast Texas to Virginia.

LANDSCAPE ZONE: 2, 4–10.

SIZE: 2–4 feet.

Perennial.

FLOWER: April–May, 3-inch head with purple to pink rays, rusty center.

SOIL: adaptable, well draining.

EXPOSURE: full sun, partial shade.

WATER: drought tolerant.

PLANTING: fall-sown seeds.

Horticulturists have worked their magic on this beautiful species and selected varieties adapted to most of the Southwest. I've seen them growing wild in deep prairie soils and equally well in caliche gardens in Central Texas. A large basal rosette of leaves sprouts in the spring, followed by tall blooming stalks crowned by the colorful flowers. You can buy coral-, crimson-, and white-flowered varieties. As summer proceeds, you'll be left with the rosette after you remove the dead stalk. For seasonal color, plant it with tall fall-blooming flowers such as goldenrod, gayfeather, and Maximilian sunflower.

Cutleaf Daisy, *Engelmannia pinnatifida*

NATIVE DISTRIBUTION: rocky, sandy soils, Texas to New Mexico, north to Kansas, Colorado; Mexico

LANDSCAPE ZONE: 1–10.

SIZE: 1–3 feet.

Perennial.

FLOWER: spring, decreasing through fall, 1-inch yellow head.

SOIL: adaptable, well draining.

EXPOSURE: full sun, partial shade.

WATER: drought tolerant.

PLANTING: fall-sown seed, transplant winter rosette.

This is no timid plant, so give it room to show off in your garden. It bursts into bloom in early spring and continues all summer. Its deep taproot makes it drought tolerant, but a little extra water will keep it blooming longer. The dense rosette of deeply lobed leaves has an ornate appeal, and the flowers form a mound of bright yellow blooms on 1- to 2-foot stalks. Use them as accent plants or borders, massed in the outskirts of your garden, or as part of a naturalized lawn. The flowers curl under during the heat of the day.

Mexican Gold Poppy

Texas Bluebell

Indian Blanket

Mexican Gold Poppy, *Eschscholtzia mexicana*

NATIVE DISTRIBUTION: desert plains, bajadas, and slopes below 4500-foot elevations; Franklin Mountains in West Texas, through New Mexico and Arizona to California, north to Utah; Mexico.

LANDSCAPE ZONE: 1–3.

SIZE: 6–18 inches tall.

Annual.

FLOWER: February–May, 2–3 inches in diameter, golden yellow.

SOIL: adaptable, well draining.

WATER: drought tolerant, 6–8 inches/year.

EXPOSURE: full sun.

PLANTING: fall- or winter-sown seeds.

This is the spectacular flower that blankets the Sonoran Desert with gold when winter rains have been sufficient. If you live in the desert portions of the Southwest, you'll want to find a place for a stand of gold poppies in your yard. The large clumps of green foliage and gorgeous flowers are guaranteed to add an eye-catching accent to any flower bed or landscape garden. They are most beautiful when planted in mass, but you can use this popular annual as a bedding plant or in mixtures. The delicate texture of the lacy foliage provides a pleasing complement for the brilliantly colored petals. Occasionally, pink or white mu-

tants will spring up. Gold poppies reseed well, but for heavy cover, you may need to sow additional seeds until a good seed bank is established in the soil. The California gold poppy, *Eschscholtzia californica*, is closely related.

* * *

Texas Bluebell or Tulip Gentian, *Eustoma grandiflorum*

NATIVE DISTRIBUTION: moist prairies, Texas, north to Colorado; Mexico.

LANDSCAPE ZONE: 1–10.

SIZE: 1–2 feet tall.

Annual or short-lived perennial.

FLOWER: June–September, blue, 2–3 inches in diameter.

SOIL: adaptable, moist, poor or well draining.

EXPOSURE: full sun, partial shade.

WATER: moderately drought tolerant.

PLANTING: fall-sown seeds on top of soil.

Pay special attention to any plant with the scientific name *grandiflorum*: it means large flowers. With their gorgeous tulip-shaped blossoms, bluebells will be the hit of your wildflower garden from summer until frost. Use them as a colorful border, as an accent group, in pots, or as long-lasting cut flowers. It's easier to buy rosettes in the spring than

to try growing the tiny seeds. Bluebells have long been cultivated, and you can choose among pink, white, rose, lilac, and double-flowered varieties. In saline areas, plant the similar species, *Eustoma exaltatum*, from West Texas.

* * *

Indian Blanket or Firewheel, *Gaillardia pulchella*

NATIVE DISTRIBUTION: sandy soils, Arizona east to Virginia; Mexico.

LANDSCAPE ZONE: 1–9.

SIZE: 1–2 feet.

Annual.

FLOWER: May–July, yellow and red, 1–2 inches across.

SOIL: adaptable, well draining.

EXPOSURE: full sun.

WATER: drought tolerant.

PLANTING: fall- or spring-sown seeds.

This vigorous flower has the reputation of being one of the easiest wildflowers to establish. Just rake the seeds into loose topsoil, then let them reseed before mowing or clearing your garden. In nature's succession of color, they will blanket your naturalized yard or decorate your garden after the March–April bloomers have faded. You can plant firewheels as a clumping border or as a member of a mixed garden. Various red, white, and yellow color selections are available. Cut the blooms for showy arrangements and to extend the flowering period. If you want a perennial, plant *Gaillardia aristata*, which is similar in appearance and habitat requirements. It has a dwarf cultivar that grows to 10 inches and comes in various color selections. Gaillardias are included in most wildflowers mixes.

Maximilian Sunflower

Heartleaf Hibiscus

Bush Morning Glory

Maximilian Sunflower, *Helianthus maximiliani*

NATIVE DISTRIBUTION: moist prairies and ditches, coastal states to Texas, central states to Canada.

LANDSCAPE ZONE: 1–10.

SIZE: 4–8 feet.

Perennial.

FLOWER: August–October, yellow, 3 inches in diameter.

SOIL: adaptable, moist, well draining.

EXPOSURE: full sun.

WATER: drought tolerant, best with 18 inches/year.

PLANTING: fall- or spring-sown seeds, root and plant division.

If you have a place in your yard for a dense mass of head-high flower stalks covered with a profusion of brilliant yellow blooms, this vigorous plant is made to order. Plant it to highlight a wall or fence, to provide a background in your garden, or to accent a corner. In marginal conditions, such as shallow dry soil, these sunflowers may reach only 3 to 4 feet, but they will bloom just as gorgeously. They spread by rhizomes and in deep, moist soil can take over 4 to 8 square feet of space. As with all perennials, dividing the plant every few years increases vigor and blooming. You'll need to remove the dead stalks in the winter. Agricultural agencies have made selections adapted for range planting to provide cover and forage for livestock, birds, deer, and other wildlife.

* * *

Heartleaf Hibiscus, *Hibiscus cardiophyllus*

NATIVE DISTRIBUTION: rocky canyons, gravelly slopes, South Texas; Mexico.

LANDSCAPE ZONE: 1–4, 6.

SIZE: 1–3 feet.

Perennial.

FLOWER: throughout year to frost, red, 2–3-inch diameter.

SOIL: adaptable, well draining.

EXPOSURE: full sun, partial shade.

WATER: drought tolerant.

PLANTING: seeds.

This delightful plant will add a splash of scarlet to your yard and is easy to contain in a limited space. The brilliant flowers nestled in the soft heart-shaped leaves cover the plant all year until it freezes back. Plant it as a border or accent plant in your landscape garden. It makes a colorful companion and is compatible in habitat to blue-eyed grass, blackfoot daisy, and sand abronia. Or you can use it as a pot plant on your patio or poolside and move it inside during freezing weather. A related hibiscus with spectacular golden blooms is desert rosemallow, *Hibiscus coulteri*, native to deserts from West Texas to Arizona. It has the same habitat and landscape requirements. Both flowers are excellent plantings for dry, rocky soils.

* * *

Bush Morning Glory, *Ipomoea leptophylla*

NATIVE DISTRIBUTION: sandy plains and mesas to 7000-foot elevations, north Central Texas to northeastern New Mexico, north to Montana.

LANDSCAPE ZONE: 1–6, 9.

SIZE: 2–3 feet tall, 3–5 feet wide.

Perennial.

FLOWER: May–July, 3 inches in diameter, 4 inches long, lavender.

SOIL: sand, sandy loam, well draining.

EXPOSURE: full sun.

WATER: drought tolerant, 10 inches/year.

PLANTING: sow fresh or packaged seeds in spring.

If you like the gorgeous flowers of morning glory vines, this plant will really capture your imagination. Spectacular trumpets cover the dense rounded bush with a coat of color that will enliven your yard. Plant it in mass for a colorful groundcover and soil binder in a sandy location or to complement a planting of mixed shrubs and perennials. You may need to give it an extra drink to ensure profuse summer blooming. This cold- and drought-tolerant plant grows from a deep taproot that gets deeper and bigger every year, so be sure you plant it in an appropriate location. Once established, it's difficult to move. In nature's scheme of succession, it dies back in late summer, making it a good companion to fall bloomers like gayfeather, goldeneye, paperflower, and cowpen daisy, which have similar habitat requirements.

Skyrocket

Standing Cypress

Gayfeather

Nuttall Gilia

Skyrocket or Scarlet Gilia, *Ipomopsis aggregata (Gilia aggregata)*

NATIVE DISTRIBUTION: dry mountain slopes 5000–9000 feet, West Texas to California, north to Canada; Mexico.

LANDSCAPE ZONE: 2, 3, 9, 10.

SIZE: 2–4 feet tall.

Biennial.

FLOWER: May–September, red, 1 inch long.

SOIL: adaptable, well draining.

EXPOSURE: full sun.

WATER: needs extra water in dry areas.

PLANTING: fall- or spring-sown seed.

You'll have to be patient to enjoy the scarlet, tube-shaped flowers of this plant, but it's worth the wait. All you'll see the first year from seed is a rosette of leaves. The second spring, the rosette sends up a single flower stalk covered with delicate red "rockets" with five spreading petals. If a nursery carries the rosettes, you can enjoy the bright flowers the first summer. For flowers every year, plant two years in a row and let the flowers reseed. For a dramatic effect, plant them in mass for a colorful array waving in the breeze, or mix them in an accent patch with different colors of penstemons. As a bonus, you'll have hummingbirds whizzing in and out all day long. At hotter low elevations, skyrocket needs extra water.

Standing Cypress, *Ipomopsis rubra*

NATIVE DISTRIBUTION: dry slopes, fields, throughout Texas to Florida.

LANDSCAPE ZONE: 1–10.

SIZE: 2–6 feet.

Biennial.

FLOWER: May–August, 1 inch long, red.

SOIL: sand, loam, rocky, well draining.

EXPOSURE: full sun, partial shade.

WATER: drought tolerant.

PLANTING: fall- or spring-sown seed.

With good garden soil and ample water, you can have 6-foot flower stalks covered with showy scarlet blooms. For the best effect, mass plant them as a background, against a garden wall, or on a sunny slope. Like most Ipomopsis, this one takes two years to bloom, but the first-year rosettes are often available from nurseries. Standing cypress reseeds itself, so after two years, all you'll have to do is sit back and enjoy your crop of flowers and the hummingbirds who come for dinner. Be sure to shake out the tiny seeds before you remove the spent stalks.

Gayfeather, *Liatris punctata*

NATIVE DISTRIBUTION: calcareous uplands from West Texas and New Mexico north to Canada.

LANDSCAPE ZONE: 1–6, 9, 10.

SIZE: 1–3 feet.

Perennial.

FLOWER: August–October, spike of small purple flowers.

SOIL: calcareous, well draining.

EXPOSURE: full sun.

WATER: drought tolerant, 12 inches/year.

PLANTING: corm division, fall seeding.

You'll need two ingredients to enjoy this striking wildflower: a sunny location and well-draining soil. I planted mine in too much shade and the stalks bloomed lying on the ground instead of erect as they normally grow. The cluster of upright stems looks like a mass of purple bottlebrushes and provides beautiful fall color for your garden. Plant them to make a perennial border, to accent a pool or patio decor, or to add color to a landscape island. Numerous species of *Liatris* grow across the Southwest, so select one native to your area, if possible. Gayfeathers are a common ingredient in meadow mixes and provide a colorful contrast against the brown of dormant fall grass in naturalized areas. Seedlings sometimes take several years to produce blooms.

Nuttall Gilia, *Linanthastrum nuttallii (Gilia nuttallii)*

NATIVE DISTRIBUTION: rocky crevices and slopes, open ponderosa pine forests, 5500–8000-foot elevations, Arizona, Colorado, and west.

LANDSCAPE ZONE: 2, 5, 9, 10.

SIZE: 6–12 inches tall.

Perennial.

FLOWER: July–November, 1 inch, white.

SOIL: adaptable, well draining.

EXPOSURE: full sun, partial shade.

WATER: drought tolerant.

PLANTING: seeds.

You may have to gather your own seeds for this beauty, but if you do it will make a perfect addition to your landscape design. Its low, compact shape, dense green foliage, and profusion of dainty white phloxlike flowers make a beautiful foreground or accent plant. You can mass plant it as a groundcover, use it to border walks, patios, or landscape gardens, or plant it in rock crevices. I haven't found out anything about propagating this desirable plant, so you're on your own here.

Blue Flax

Cardinal Flower

Blue Flax, *Linum lewisii*

NATIVE DISTRIBUTION: prairies, mesas, mountains, usually above 3500 feet, Texas to California, north to Alaska; Mexico.

LANDSCAPE ZONE: 1–10.

SIZE: 1–2 feet tall.

Short-lived perennial.

FLOWER: March–July and fall, 1 inch, blue.

SOIL: adaptable, well draining.

EXPOSURE: full sun, partial shade.

WATER: drought tolerant.

PLANTING: fall-sown seeds.

A profusion of sky-blue flowers covers the slender stems of this erect plant. Each wand-like stem branches near the top and displays a bouquet of blooms and buds. The dainty blossoms fade and drop by afternoon, but new ones replace them the next morning. The petals can vary from light to dark blue to almost white, with darker lines (nectar guides for insects) leading to the contrasting yellow centers. Flax lives for one or two years and reseeds itself readily. You can expect to see it in most seed mixtures you buy. Trimming it back and giving it extra water in the summer encourages fall blooming. In addition to this and other blue-flowered species, numerous yellow species grow throughout the Southwest.

Cardinal Flower, *Lobelia cardinalis*

NATIVE DISTRIBUTION: moist meadows, streambanks, throughout United States; Canada, Mexico.

LANDSCAPE ZONE: 1–10.

SIZE: 2–4 feet tall.

Perennial.

FLOWER: May–October, spike of 2-inch red flowers.

SOIL: adaptable, moist, poor to well draining.

EXPOSURE: partial shade, full sun.

WATER: regular moisture.

PLANTING: fall-sown seeds, cuttings, layering, division.

This tall plant with crimson flowers thrives in moist, rich soil and partly sunny locations, such as pond sides. However, it does surprisingly well in a regular garden setting that's dry but not parched. If you plant it in an arid location, it will need more shade and regular watering. The tall leafy stems, with their brilliant scarlet flowers, make an eye-catching accent plant, or mass plant it for background color throughout the summer and fall. If you bend down a stem and cover it with soil, it will root at the leaf nodes. Then transplant it in the spring. Plant cardinal flowers and you'll get a bonus: hummingbirds.

Bluebonnet

Bluebonnet, *Lupinus* species

NATIVE DISTRIBUTION: sandy, rocky desert soils and mountain slopes of the western United States.

LANDSCAPE ZONE: 1–10.

SIZE: 1–2 feet.

Annual.

FLOWER: March–April, spike of blue flowers.

SOIL: alkaline, well draining.

EXPOSURE: full sun.

WATER: drought tolerant.

PLANTING: fall-sown seeds.

The Southwest abounds with lupines, but none is as famous as the state flower of Texas, *Lupinus texensis*. In the spring, bluebonnets blanket roadsides, hills, pastures, and prairies across the state, thanks to the decades-old planting program of the Texas Highway Department. The erect spikes of fragrant pea-like flowers thrive in sunny, well-draining loca- tions and make dramatic naturalized mass plantings or accent patches in your yard or garden. All lupines have a tough seed coat adapted to harsh and unpredictable growing conditions, allowing the seeds to germinate periodically over a several-year period. Soaking your seeds one to two days will ensure that some germinate immediately. Dusting the wet seeds with the bacterial inoculant Rhizobium may produce hardier plants. Plant in the fall ¼ to ½ inch deep in lightly tilled soil. Twelve seeds per square foot will give a dense display. The seeds overwinter as a small rosette, so water them if fall rains fail. In the spring, don't mow until the seeds have matured and dispersed, and you will have a colorful show every spring. In the Sonoran Desert and the high-desert zones, plant *Lupinus arizonica* or *Lupinus sparsiflorus*. In the Chihuahuan Desert, plant *Lupinus havardii*. In the high plateau zone, plant a mountain species, such as *Lupinus palmeri*, which occurs at 4000- to 8000-foot elevations in New Mexico and Arizona.

Giant Four-O'Clock

Lemon Mint

Fluttermill

Prairie Primrose

Giant Four-O'Clock, *Mirabilis multiflora*

NATIVE DISTRIBUTION: dry, sandy, rocky plains and pinyon grasslands, 2500–6500-foot elevations, West Texas to Arizona, Colorado to Nevada; Mexico.

LANDSCAPE ZONE: 1–6, 9.

SIZE: 2 feet tall, 4 feet wide.

Perennial.

FLOWER: May–September, purplish red, 1 inch across, 2 inches long.

SOIL: adaptable, well draining.

EXPOSURE: sun.

WATER: drought tolerant.

PLANTING: scarify seeds, stratify one month, plant in spring; soft cuttings.

The mass of vivid, tubular flowers nestled against the bright green heart-shaped leaves creates a spectacular sight in your yard. With dense foliage and a rounded profile, this robust plant presents a commanding appearance when used as a mounding groundcover or border plant. Its extensive tubular root system helps it stabilize slopes and prevent erosion, but it also enables it to crowd out less vigorously growing plants. So give it plenty of room. Each cluster of the majestic flowers has three to six blooms, which close during the heat of the day. The plant dies back in the winter.

Lemon Mint or Horse Mint, *Monarda citriodora*

NATIVE DISTRIBUTION: sandy and rocky hills and prairies throughout Texas, north to Kansas; Mexico.

LANDSCAPE ZONE: 1–8.

SIZE: 1–2 feet tall.

Annual or biennial.

FLOWER: May–July, ¾-inch pink to purple flowers on 6 inch spike.

SOIL: adaptable, alkaline, well draining.

EXPOSURE: full sun, partial shade.

WATER: drought tolerant.

PLANTING: fall- or spring-sown seed.

This picturesque plant is outstanding in its field, or any field for that matter. It forms dense colonies in prairies, pastures, and naturalized areas. It flowers after the early-spring bloomers and until midsummer. It will bloom with Indian blanket, cutleaf daisy, and bluebell. The showy spikes of flowers make good borders, background plantings, or cut flowers, and the leaves and flowers make a strong herbal tea. Supplemental water in the spring and summer will ensure flowering if rains fail. Delay mowing to give this annual a chance to reseed itself, and you'll have a colorful display every year. For altitudes above 5000 feet, plant beebalm, *Monarda menthifolia.*

Fluttermill or Missouri Evening Primrose, *Oenothera macrocarpa* (*O. missouriensis*)

NATIVE DISTRIBUTION: limestone soils, prairies and hillsides, Central Texas north to Missouri, Nebraska.

LANDSCAPE ZONE: 1–7, 9, 10.

SIZE: 6–12 inches tall, 1–2 feet wide.

Perennial.

FLOWER: April–August, yellow, 4 inches across.

SOIL: adaptable, alkaline, well draining.

EXPOSURE: full sun.

WATER: drought tolerant.

PLANTING: fall-sown seeds.

The tissuelike buttery yellow flowers and slender dark green leaves create a cheerful color combination for your landscape decor. This low-sprawling plant makes a delightful border flower for your entry or patio garden or a colorful accent in your rock garden. The stems may spread out over 2 feet, so give it enough room to show off. The showy blooms open in the evening and close during the heat of the next day. The distinctive seed pod has four large wings, hence its common name, fluttermill. This flower is a common constituent of commercial seed mixes.

Prairie Primrose or Pink Evening Primrose, *Oenothera speciosa*

NATIVE DISTRIBUTION: prairies and roadsides throughout Texas, north to Kansas; Mexico.

LANDSCAPE ZONE: 1–10.

SIZE: 1 foot.

Perennial.

FLOWER: March July, 2-inch diameter, pink.

SOIL: adaptable, well draining.

EXPOSURE: full sun.

WATER: drought tolerant.

PLANTING: fall sown seeds.

Plant this flower and watch colorful waves of rosy pink spread across your yard. This sprawling plant forms colonies so dense that the vivid flowers obscure the ground. It blooms heaviest in the spring and on through the summer until burnt back by heat and drought. Give it extra water and it's almost evergreen. Use it as bedding plant or groundcover, or to add color to a naturalized yard. Since this vigorous grower spreads by rhizomes, be careful about planting it in a flower bed with rich garden soil.

Limoncillo

Scarlet Bugler

Rocky Mountain Penstemon

Bush Penstemon

Limoncillo, *Pectis angustifolia*

NATIVE DISTRIBUTION: dry, calcareous soils, West Texas, New Mexico and Arizona at 3500–7000-foot elevations; Colorado, Nebraska, Mexico.

LANDSCAPE ZONE: 1–6, 9.

SIZE: 8 inches tall.

Annual.

FLOWER: summer–fall, ½ inch, yellow.

SOIL: adaptable, alkaline, well draining.

EXPOSURE: full sun, partial shade.

WATER: drought tolerant.

PLANTING: fall- or spring-sown seeds.

With this little herbaceous wildflower, what you see is only half of what you get. Pinch the leaves and smell the lemon scent, and you won't know whether to plant it in your herb garden or use it as a landscape plant. Do both. The delicate leaves and abundant yellow flowers form a thick mat of contrasting colors that will accent your rock garden or flower bed. And after a hard day's work in the yard, use a twig of leaves to brew a refreshing lemon-flavored tea — iced or hot. The leaves also make a good seasoning for soups, stews, and fish. About a dozen other species with similar characteristics grow throughout the Southwest. Chinchweed, *Pectis papposa*, is particularly showy in southern Arizona after summer rains.

Beard Tongues, *Penstemon* species

LANDSCAPE ZONE: 1–10.

SIZE: 1–4 feet.

Perennial.

FLOWER: spring–summer.

SOIL: adaptable, well draining

EXPOSURE: partial shade, full sun.

WATER: drought tolerant.

PLANTING: fall-sown seeds.

With stately spikes of tubular flowers, penstemons are truly one of the aristocrats of the garden, and we have scores of species in the Southwest to choose from. These plants grow from the low deserts to mountain peaks, from sandy, arid hillsides to boreal forests, so you can choose species suited for your growing conditions no matter where you live. Some are 6 feet tall, some 1 foot short, and they come in a rainbow of reds, pinks, oranges, blues, purples, and whites. Don't bypass penstemons when making your selections for a perennial garden. Use them to accent your rock garden, as border plants, or in a mass planting for a stunning effect. If you like hummingbirds, plant penstemons in profusion, and you'll have them visiting your yard all summer. When they're not blooming, they have an attractive basal rosette of leaves. Below just a few penstemons representative of the various species and colors usually available.

Red Penstemons

Scarlet bugler, *Penstemon barbatus*: West Texas to northern Arizona, Utah, Colorado, 4000–10,000 feet; June–September; 2–4 feet tall.

Cardinal penstemon, *Penstemon cardinalis*: Guadalupe Mountains of Texas and New Mexico; May–July; 3 feet tall.

Firecracker penstemon, *Penstemon eatoni*: mesas and mountains, 2000–7000 feet, southern Colorado to central Arizona, California, Utah; April–June; 2 feet tall.

Big Bend (Havard) penstemon, *Penstemon havardii*: Chihuahuan Desert, mountain slopes, grasslands, Texas's Trans-Pecos area; April–October; 2–4 feet tall.

Pineleaf penstemon, *Penstemon pinifolius*: rocky slopes 6000–8500 feet, New Mexico, southwestern Arizona; summer, fall; 6–18 inches tall.

Parry's penstemon, *Penstemon parryi*: Sonoran Desert, rocky slopes, grasslands, 1500–5,000 feet; March–April; 1–3 feet tall.

Desert penstemon, *Penstemon pseudospectabilis*: southwestern New Mexico to southern California, below 6000 feet; late spring, summer; 2–4 feet.

Blue Penstemons

Pagoda penstemon, *Penstemon angustifolius*: mesas, sandy grasslands, northern Arizona, New Mexico; May–June; 1 foot tall.

James penstemon, *Penstemon jamesii*: mesas, mountains 4500–7000 feet, western New Mexico, northern Arizona; May–June; 1 foot tall.

Rocky Mountain penstemon, *Penstemon strictus*: mesas, mountains 7000–8000 feet, northern New Mexico, northeastern Arizona; June–July; 2–3 feet.

Gulf Coast penstemon, *Penstemon tenuis*: poorly drained soils, Texas Gulf Coast, Louisiana, Arkansas; April–May; 1½–3 feet.

White to Pinkish Penstemons

Bush penstemon, *Penstemon ambiguus*: sandy soils, Panhandle and West Texas to California; May–October; 1–4 feet.

Foxglove (Wild Snapdragon), *Penstemon cobaea*: loamy soils from Texas Panhandle to Gulf coast, north to Nebraska, escaped from cultivation near Flagstaff; April–May; 1–2 feet.

Palmer penstemon, *Penstemon palmeri*: gravelly washes, mesas, 2000–6500 feet, Arizona, Utah, California; May–June; 2–3 feet.

False Dragonhead

Paperflower

Drummond Phlox, *Phlox drummondii*

NATIVE DISTRIBUTION: sandy prairies and roadsides in eastern half of Texas.

LANDSCAPE ZONE: 1–10.

SIZE: 6–18 inches tall.

Annual.

FLOWER: spring, 1-inch diameter, red to pink.

SOIL: adaptable, slightly acid to neutral, well draining.

EXPOSURE: full sun, partial shade.

WATER: drought tolerant.

PLANTING: fall-sown seeds, spring-planted seedlings.

Since this famous annual was named in 1834, it has been domesticated and planted around the world. You can buy dwarf and tall varieties, ones with rounded or star-shaped petals, and varieties with white, maroon, coral, pink, or red flowers and different-colored centers, or eyes. Mass plant them and the dense clusters of brilliant flowers will paint your yard or flower bed with a multitude of rosy hues. Use them as borders or accent patches, or sow them in a naturalized area. They die after flowering; for continual cover, plant them with summer-flowering species such as limoncillo, blue flax, and desert marigold. Though preferring sandy, acid soil, this phlox adapts to most well-drained sites, including the alkaline soils common throughout the Southwest. Dozens of annual and perennial phlox species grow throughout the Southwest, so choose one to grace your landscape.

* * *

False Dragonhead or Obedient Plant, *Physostegia virginiana* subsp. *praemorsa*

NATIVE DISTRIBUTION: prairies, ditches, moist soil, East to north Central Texas, canyons in Guadalupe Mountains; eastern United States; Canada.

LANDSCAPE ZONE: 2, 4–10.

SIZE: 2–4 feet tall.

Perennial.

FLOWER: August–November, 10-inch spike of 1-inch pink funnel-shaped flowers.

SOIL: adaptable, moist, rich.

EXPOSURE: partial shade, full sun.

WATER: moderately drought tolerant.

PLANTING: root division, seeds.

False dragonheads have been garden favorites for decades, especially this fall-blooming species. Its tall wandlike stems crowned with a dense spike of flamboyant flowers will turn your garden into a showplace. Use it as a thick border plant or as a background. It spreads by slender rhizomes to form a dense, but controllable, patch of color and dies back in the winter. In dry locations, plant it in partial shade to keep it from drying out. Several other native physostegias bloom in the spring and summer. Our fall-blooming native has been lumped with the wider-ranging species *Physostegia virginiana*, common in the nursery trade.

Paperflower, *Psilostrophe tagetina*

NATIVE DISTRIBUTION: desert plains, mesas to 7000 feet, West Texas to southern Arizona; Mexico.

LANDSCAPE ZONE: 1–6, 9.

SIZE: 1–2 feet tall, 3 feet wide.

Short-lived perennial.

FLOWER: spring–fall, 1-inch diameter, yellow.

SOIL: adaptable, well draining.

EXPOSURE: full sun.

WATER: drought tolerant.

PLANTING: fall-sown seeds.

This densely branching perennial will form a rounded mass of bright yellow in your yard for most of the year. The butter-colored flowers cover the plant so thickly that you won't be able to see the grayish green foliage. The compact shape suits it for a border or accent plant, or you can mass them for a colorful background against a wall or fence. When the vibrant flowers fade with age and become papery, you can use them in dried-flower arrangements. Six species of paperflower grow through the desert Southwest, all with similar habitat requirements and landscape applications.

Mexican Hat

Brown-eyed Susan

Wild Petunia

Red Sage

Mexican Hat, *Ratibida columnaris*

NATIVE DISTRIBUTION: calcareous soils, prairies, grasslands, mesas to 7000 feet, Texas to Arizona, north to Illinois, Montana; Mexico.

LANDSCAPE ZONE: 1–10.

SIZE: 1–3 feet.

Perennial.

FLOWER: May–July, 2 inches, red to yellow or blotched petals with a tall central cone.

SOIL: adaptable, well draining.

EXPOSURE: full sun, partial shade.

WATER: drought tolerant.

PLANTING: fall- or spring-sown seeds.

In any one field of Mexican hats, you'll find flowers with red to maroon petals, yellow petals, and solid and mixed colors of every hue. Maybe it's nature's way of showing us how beautiful a diversity of colors can be. If you can spread seed, you can grow this robust flower in your yard. It's one of the most common ingredients in wildflower mixes for the Southwest. A stand of these tall flowers swaying in the breeze adds not only color but also a dynamic dimension to naturalized areas, borders, background beds, and accent patches. Extra water in the summer will extend the bloom into the fall. The unusual flowers, with their drooping, multicolored petals and protruding cones, make an attractive addition to cut-flower arrangements.

Brown-eyed Susan, *Rudbeckia hirta*

NATIVE DISTRIBUTION: prairies, fields, throughout Texas except the Trans-Pecos, east to Florida, north to Canada; Mexico.

LANDSCAPE ZONE: 1–10.

SIZE: 1–3 feet.

Short-lived perennial.

FLOWER: May–October, 2–3-inch diameter, yellow with brown center.

SOIL: adaptable, well draining.

EXPOSURE: full sun, partial shade

WATER: drought tolerant.

PLANTING: fall- or spring-sown seeds.

A rounded clump of these bright lemon yellow flowers with contrasting centers will add color to your flower bed or naturalized area all summer. This long-blooming species begins blooming after the early-spring flowers fade and continues until the fall species begin their show. Give it extra water to keep it dense and lush and covered with a profusion of gold and brown. Though living only one or two years, this hardy flower readily reseeds itself to ensure an annual bloom. Let the seed heads fully mature and disperse before mowing, and don't remove the shredded mulch. A domesticated related species, goldenglow, *Rudbeckia laciniata*, has double rays and a yellow center.

Wild Petunia, *Ruellia nudiflora*

NATIVE DISTRIBUTION: pastures, prairies, stream banks, throughout Texas except Panhandle.

LANDSCAPE ZONE: 1–4, 6–8.

SIZE: 1–2 feet tall.

Perennial.

FLOWER: April–October, 2-inch diameter, purple to lavender, sometimes white.

SOIL: adaptable, well draining.

EXPOSURE: partial shade.

WATER: drought tolerant.

PLANTING: fall-sown seeds.

This shade-loving plant starts blooming as a small plant in the spring and keeps growing and blooming until fall. The clusters of crinkly, delicate flowers resemble the unrelated domesticated petunia. This is the perfect plant for those troublesome shady spots where your favorite sun-loving flowers just won't grow. Give wild petunia dappled shade and a little extra water, and it will bloom all summer. Use it as a border or in your entry, pool, or patio flower bed. Several other native and naturalized species of *Ruellia* with similar landscape applications are sold in the nursery trade. Blue shade, *Ruellia caroliniensis* and *R. malacosperma*, are native species, and narrow leaf wild petunia, *R. brittoniana*, a native of Mexico, is widely naturalized throughout the southern states.

Red Sage, *Salvia coccinea*

NATIVE DISTRIBUTION: sandy soils in prairies, woods, thickets, South and East Texas to South Carolina; Mexico.

LANDSCAPE ZONE: 2–8.

SIZE: 1–3 feet tall.

Perennial.

FLOWER: February–November, 1 inch long, tube shaped, red.

SOIL: adaptable, well draining.

EXPOSURE: partial shade, full shade.

WATER: drought tolerant.

PLANTING: fall- or spring-sown seeds.

Hummingbirds love the scarlet flowers that whorl around the erect stalk of this long-blooming plant. The flowers first appear in the spring, but fall is its time of glory. Mass plant them and the flowers will look like a field of tiny red flags waving in the breeze. The light green leaves provide a dense groundcover, one you will especially appreciate under trees or in shady areas around your house. You can plant it in a mixed garden with other shade-loving flowers, such as wild petunia, spiderwort, and violets. Trimming it back during the year keeps it compact. A smaller shade lover, cedar sage, *Salvia roemeriana*, grows in Central Texas and has similar landscape appeal.

Mealy Blue Sage

Blue-eyed Grass

Goldenrod

Mealy Blue Sage, *Salvia farinacea*

NATIVE DISTRIBUTION: prairies, woods, throughout Texas.

LANDSCAPE ZONE: 1–9.

SIZE: 2–3 feet tall, to 3 feet wide.

Perennial.

FLOWER: April–September, bluish, ½ inch long.

SOIL: adaptable, well draining.

EXPOSURE: full sun, partial shade.

WATER: drought tolerant.

PLANTING: seeds, cuttings.

This fast-growing plant forms a rounded mound of grayish green foliage with numerous spikes of crowded, tiny, tube-shaped flowers. The purple to light blue flowers whorl around a leafless 1- to 2-foot stem and provide color for your garden through the summer and into the fall. They have a tendency to get leggy. You may have to trim back the flowering stalks during the summer to have a thick fall bloom. They seed themselves easily, so you'll have either a garden full of mealy sage or plenty of starts for your friends. You can mass plant them for a background plant or border. They freeze in cold climates. Several varieties, including one with white flowers, are available. A number of other blue sages grow in the Southwest and have similar landscape applications.

Blue-eyed Grass, *Sisyrinchium* species

NATIVE DISTRIBUTION: various species throughout North America.

LANDSCAPE ZONE: 1–10.

SIZE: 6–18 inches.

Perennial, bulb.

FLOWER: spring, 1 inch across, blue with yellow eye.

SOIL: adaptable, well draining.

EXPOSURE: full sun, partial shade.

WATER: drought tolerant.

PLANTING: fall-sown seeds, clump division.

They're not a grass and not always blue, but they're always a dainty addition to your landscape. These members of the iris family display a dense bouquet of blue, violet, lavender, pink, purple, rose, or even white or yellow flowers in your garden. The dainty blooms cover the symmetrical bundle of grasslike leaves and stems and make a perfect border or accent plant. Or you can mass them together for a spectacular patch of color in your wildflower garden or around a tree. After their month of glory, they die back and disappear like the other iris species, their bulbs waiting till next spring. Numerous species of blue-eyed grass grow throughout the Southwest.

Goldenrod, *Solidago* species

NATIVE DISTRIBUTION: throughout United States.

LANDSCAPE ZONE: 1–10.

SIZE: 1–6 feet.

Perennial.

FLOWER: summer, fall, spike of small yellow flowers.

SOIL: adaptable, poor to well draining.

EXPOSURE: full sun, partial shade.

WATER: some species drought tolerant.

PLANTING: fresh seeds, root division when dormant.

From deserts to mountains and in marshes and prairies, you'll find numerous species of goldenrod throughout the Southwest. The large flowering spike crowning a waving stalk makes them among the most conspicuous fall wildflowers. Because of the diversity in size and aggressiveness within the genus, choose your species and where you plant carefully. Some grow head-high, while others are waist-high, or only knee-high. They make a colorful complement for meadows and naturalized areas, but tend to spread like weeds in garden settings. They spread by rhizomes, so don't plant them where you have to worry about control. Mass plant goldenrods to get extended color, since each plant has a short blooming period. My favorite species is sweet goldenrod, *Solidago odora*, whose leaves make a delicious licorice-flavored tea or spice. Contrary to popular belief, these plants seldom cause hay fever. Wind-pollinated ragweed, which blooms congruently, is the major culprit.

Desert Globemallow

Greenthread

Spiderwort

Desert Globemallow, *Sphaeralcea* species

NATIVE DISTRIBUTION: sandy, rocky soils, deserts and mesas, West Texas to California; Mexico.

LANDSCAPE ZONE: 1–7, 9, 10.

SIZE: 1–6 feet tall.

Perennial.

FLOWER: throughout year, 1 inch across; red, pink, or lavender.

SOIL: adaptable, well draining.

EXPOSURE: full sun.

WATER: drought tolerant.

PLANTING: fall-sown seed.

If you like hollyhocks, you'll want these miniature versions for your desert garden. Plant these graceful plants as a silhouette along a wall or fence line. The cuplike flowers bloom all along the upper portion of the stalk and range from orange to pink, peach, red, and lavender. These vigorous growers send up numerous stems from a single root. If you can't find globemallows at a nursery, don't despair. Pick a few ripe seed heads from these flowers so abundant in desert soils, and you'll have your own specimens in a few months. The most common species seen are *Sphaeralcea ambigua*, *S. angustifolia*, *S. coccinea*, *S. grossulariaefolia*, *S. incana*, and *S. digitata*.

Greenthread, *Thelesperma filifolium*

NATIVE DISTRIBUTION: dry soils, throughout Texas into Arkansas, Oklahoma, Louisiana.

LANDSCAPE ZONE: 1–9.

SIZE: 1–2 feet.

Annual or short-lived perennial.

FLOWER: February–December, 1–2-inch diameter, yellow with brown center.

SOIL: adaptable, calcareous, well draining.

EXPOSURE: full sun.

WATER: drought tolerant.

PLANTING: fall- or spring-sown seeds.

The dense mass of finely textured, filamentlike leaves with contrasting yellow and rusty red flowers makes this a gorgeous plant for your flower bed. The bright flowers sit perched atop leafless stalks growing out of the bright green foliage. The center color can vary from reddish brown to yellow. Plant greenthread in mass for a spectacular blanket of golden color or in a naturalized area or as an accent in your flower garden. It bursts into color in the spring and may bloom intermittently later if given extra water. Once established, this flower reseeds itself well. The similar, but perennial, *Thelesperma ambiguum* is often available from native-seed nurseries.

Spiderwort, *Tradescantia occidentalis*

NATIVE DISTRIBUTION: sandy soils, prairies, plains throughout Texas to Arizona, north to Montana.

LANDSCAPE ZONE: 1–10.

SIZE: 1–2 feet tall.

Perennial.

FLOWER: February–July, clusters of blue to rose, 1-inch flowers.

SOIL: adaptable, well draining.

EXPOSURE: full shade, partial shade.

WATER: drought tolerant.

PLANTING: fresh seeds, root division.

This is one of the most picturesque flowers I know. The three symmetrical royal blue petals with contrasting golden anthers glisten in the mottled sunlight of their shady habitat. Each cluster of flowers nestles above nodding unopened buds atop a slender stalk. The three-petaled blossoms fade in one day, but are replaced by one of the waiting buds. Spiderworts are ideal for shady borders or groundcovers under trees, or in a foundation garden. The tidy clumps and arching bladelike leaves make an eye-catching addition to your perennial flower bed. Dozens of species of *Tradescantia* grow throughout the United States, with numerous garden varieties, some with white flowers.

Golden Crownbeard

Woolly Ironweed

Prairie Verbena

Prairie Verbena or Dakota Vervain, *Verbena bipinnatifida*

NATIVE DISTRIBUTION: sandy, rocky soils, fields, prairies, mesas and uplands to 10,000 feet, Texas to Arizona, north to South Dakota; Mexico.

LANDSCAPE ZONE: 1–10.

SIZE: 6–12 inches high, 1–3 feet wide.

Short-lived perennial.

FLOWER: March–October, round cluster of ¼-inch purple flowers.

SOIL: adaptable, well draining.

EXPOSURE: full sun.

WATER: drought tolerant.

PLANTING: fresh seeds, basal stem cuttings.

Maybe you've seen the low-growing, rounded clusters of verbena growing in the wild and thought it would make an ideal landscape plant. You were right. With abundant brilliant flowers and fine-textured leaves, this plant fits a multitude of landscape niches. You can use it as an attractive border for walks and patios, as a foreground plant in your perennial bed, or as a patch of color in your rock garden. For a long-blooming groundcover, plant them 2 feet apart. The reclining stems root in loose soil to form matlike colonies that stabilize slopes and bare spots, and the plant reseeds itself readily. The flower color may vary from rose to lavender, purple, and maroon. For a striking color combination, plant them with prairie evening primrose, Indian blanket, or sand verbena. Several other low-growing verbenas grow in arid soils in the Southwest, including *Verbena gooddingii* and *V. wrightii*. Nurseries also carry red and purple flowering hybrids.

Golden Crownbeard or Cow Pen Daisy, *Verbesina encelioides*

NATIVE DISTRIBUTION: sandy, disturbed soils, roadsides, deserts to 7000 feet, Florida to California; Mexico.

LANDSCAPE ZONE: 1–10.

SIZE: 2–3 feet tall.

Annual.

FLOWER: February–December, 2 inches across, yellow.

SOIL: adaptable, well draining.

EXPOSURE: full sun

WATER: drought tolerant.

PLANTING: fall- or spring-sown seeds.

This rapidly growing annual will begin adding color to your landscape early in the spring, but it really puts on its show in the fall. Masses of lemon yellow flowers with yellow centers cover the tall, spreading plant. Use it as a background or a border along a wall or fence. It's too rangy looking for a formal garden, so keep it in the outskirts. It normally colonizes waste places, so you can use it as a tall component for a naturalized planting. It readily reseeds itself. Dwarf crownbeard, *Verbesina nana*, grows to about 6 inches tall with showy 1½-inch flowers and would make an excellent groundcover, accent, or foreground plant.

Woolly Ironweed, *Vernonia lindheimeri*

NATIVE DISTRIBUTION: dry, rocky hills, Central and West Texas.

LANDSCAPE ZONE: 1–9.

SIZE: 8–30 inches tall.

Perennial.

FLOWER: June–September, head with clusters of tiny pink flowers.

SOIL: adaptable, well draining.

EXPOSURE: full sun.

WATER: drought tolerant.

PLANTING: fall-sown seeds.

Landscapers choose this plant and its close relatives for the plant's outstanding summer and fall color. Dense clusters of tiny pink to purple flowers on erect stems bloom from summer until frost. You can plant them as a background or border, but use them with caution, especially in garden settings. These robust, invasive growers spread by underground roots and will spread like weeds in rich garden or prairie soil. This species has narrow leaves with woolly undersides. Two taller ironweeds, *Vernonia baldwinii* and *V. missurica*, have wide leaves and are often available.

63

Goldeneye

Missouri Violet

Rocky Mountain Zinnia

Goldeneye, *Viguiera dentata*

NATIVE DISTRIBUTION: dry limestone hills, canyons, woods, to 7000 feet, Central Texas through Arizona; Central America.

LANDSCAPE ZONE: 1–7, 9, 10.

SIZE: 3–6 feet.

Perennial.

FLOWER: September–November, 1 inch, yellow.

SOIL: adaptable, well draining.

EXPOSURE: full sun, partial shade.

WATER: drought tolerant.

PLANTING: fall- or spring-sown seeds.

If you want a waist- to head-high mass of color or to border a fence, to provide a background in your perennial garden, or to cover a naturalized area, plant goldeneye. This vigorous grower needs elbow room or it will run over its neighbors, but let it spread and it's spectacular. It is large enough to make a colorful companion to fall-blooming shrubs, such as cenizo, shrubby boneset, Turk's cap, autumn sage, and mountain sage. A similar species, showy goldeneye, *Viguiera multiflora*, is sometimes available from native-seed sources.

Missouri Violet, *Viola missouriensis*

NATIVE DISTRIBUTION: stream banks and woodlands, mountains at 5000–6500-foot elevations, Texas to New Mexico, Illinois to Colorado.

LANDSCAPE ZONE: 2, 4–9.

SIZE: 3–6 inches tall.

Perennial.

FLOWER: February–May, 1 inch across, light blue to white.

SOIL: adaptable, well draining.

EXPOSURE: light shade.

WATER: moderately drought tolerant.

PLANTING: root division, fall-sown seeds.

Do you have a spot in your yard or garden that gets mottled shade and regular moisture? If you can simulate the habitat of a creek bed or mountain woodland, plant a dainty violet. The dense rosette of basal leaves with their exquisite little flowers make delightful accent plants for a shady patio garden, a filler between rocks, or a small-scale groundcover under a tree or shrub. They go dormant and disappear in the summer, but come back in the cool of the year. Numerous species of violets are available in the nursery trade, so don't deplete our wild populations.

Rocky Mountain Zinnia or Plains Zinnia, *Zinnia grandiflora*

NATIVE DISTRIBUTION: dry, calcareous slopes, plains, mesas, pinyon-juniper woodlands, 3000–6500-foot elevations; West Texas to Arizona, Colorado, Kansas; Mexico.

LANDSCAPE ZONE: 1–6, 9.

SIZE: 4–8 inches high, 8–10 inches wide.

Perennial.

FLOWER: June–October, 1–2-inch diameter, yellow.

SOIL: adaptable, alkaline, well draining.

EXPOSURE: full sun.

WATER: drought tolerant, 6–8 inches/year.

PLANTING: spring-sown seeds, plant division.

If you've ever seen this plant, you'll agree that it belongs in a garden. Compact in size, covered with lemon yellow flowers, and long blooming, it's everything you could ask for in a perennial. Use it as a bedding or border plant or for a touch of color in a rock garden. Set them about 8 inches apart for a mass planting to make a groundcover, a border, a walk, or garden, or to stabilize a slope or bare spot. They grow rapidly from seed, with their most profuse flowering in the fall. After blooming, the petals dry to a straw color, revealing the light green needlelike leaves that densely cover the plant. The rounded mounds of bright yellow perfectly complement another wonderful perennial, blackfoot daisy.

Catclaw Acacia

Huisache

Catclaw Acacia, *Acacia greggii*

NATIVE DISTRIBUTION: washes, mesas to 5000 feet, South, Central, and West Texas to southern Arizona, California; Mexico.

LANDSCAPE ZONE: 1–7.

SIZE: shrubby to 15 feet.

LEAVES: deciduous.

FLOWER: April–October; creamy yellow spikes; fruit, 5-inch flat pods.

SOIL: sand, limestone, alkaline, well draining.

EXPOSURE: full sun, partial shade.

TEMPERATURE TOLERANCE: cold hardy.

WATER: drought tolerant, 8 inches/year.

PROPAGATION: scarified seeds.

This shrubby acacia makes a delightful single- or multi-trunked ornamental tree, but you'll probably have to prune it to the desired shape. In the wild it often forms impenetrable thickets of thorny waist- to head-high shrubs. You can grow it in the same way in your yard if you want a security hedge with vicious catclaw thorns. Blossoms cover the tree in the spring and continue blooming to a lesser extent into fall. Its fragrant flowers and twisted pods accent mixed plantings and make it an appealing specimen plant for a small area. Its feathery foliage and irregular crown provide filtered shade. The closely related Wright acacia, *Acacia wrightii*, is more treelike and cold hardy. It grows in South and West Texas, north almost to Wichita Falls. A beautiful example is growing in the courtyard of the Alamo in San Antonio.

Huisache or Sweet Acacia, *Acacia smallii (A. farnesiana)*

NATIVE DISTRIBUTION: hillsides, desert grasslands to 5000-foot elevations, South Texas north to Austin, west to southern Arizona, California; Mexico.

LANDSCAPE ZONE: 1–4, 6.

SIZE: 15–25 feet tall, vaselike shape, multiple trunks.

LEAVES: deciduous.

FLOWER: February–April, round, golden, fragrant; fruit, seed pods, round, 2–3 inches long.

SOIL: adaptable, well or slow draining.

EXPOSURE: full sun.

TEMPERATURE TOLERANCE: 20 degrees F.

WATER: drought tolerant, 8 inches/year.

PROPAGATION: scarified seed.

In the spring, the barren limbs of huisache turn into golden wands and perfume the air with a profusion of flowers. Its fernlike foliage and rounded crown cast dense shade as the tree matures. Lower branches tend to droop and require pruning. Its moderate size makes it appropriate for small areas unsuitable for a large tree. You can trim huisache into a densely foliated shrub or sheared hedge. The numerous slender branches have pairs of pinlike thorns, making it an effective physical barrier hedge. In the northern extremes of its range, hard freezes nip flower production, cause limb loss, or freeze to the ground. Huisache has been planted ornamentally since the 1600s.

Southern Sugar Maple

Bigtooth Maple

Southern Sugar Maple, *Acer barbatum*

NATIVE DISTRIBUTION: East Texas piney woods; north to Missouri, east to Florida; Canada.

LANDSCAPE ZONE: 5, 7, 8.

SIZE: 30–90 feet tall.

LEAVES: deciduous, brilliant fall colors.

FRUIT: spring, winged seeds on female trees.

SOIL: moist, rich, well draining.

EXPOSURE: full sun.

TEMPERATURE TOLERANCE: cold hardy.

WATER: moisture loving, 20–48 inches/year.

PROPAGATION: freshly gathered seed.

The flamboyant fall colors make this maple a prized landscape tree for home and street plantings in East and North Texas. Saplings propagated from North Texas and Oklahoma trees survive well as far west as the Panhandle of Texas. The rounded canopy provides dense shade throughout the summer. You can hang a hammock, but don't plant sun-loving plants, beneath one. In the fall, the leaves turn brilliant hues of yellow, orange, and scarlet. Red maple, *Acer rubrum*, has most of the same landscape qualities and is suitable for planting in Zone 8 in either moist or well-draining soil. Another maple for Zone 8 is the chalk maple, *Acer leucoderme*, but its use is limited by its availability. It has multiple trunks and distinctive white bark and averages 15 feet tall. It occurs in the Sabine National Forest in extreme East Texas, where it grows as an understory tree, so it is shade tolerant.

Bigtooth Maple, *Acer grandidentatum*

NATIVE DISTRIBUTION: protected canyons of Central Texas and mountain canyons west to Arizona, north to Wyoming; Mexico.

LANDSCAPE ZONE: 2, 3, 5–7.

SIZE: to 50 feet.

LEAVES: deciduous, brilliant fall colors.

FRUIT: spring, winged seeds on female trees.

SOIL: limestone, igneous, well draining.

EXPOSURE: full sun.

TEMPERATURE TOLERANCE: cold hardy.

WATER: drought tolerant, 16 inches/year.

PROPAGATION: freshly gathered seeds, but extremely poor viability.

As its availability increases, the bigtooth maple is becoming one of the premier landscape trees in the Southwest. It is the western counterpart of the eastern sugar maple and in the autumn paints the landscape with equally beautiful hues of red, orange, and gold. Its large crown provides shade cooling for yards, walkways, parking lots, and the southwest sides of buildings. Bigtooth maples are hardy and grow as much as 3 feet per year. Specimens four years old at Lost Maples State Natural Area in Texas had grown 8 feet tall. The trees should thrive in areas with at least 16 inches of rain, cold winters, and about a 225-day growing season. For their autumn colors to develop fully, they require cold nights and sunny days in the fall. To get the best color display, be sure the trees you buy come from your area. Poor seed viability limits availability, but some nurseries have the tree in quantity. One rancher-turned-nurseryman fences off his "mother trees" to keep the deer from browsing the seedings.

Texas Madrone

Pecan

Texas Madrone, *Arbutus texensis* (*A. xalapensis*)

NATIVE DISTRIBUTION: Central Texas, the Trans-Pecos, southeastern New Mexico mountains at 4000–7000-foot elevations; Mexico.

LANDSCAPE ZONE: 2, 3, 5, 6.

SIZE: 15 to 30 feet tall.

LEAVES: evergreen.

FLOWER: February–March, creamy clusters of tiny blooms; fruit, ornate red berries in fall.

SOIL: limestone or igneous, well draining.

EXPOSURE: full sun.

TEMPERATURE TOLERANCE: cold hardy.

WATER: drought tolerant, 16 inches/year.

PROPAGATION: seed, cuttings.

Few trees in the Southwest have the ornamental beauty of the madrone. The vibrant shiny leaves form a dense crown accented in the spring by clusters of creamy white flowers and in the fall by bright red berries. Wildlife love the succulent fruit. In the spring, the smooth white bark peels away in paper-thin layers to reveal the striking pinkish red new bark. The twisting multiple trunks and ornate bark make this tree a classic landscape choice. With evergreen foliage, abundant flowers, and colorful fruit, a madrone will enliven small front and side yards, patios, and commercial plantings. At its eastern limit in the hills of western Travis County, it seems to be very specific to certain strata of limestone. The northern limit of its range is near Lubbock. A beautiful specimen grows in the courtyard of Indian Lodge in Davis Mountains State Park, Texas. The Arizona madrone, *Arbutus arizonica*, grows at 4000- to 8000-foot elevations in southern New Mexico and Arizona. Don't use fertilizers containing copper, since madrones have a symbiotic relationship with root fungi. Seedlings take years to become fully established.

Pecan, *Carya illinoinensis*

NATIVE DISTRIBUTION: moist woodlands and river bottoms of Central and Northwest Texas, east to Alabama, north to Iowa.

LANDSCAPE ZONE: 6–8.

SIZE: to 90 feet.

LEAVES: deciduous.

FRUIT: fall, delicious nuts.

SOIL: deep, well draining.

EXPOSURE: full sun.

TEMPERATURE TOLERANCE: cold hardy.

WATER: moisture loving, 24 inches/year.

PROPAGATION: seeds, cuttings, budding, grafting.

If you have deep, well-draining soil and a lot of space, treat yourself to the state tree of Texas. The Indians and everyone after them have prized the pecan for its abundant, delicious nuts. Early settlers had contests to find the tree with the largest nuts. Today you can choose from more than one hundred varieties; be sure to plant one adapted to your area. Pecans grow moderately fast and mature with a crown spread of 50 feet, so plant them only in areas suitable for a large-proportioned shade tree. Native trees begin bearing in about twenty years, at 30 to 40 feet tall, and bear fruit for three hundred years. Many horticultural varieties mature in six to nine years and have a larger nut. Popular varieties include desirable, Choctaw, Cheyenne, Mohawk, Caddo, Shawnee, Kiowa, and Sioux. Select varieties that fruit early in the season if you live in the northern parts of its range. Native trees usually skip several years between large crops, while the horticultural varieties produce more regularly. The allergenic pollen can cause severe hay fever in the spring. Pests that attack pecans include bark beetles, which require a systemic poisoning, and tent caterpillars, which should be sprayed or have their web tents physically destroyed.

Netleaf Hackberry

Blue Palo Verde

Netleaf Hackberry, *Celtis reticulata*

NATIVE DISTRIBUTION: hills, canyons, streams throughout Texas, Arizona, southern New Mexico; Oklahoma to Washington, Mexico.

LANDSCAPE ZONE: 2–8

SIZE: 30–40 feet tall.

LEAVES: deciduous.

FRUIT: fall, round fleshy red drupes.

SOIL: adaptable, well draining.

EXPOSURE: full sun, partial shade.

TEMPERATURE TOLERANCE: cold hardy.

WATER: drought tolerant, 12 inches/year.

PROPAGATION: seeds.

Perhaps the most abundant and widespread tree in Texas, hackberry grows from the Panhandle to the southern tip of the state in clay, sandy, and rocky soils. Many consider these fast-growing trees a weed, but hackberries definitely have a place in the landscape. They grow almost anywhere, provide abundant shade, and produce tiny fruit that makes excellent forage for birds, advantages that may outweigh their short life of about fifty years. A closely related species, *Celtis laevigata*, grows in the eastern two-thirds of Texas. You can plant it east of Del Rio and Wichita Falls. The shrubby desert hackberry, *Celtis pallida*, is extremely drought tolerant and can be trimmed into an attractive shrub or multi-trunked tree.

Blue Palo Verde, *Cercidium floridum*

NATIVE DISTRIBUTION: desert washes and valleys to 4000-foot elevations, New Mexico to California; Mexico.

LANDSCAPE ZONE: 1, 2

SIZE: 15 to 25 feet tall and wide.

LEAVES: deciduous in cold and drought.

FLOWER: April–July, abundant yellow flowers; fruit, 2–3-inch seed pods.

SOIL: sandy, well draining.

EXPOSURE: full sun.

TEMPERATURE TOLERANCE: hardy to 10 degrees F.

WATER: drought tolerant, 8 inches/year.

PROPAGATION: scarified seeds.

This fast-growing tree is one of the most popular landscape trees in Phoenix and Tucson, and for good reasons. From March through July, depending on moisture, lemon yellow flower clusters obscure the branches. Once you see a blue palo verde in full bloom, you'll know why it was designated the state tree of Arizona. The graceful, spreading shape and smooth bluish green trunk and limbs add to the ornamental effect. This truly drought-tolerant plant loses its tiny leaves during dry summers, but its dense array of slender branches still provides filtered shade. The similar little-leaf palo verde, *Cercidium microphyllum*, has equal landscape value. The Texas palo verde, *Parkinsonia texana*, is a landscaping counterpart and is commonly used in Landscape Zones 3, 4, and 6.

Redbud

Desert Willow

Redbud, *Cercis canadensis* and *Cercis occidentalis*

NATIVE DISTRIBUTION: *C. canadensis:* sandy forests, rocky hills, mountains, East Texas through the Trans-Pecos; eastern United States. *C. occidentalis:* desert hillsides and streams, Arizona, California, Utah, Nevada.

LANDSCAPE ZONE: 1–9.

SIZE: 15–30 feet tall.

LEAVES: deciduous.

FLOWER: March–May, tiny red flowers before leaves; fruit, 2–3-inch pods.

SOIL: adaptable, well draining.

EXPOSURE: full sun, partial shade.

TEMPERATURE TOLERANCE: cold hardy.

WATER: moderately drought tolerant, depending on variety, 12–35 inches/year.

PROPAGATION: stratified, scarified seed.

The redbud greets spring with a blaze of color. In early March, tiny scarlet blossoms cover the bare limbs, and by the time the leaves emerge, the petals blanket the ground like red snow. Redbuds grow rapidly and have an upright rounded to flat-topped crown that provides moderately dense shade. They are perfect for adding spring color to a limited space, such as a side yard, patio, or isolated corner. Use them as a border along drives or in group plantings. In East Texas, their size and colorful flowers make them ideal companion plants for flowering dogwood, while farther west they complement Mexican plum, Mexican buckeye, retama, and palo verde. In low-desert areas, redbud may sunburn if planted in southern exposures.

The eastern redbud, *Cercis canadensis* var. *canadensis*, grows in the deep, rich soils of the eastern woodlands and northern central Texas, where it receives at least 35 inches rainfall per year. Texas redbud, *C. canadensis* var. *texensis*, grows on calcareous soil of the Edwards Plateau and north Central Texas into the Panhandle and Oklahoma, where it gets 20 to 30 inches of rain annually. Mexican redbud, *C. canadensis* var. *mexicana*, is prevalent west of the Pecos River, where the rainfall is 12 to 20 inches annually. Western redbud, *C. occidentalis*, requires winter temperatures below 28 degrees F. to trigger profuse flowering. Several forms of the Eastern and Texas redbud are available, including ones with double, pink, or white flowers and red leaves. Be sure you purchase a variety adapted to your area.

✳ ✳ ✳

Desert Willow, *Chilopsis linearis*

NATIVE DISTRIBUTION: dry washes at elevations of 1500–5000 feet, West Texas to California; Mexico.

LANDSCAPE ZONE: 1–7.

SIZE: 10–25 feet.

LEAVES: deciduous.

FLOWER: May–June, fall, clusters of orchidlike blossoms; fruit, 4–12-inch seed pods.

SOIL: adaptable, well draining.

EXPOSURE: full sun, partial shade.

TEMPERATURE TOLERANCE: heat and cold hardy.

WATER: drought tolerant, 12 inches/year.

PROPAGATION: fresh seeds, semi-hardwood and dormant cuttings.

This premier, fast-growing plant brings spectacular trumpet-shaped flowers and bright green willowlike foliage to your yard. Clusters of up to five blossoms dangle from the branch tips all summer. Grow it as a large shrub; its many branches and thick foliage suit it for background, windbreak, screen, or specimen plantings. Or you can train it into a small tree with an upright shape and single or multiple trunks. Horticulturists have developed a number of varieties and cultivars with flower colors from the natural pinkish purple to pink, burgundy, and white. Since flowers grow on new wood, pruning encourages profuse blooming. Well-draining soil is a necessity, especially in areas that receive more than 30 inches of rain annually. Desert willow is used in shelter-belt plantings as far north as Kansas. It freezes to the ground, but recovers rapidly and regains its height.

Fringe Tree

Brasil

Wild Olive

Fringe Tree, *Chionanthus virginicus*

NATIVE DISTRIBUTION: moist woods, East Texas to Florida, north to Missouri, Pennsylvania.

LANDSCAPE ZONE: 7, 8.

SIZE: 10–20 feet.

LEAVES: deciduous.

FLOWER: March–June, dangling 6-inch white tassels; fruit, bluish black drupe.

SOIL: adaptable, acidic, poor to well draining.

EXPOSURE: partial shade.

TEMPERATURE TOLERANCE: cold hardy.

WATER: regular moisture, 40 inches/year.

PROPAGATION: double-stratified seeds, softwood cuttings, layering, grafting, budding.

This small tree has its moment, or several weeks, of glory in early spring when white tassellike fragrant flowers cover it like foil icicles on a Christmas tree. This elegant tree grows rapidly, typically with a dense rounded crown. Use it as a specimen plant or in a mixed planting. Imagine the spring beauty of a screen planting of a fringe tree with redbuds and dogwoods. As an understory forest tree, it does well in dappled shade under taller trees. Its leaves may persist through the winter or turn yellow and drop, depending on the temperature.

Brasil or Bluewood, *Condalia hookeri*

NATIVE DISTRIBUTION: dry soils of West, Central, and South Texas below 2000 feet; Mexico.

LANDSCAPE ZONE: 4, 6.

SIZE: 8–15 feet.

LEAVES: evergreen.

FRUIT: spring–fall, small, fleshy drupe maturing black, edible.

SOIL: adaptable, well draining.

EXPOSURE: sun, partial shade.

TEMPERATURE TOLERANCE: moderately cold hardy.

WATER: drought tolerant, 18 inches/year.

PROPAGATION: fresh or stratified seeds.

The dense branching habit and evergreen foliage make brasil effective for screen and background applications, and its stiff, thorny branches make an effective physical barrier hedge. You can shape it into a beautiful specimen shrub, but I like it best when it's grown as a picturesque multi-trunked tree with an irregular, spreading crown. The small bright green leaves with contrasting ¼-inch black fruit add an airy touch to your yard, and birds love the fruit. In South Texas, it forms impenetrable thickets and is one of the most important plants for wildlife food and cover.

Wild Olive or Anacahuita, *Cordia boissieri*

NATIVE DISTRIBUTION: brushlands, southern tip of Texas; Mexico.

LANDSCAPE ZONE: 2–4.

SIZE: 10 to 15 feet.

LEAVES: evergreen.

FLOWER: April–June, throughout year, white, trumpet shaped with yellow throat, 2 inches across; fruit, 1 inch, white to brownish.

SOIL: adaptable, well draining.

EXPOSURE: full sun, partial shade.

TEMPERATURE TOLERANCE: hardy to 20 degrees F.

WATER: moderately drought tolerant, 16–20 inches/year.

PROPAGATION: fresh or double-stratified seed, softwood or semihardwood cuttings.

The 5-inch evergreen leaves, spectacular flowers, and small size make wild olive an addition to your landscape you'll always be proud of. The tree grows moderately fast, developing a thick, rounded crown. Dramatic clusters of white tissuelike flowers cover the tree from spring into the winter. The white flowers contrasted by the dark green foliage beautifully accent a pool or patio, an entrance way, or the corner wall of a house. Its compact size is ideal for small yards, formal gardens, and areas where a tree for accent, not shade, is desired. It even can be pruned into a low shrub. The olivelike fruit ripens in the late summer. In Texas, wild olive is planted as far north as San Antonio, but it occasionally freezes back.

Flowering Dogwood

Arizona Cypress

Flowering Dogwood, *Cornus florida*

NATIVE DISTRIBUTION: woodlands, East Texas to Florida, north to Canada.

LANDSCAPE ZONE: 7–10.

SIZE: 15–25 feet.

LEAVES: deciduous.

FLOWER: March–June, 2-4-inch showy white bracts; fruit, scarlet drupes in fall.

SOIL: sandy, acid, well draining.

EXPOSURE: shade and filtered sun.

TEMPERATURE TOLERANCE: cold hardy.

WATER: moisture loving, 24 inches/year.

PROPAGATION: seeds, cuttings, layering.

East Texans are as proud of their dogwoods as they are of their native heritage. Touring one of the "dogwood trails" is a spring tradition. For about two weeks, yards come alive with gorgeous colors from cultivars with pink, red, and the traditional white flowers. Dappled sunlight filtering through the larger trees highlights the blossom-covered branches. For its spreading limbs to have the natural, airy, irregular appearance, dogwoods must be planted in dappled shade. They make an ideal informal accent for small yards or patios. Or you can group them as a background planting. For a colorful combination, mix them with redbud or magnolia. In the fall, the leaves turn scarlet and clusters of red berries decorate the barren limbs and attract hungry birds. Dogwoods have a sensitive network of surface feeding roots easily damaged by drought, tilling, or adding a thick layer of soil; however, light mulching will preserve moisture. If you live in the Southwest mountains outside the dogwood's native range, be sure to choose a variety adapted to your climate.

Arizona Cypress, *Cupressus arizonica*

NATIVE DISTRIBUTION: mountains at 3000–7000-foot elevations, Texas to California; Mexico.

LANDSCAPE ZONE: 2–7, 9.

SIZE: 20–50 feet tall, 20 feet wide

LEAVES: evergreen.

FRUIT: 1-inch cones.

SOIL: adaptable, well draining.

EXPOSURE: full sun.

TEMPERATURE TOLERANCE: cold hardy to about 0 degrees F.

WATER: drought tolerant, 16 inches/year.

PROPAGATION: cuttings.

Its grayish green juniperlike foliage and classic Christmas tree shape make Arizona cypress a popular yard tree throughout the Southwest. When planted close together, younger specimens make a striking head-high or taller border hedge or background planting. Use a row planting as a sun screen, to provide visual privacy, or as a windbreak. As the tree matures, it develops a rounded crown, often with spreading branches. You can remove lower limbs to reveal the scaly red bark and shape the plant into a large shade tree. Growing rapidly when young, it is considered short-lived, thirty to fifty years, though seven hundred-year-old specimens are known. Various varieties and forms have been segregated, including beautiful Arizona cypress (var. *bonita*), a silvery foliated variety (var. *glauca*), a compact form (*forma compacta*), a dwarf form (*forma nana*), and a pyramid-shaped form (*forma pyramidalis*). Arizona cypress survives well to the southern portion of Landscape Zone 5 and east to Dallas.

71

Texas Persimmon

Anacua

Texas Persimmon, *Diospyros texana*

NATIVE DISTRIBUTION: rocky hills, woodlands of Central, South, West Texas; Mexico.

LANDSCAPE ZONE: 1–7.

SIZE: 8–15 feet.

LEAVES: almost evergreen.

FLOWER: spring, fragrant, tiny, white; fruit, 1 inch, black, edible, on female trees.

SOIL: adaptable, well draining.

EXPOSURE: sun, partial shade.

TEMPERATURE TOLERANCE: cold hardy.

WATER: drought tolerant, 12 inches/year.

PROPAGATION: fresh seed.

Once you see this tree's smooth white to gray bark and ornately contorted trunk, you'll start looking for a place to plant one in your yard. Its flowers, fruit, and peeling bark make it one of the premier landscaping small trees in the Southwest. Its narrow crown is perfect for patio and pool plantings or as an accent for a small area. Even though the tree is intricately branched and densely foliated, it is seldom large enough to provide much shade. Tiny fragrant bell-shaped flowers cover the tree in the spring, and in late summer female plants bear sweet, juicy fruit that makes delicious jelly. It's evergreen during mild winters. Seedlings take about ten years to develop the distinctive bark. A three-year-old specimen planted at Santa Ana National Wildlife Refuge, Texas, was 5 feet high and flowered for the first time.

* * *

Anacua, *Ehretia anacua*

NATIVE DISTRIBUTION: alluvial woods, South Texas, north to Austin; Mexico.

LANDSCAPE ZONE: 4, southern 6–7.

SIZE: 15–40 feet.

LEAVES: evergreen.

FLOWER: March–April, fragrant clusters of white flowers; fruit, edible yellow to red drupes, summer.

SOIL: moist, rich, well draining.

EXPOSURE: sun, partial shade.

TEMPERATURE TOLERANCE: dies back in hard freeze.

WATER: moderately drought tolerant, 24 inches/year.

PROPAGATION: seed, root suckers.

Anacua trees have something for your landscape all year long. The sandpaper-rough evergreen leaves provide winter color, and in the spring the tree is almost entirely obscured by tight bouquets of tiny white flowers. In the fall, dense clusters of showy yellow to red fruit cover the tree until devoured by wildlife.

White Ash

Mature trees have dense, rounded crowns, often with multiple trunks. Its moderate size suits it for small front and side yards and commercial plantings with limited space. Its only disadvantage is that the abundant berries can cause messy litter on walks, drives, and patios. Anacuas grow slowly and spread by root suckers. You can grow the tree as far north as Dallas and east to Houston, but it dies back in hard winters. Mature examples of the tree grow on the grounds of Goliad State Historic Park in Goliad, Texas.

* * *

White Ash, *Fraxinus americana*
Green Ash, *Fraxinus pensylvanica*

NATIVE DISTRIBUTION: alluvial woods in the eastern half of Texas, eastern United States; Canada.

LANDSCAPE ZONE: 7, 8.

SIZE: 30–80 feet.

LEAVES: deciduous.

FRUIT: winged seeds in summer on female trees.

SOIL: adaptable.

EXPOSURE: full sun.

TEMPERATURE TOLERANCE: cold hardy.

WATER: moisture loving, 35 inches/year.

PROPAGATION: seeds.

White ash and green ash are popular deciduous shade trees for home, street, and park planting in the eastern United States. They grow fast, live long, and are relatively disease free. The green ash tends to have spreading limbs and the white ash more of an upright profile. Both have dense rounded crowns casting extensive shade and will eventually shade and dominate the entire yard. You can use shade-tolerant shrubs with them, such as flowering dogwood, American beautyberry, and yaupon. If you have deep, rich, moist soil, white and green ash are two of your best choices for a large shade tree.

Texas Ash, *Fraxinus pensylvanica* var. *texensis*

NATIVE DISTRIBUTION: limestone hills in Central Texas, Del Rio to Dallas, Oklahoma.

LANDSCAPE ZONE: 2–7.

SIZE: 30 feet.

LEAVES: deciduous with fall colors.

FRUIT: winged seeds in summer on female trees.

SOIL: adaptable, alkaline, well draining.

EXPOSURE: full sun, partial shade.

TEMPERATURE TOLERANCE: cold hardy.

WATER: drought tolerant, 12 inches/year.

PROPAGATION: seeds.

The leaves of Texas ash provide lustrous shades of bright green in the spring, while in the fall they brighten the landscape with hues of yellow, gold, and red. Its medium size makes it suitable for the small home lots so prevalent today. In landscapes large enough for two small- to medium-sized trees, wild olive, flame leaf sumac, soapberry, and Mexican plum make colorful companions. The Texas ash is the only truly drought-tolerant large ash in the Southwest and deserves greater attention as a shade tree. The Arizona ash, *Fraxinus velutina* var. *glabra*, so common in the nursery trade, is often planted in monotonous profusion in subdivisions, yet it lacks the heat and drought tolerance and many of the fine landscape qualities of its underused relative. If you decide to plant Arizona ash, use the "Rio Grande" cultivar, which is more heat and drought tolerant.

❊ ❊ ❊

Fragrant Ash, *Fraxinus cuspidata*

NATIVE DISTRIBUTION: rocky mountain slopes 2400–7000 feet, the Trans-Pecos to northern Arizona; Mexico.

LANDSCAPE ZONE: 2–7, 9.

SIZE: 10–20 feet.

LEAVES: deciduous.

FLOWER/FRUIT: April–May, 2–4-inch

Fragrant Ash

clusters of showy white flowers; clusters of winged seeds.

SOIL: adaptable, moderate to well draining.

EXPOSURE: full sun, partial shade.

TEMPERATURE TOLERANCE: cold hardy.

WATER: drought tolerant, 16 inches/year.

PROPAGATION: fresh or stratified seed.

In the spring as the leaves emerge, bundles of feathery white flowers cover the fragrant ash, drooping gracefully from the branch tips. This is our only ash with showy flowers. The small size adapts it to yards or commercial plantings where large trees are unsuitable. It makes an attractive specimen plant or an addition to a patio or courtyard. In mass plantings, fragrant ash is a colorful companion and compatible in size and habitat with western redbud, anacacho orchid tree, golden ball leadtree, and Mexican buckeye. A larger flowered variety, *macropetala*, occurs in the Grand Canyon area in Arizona.

❊ ❊ ❊

Gregg Ash, *Fraxinus greggii*

NATIVE DISTRIBUTION: limestone hills, dry streams, the Trans-Pecos area of Texas, southern Arizona at 4000–5000-foot elevations; Mexico.

LANDSCAPE ZONE: 1–4, 6.

Gregg Ash

SIZE: 10–15 feet.

LEAVES: evergreen.

FRUIT: winged seeds.

SOIL: limestone, well draining.

EXPOSURE: full sun, partial shade.

TEMPERATURE TOLERANCE: withstands moderate freezing within native range.

WATER: drought and heat tolerant, 8 inches/year.

PROPAGATION: fresh or stratified seeds.

The compact, upright shape and evergreen foliage make Gregg ash a good choice if you want a small tree or large shrub. You can plant it in a large planter box to accent pools and patios or as a specimen plant. With year-round foliage color, it makes a good component for a row planting or visual screen. In group plantings, its foliage, size, and habitat are compatible with desert yaupon, Texas mountain laurel, brasil, and black brush.

❊ ❊ ❊

Honey Locust, *Gleditsia triacanthos* var. *inermis*

NATIVE DISTRIBUTION: eastern half of Texas, eastern United States.

LANDSCAPE ZONE: 1–9.

SIZE: 30–70 feet.

LEAVES: deciduous.

Honey Locust

FLOWERS: May–June, green, pealike, 2–5-inch-long clusters; fruit, 12-inch seed pods.

SOIL: adaptable.

EXPOSURE: full sun.

TEMPERATURE TOLERANCE: heat tolerant, cold hardy.

WATER: drought tolerant, 8 inches/year.

PROPAGATION: scarified seeds, cuttings.

This fast-growing erect tree has compound leaves with small leaflets. It provides only moderate shade, an important consideration if you want to plant lawn grass or shrubs around it. The small leaves minimize raking chores, but the large pods can cause considerable litter. Plant this thornless variety, or you will have to contend with vicious three-pronged spines up to 12 inches long. The roots can cause pavement heaving when planted close to walks and drives. Young trees need supplemental watering, but when established honey locust requires little maintenance even in hot, dry areas. It is widely planted in the Panhandle of Texas and westward. Numerous forms with a variety of shapes and foliage colors exist.

American Holly

Little Walnut

Eastern Black Walnut

American Holly, *Ilex opaca*

NATIVE DISTRIBUTION: post oak savannah and piney woods of East Texas; east to Florida, north to Massachusetts and Wisconsin.

LANDSCAPE ZONE: 7, 8.

SIZE: 20–50 feet.

LEAVES: evergreen.

FRUIT: fall, poisonous red berries on female trees.

SOIL: sand, loam, acid, well draining.

EXPOSURE: full sun, shade.

TEMPERATURE TOLERANCE: cold hardy.

WATER: moisture loving, 36 inches/year.

PROPAGATION: seed, cuttings.

The natural elegance of American holly makes it one of the most ornamental trees in North America. Its stiff evergreen leaves have a dark green color and sharp spines along the edges. Bright red berrylike drupes, a favorite Christmas decoration, accent the rich green foliage in November and December. When grown alone in sun, the tree develops a picturesque pyramidal shape, with the lower limbs extending to the ground. In the wild, it is an understory tree, so you can plant it under large canopy trees. In shade it develops a more spreading form, often with several trunks. You can prune it into a thick shrub or a dense barrier hedge with spiny leaves. American holly is a vigorous, healthy tree, but slow to moderate growing. More than three hundred varieties have been developed, so choose one most adapted to your soil, climate, and landscape needs.

* * *

Little Walnut, *Juglans microcarpa*
Arizona Walnut, *Juglans major*

NATIVE DISTRIBUTION: stream beds from Central Texas west to Arizona in upper deserts, grasslands, oak woodlands at 3500–7000 feet; Mexico.

LANDSCAPE ZONE: 2–7.

SIZE: 15–45 feet.

LEAVES: deciduous.

FRUIT: ½- to 1-inch diameter nuts in fall.

SOIL: deep, well draining.

EXPOSURE: full sun.

TEMPERATURE TOLERANCE: heat tolerant, cold hardy.

WATER: drought tolerant, 16–24 inches/year.

PROPAGATION: seeds.

These two species are so closely related that some botanists consider them varieties, but they do have slightly different growth characteristics. Little walnut often has a shrubby appearance with multiple trunks. It reaches about 20 feet, with trunks that spread from the base to form a pleasing shade tree. Arizona walnut grows to 45 feet from a single trunk with a rounded canopy of dark green leaves. Both grow rapidly, live long, and provide sweet, but hard-shelled, nuts for wildlife and human consumption. The Arizona walnut grows better at higher elevations in the West and should be used there, but you can use either in Texas. Both bear good crops every two to three years.

* * *

Eastern Black Walnut, *Juglans nigra*

NATIVE DISTRIBUTION: deep, rich limestone soils, East Texas to Florida, north to the Great Lakes.

LANDSCAPE ZONE: 7, 8.

SIZE: 30–80 feet.

LEAVES: deciduous.

FRUIT: fall, 1½- to 2½-inch nuts.

SOIL: deep, moist, nearly neutral, rich with calcium.

EXPOSURE: full sun.

TEMPERATURE TOLERANCE: cold hardy.

WATER: moisture required, 35 inches/year.

PROPAGATION: seed.

Black walnut has a densely foliated, rounded crown and provides deep shade for your yard. Give it ample space to grow because of its size and the toxic substance, juglone, contained in the roots, leaves, and seed husks. The secretion suppresses growth or kills some plants. Black walnut is sensitive to soil types and grows best in deep, moist, fertile limestone soil with a nearly neutral pH. In favorable locations, the tree will grow 3 to 4 feet a year, attaining 40 to 50 feet in twenty years. Though encased in a stone-hard shell, the nut meat is unexcelled in sweetness and is a favorite addition to cake and cookie recipes. Walnuts mature in about twelve years and bear good crops every two to three years. More than one hundred horticultural varieties exist for commercial walnut production. The beautiful black wood, which gives the tree it species name, is prized for fine furniture and woodworking.

Alligator Juniper

Rocky Mountain Juniper

Eastern Red Cedar

Photo © Dan Huff

Alligator Juniper, *Juniperus deppeana*

NATIVE DISTRIBUTION: 4500–8000 feet in mountains of the Trans-Pecos in Texas, central and southern New Mexico and Arizona; Mexico.

LANDSCAPE ZONE: 2, 3, 5–7, 9, 10.

SIZE: 25–50 feet.

LEAVES: evergreen, scalelike.

FRUIT: bluish berrylike cones on female trees.

SOIL: adaptable, well draining.

EXPOSURE: full sun.

TEMPERATURE TOLERANCE: heat tolerant, cold hardy.

WATER: drought tolerant, 16 inches/year.

PROPAGATION: seed.

Unlike most junipers, this tree has an upright stature with a stout trunk and a rounded crown. Reddish brown berrylike fruit accent the bluish green foliage, and the checkered bark resembles the back of an alligator, hence its common name. The thick evergreen foliage and pyramid shape make alligator juniper suitable for windbreaks and screen plantings along fences, drives, or property lines or as a specimen plant. The lower branches often grow almost to the ground, but you can remove them for a more open appearance. You also can prune it into an attractive hedge or

shrub. The male trees produce mildly allergenic pollen in the spring. Judging from its natural range, it seems to prefer acid igneous soil, but this adaptable tree is surviving well in alkaline clay in Dallas.

* * *

Rocky Mountain Juniper, *Juniperus scopulorum*

NATIVE DISTRIBUTION: moist soils, Texas Panhandle, mesas and mountains 5000–9000 feet in Arizona and New Mexico, west to Oregon, north to Canada.

LANDSCAPE ZONE: 2–10.

SIZE: to 35 feet.

LEAVES: evergreen, scalelike.

FRUIT: bright blue berrylike cone on female trees.

SOIL: adaptable, well draining.

EXPOSURE: full sun.

TEMPERATURE TOLERANCE: cold hardy.

WATER: drought tolerant, 16 inches/year.

PROPAGATION: stratified seed, cuttings.

This is one of the most commonly planted junipers in the western United States. Horticulturists have developed numerous varieties to fit almost any landscape need. You can choose forms with silver, green, gray, or bluish

foliage; a pyramid, round, or columnar shape; or erect or weeping branches. The size varies from 35 feet in height to a medium-sized shrub or a 10-inch groundcover. So be sure to select the variety compatible with your landscape design and suitable for your climate. As with all junipers, plant Rocky Mountain juniper in an area large enough for the mature tree, because heavy pruning destroys the natural shape. The male trees produce a mildly allergenic pollen.

* * *

Eastern Red Cedar, *Juniperus virginiana*

NATIVE DISTRIBUTION: from the Panhandle of Texas east to Georgia, north to Canada.

LANDSCAPE ZONE: 5–8.

SIZE: 20–50 feet.

LEAVES: evergreen, scalelike.

FRUIT: bluish berrylike cones on female trees.

SOIL: adaptable, well draining.

EXPOSURE: full sun.

TEMPERATURE TOLERANCE: heat tolerant, cold hardy.

WATER: moderately drought tolerant, 20–35 inches/year.

PROPAGATION: stratified, scarified seed.

The symmetrical shape and dense evergreen foliage of the eastern red cedar complement many landscape designs. Besides the natural pyramid shape, you can choose cultivars with columnar, drooping, rounded, and even prostrate forms. Though slow to moderately fast growers, red cedars need plenty of room or they will crowd gardens or walks with their spreading branches. Try to avoid severe pruning, which destroys their natural shape. Because of their narrow, pointed crown, red cedars are not good shade trees and are generally used as accent plants, row plantings, windbreaks, and hedges. They make a good sheared hedge if planted 1 to 2 feet apart and can be kept at any height by trimming. The male trees produce mildly allergenic pollen.

Goldenball Leadtree

Sweet Gum

Southern Magnolia

Goldenball Leadtree, *Leucaena retusa*

NATIVE DISTRIBUTION: dry hills of Central and West Texas; Mexico.

LANDSCAPE ZONE: 2–4, 6, 7.

SIZE: 15–25 feet.

LEAVES: deciduous.

FLOWER: April–October, yellow, round, 1 inch; fruit, 3–10-inch pods.

SOIL: adaptable, well draining.

EXPOSURE: full sun, partial shade.

TEMPERATURE TOLERANCE: cold hardy to about 0 degrees F.

WATER: drought tolerant, 12 inches/year.

PROPAGATION: seed, cuttings.

Few trees can give your yard more beauty and visual interest than the goldenball leadtree. From April to July, 1-inch lemon yellow flower balls cover the tree with a profusion of color. Its feathery bright green foliage casts moderate shade, allowing you to plant flowers and shrubs under it. It grows rapidly, often with multiple trunks, and a typical specimen of 15 feet has a crown spread of 10 feet. The moderate size of this tree makes it suitable for planting near buildings, along drives and walks, and in courtyards and other areas of limited space. A beautiful specimen grows at the state capitol in Austin. The great leadtree, *Leucaena pulverulenta*, has similar landscape qualities and is widely planted in the lower Rio Grande valley of South Texas.

* * *

Sweetgum, *Liquidambar styraciflua*

NATIVE DISTRIBUTION: wet woodlands, East Texas to Florida, north to Connecticut; Central America.

LANDSCAPE ZONE: 7, 8.

SIZE: 50–100 feet.

LEAVES: deciduous with brilliant fall colors.

FRUIT: 1-inch spiny fruit ball in fall.

SOIL: sandy, loam, deep, moist.

EXPOSURE: full sun, partial shade.

TEMPERATURE TOLERANCE: cold hardy.

WATER: moisture loving, 40 inches/year.

PROPAGATION: fresh or stratified seed, semihardwood cuttings.

If you live in the eastern half of Texas, the autumn foliage of sweet gum will paint your landscape with brilliant hues of red, orange, yellow, and burgundy. Unfortunately, after the colorful pageant, you have to rake up the abundant large star-shaped leaves. Sweet gum develops into a tall, full-crowned tree that provides dense shade, so don't plant sun-loving flowers or shrubs around it. It grows rapidly and is good for planting along street easements for neighborhood beautification. The gumball-sized fruit capsules dangle from the tree like Christmas ornaments and birds and squirrels eat the seeds. Sweet gum adds dazzling fall color to your yard and provides a particularly beautiful contrast when planted with evergreen species such as magnolia and pines.

* * *

Southern Magnolia, *Magnolia grandiflora*

NATIVE DISTRIBUTION: moist woodlands of deep East Texas, east to Florida, north to North Carolina.

LANDSCAPE ZONE: 7, 8.

SIZE: 30–100 feet.

LEAVES: evergreen.

FLOWER: April–August, showy white 6–9-inch flowers; fruit, cone with exposed red seeds.

SOIL: moist, rich, neutral to slightly acid, well draining.

EXPOSURE: full sun.

TEMPERATURE TOLERANCE: cold hardy.

WATER: moisture loving, 40 inches/year.

PROPAGATION: fall-sown seeds, semihardwood cuttings.

Magnolia, the queen of landscape trees in the South, brings to mind plantations and Southern belles. Its large evergreen leaves, spectacular white flowers, and dense foliage give it an elegant appearance throughout the year. In the late summer, the cones ripen, with forty to sixty bright red seeds exposed on the sides. When planted in an open location, the tree develops a dense network of lower limbs and its classic pyramid shape. You can use magnolia as the dominant feature in your yard or as a focal point for an expansive open area. Magnolias grow moderately slowly. Fortunately, young trees bloom profusely. With time, the tree will cover an area 20 feet wide or more, so plant it with ample space to develop its picturesque shape. Magnolias are widely planted throughout the Southwest, but may develop iron chlorosis in alkaline soils and suffer from heat and moisture stress, requiring supplemental watering, fertilizer, and soil amendments.

Retama

Red Bay

Colorado Blue Spruce

Retama, or Jerusalem Thorn, *Parkinsonia aculeata*

NATIVE DISTRIBUTION: sandy, gravelly soils, along Rio Grande in Texas, west through southern Arizona in deserts and grasslands at 3000–4500-foot elevations; Mexico.

LANDSCAPE ZONE: 1–4, 6, 7.

SIZE: 20–40 feet.

LEAVES: deciduous

FLOWER: spring–fall, ½ inch, yellow, in clusters; fruit, 2–4-inch pods.

SOIL: adaptable, moderate to well draining, salt tolerant.

EXPOSURE: full sun, partial shade.

TEMPERATURE TOLERANCE: young trees hardy to about 15 degrees F.

WATER: drought tolerant, 10–12 inches/year.

PROPAGATION: seeds, semihardwood cuttings.

The flamboyant 6-inch flower clusters, long blooming season, ornate smooth green bark, and unusual feathery foliage make retama a popular landscape tree throughout the arid Southwest. Retama grows fast, forms a rounded crown, and provides filtered shade. You can use this medium-sized tree to accent patios, courtyards, and commercial plantings, and its light shade is compatible with desert gardens. But it has disadvantages: its needle-sharp spines give it the common name, Jerusalem thorn, and it produces considerable seed litter.

* * *

Red Bay, *Persea borbonia*

NATIVE DISTRIBUTION: woods, along streams, eastern, and coastal Texas to Florida, north to Delaware.

LANDSCAPE ZONE: coastal 4, 7, 8.

SIZE: 15–25 feet

LEAVES: evergreen.

FRUIT: ½-inch bluish black drupe.

SOIL: adaptable, moderate to well draining.

EXPOSURE: full sun, partial shade.

TEMPERATURE TOLERANCE: cold hardy.

WATER: moisture loving, 40 inches/year.

PROPAGATION: fresh or stratified seeds.

Someday, red bay may be a prized tree for landscape planting. Its elliptical 4-inch evergreen leaves, small, dense growth habit, and distinctive fruit provide excellent ornamental qualities. As a bonus, if you have one in your yard, you'll never lack bay leaves for seasoning soups and sauces. As an understory tree in nature, red bay grows well in either full sun or filtered light, both as a tree and, trimmed, as a bush. The disjointed range of red bay in Texas puzzles botanists. Besides populations in both swampy and dry areas in East Texas and along the coast, an aged population exists in rocky limestone soil along Hamilton Creek in western Travis County in Central Texas. Did Indians transport the seeds because they valued the leaves? We still have much to learn about the habitat requirements and landscape range of this apparently adaptable tree.

* * *

Colorado Blue Spruce, *Picea pungens*

NATIVE DISTRIBUTION: mountains at 6500–11,000-foot elevations from New Mexico, Arizona, north to Wyoming.

LANDSCAPE ZONE: 2, 5, 9, 10.

SIZE: 80–100 feet.

LEAVES: evergreen needles.

FRUIT: 3–4-inch cone.

SOIL: clay, loam, well draining.

EXPOSURE: full sun.

TEMPERATURE TOLERANCE: cold hardy.

WATER: moisture loving, 30 inches/year.

PROPAGATION: stratified seeds.

With more than a dozen varieties of this popular conifer to choose from, you can select the exact size, shape, and color best suited for your landscape. Foliage colors include dark green and various shades of bluish green, gold, yellow, and silver. The size and shape vary from the natural tall pyramid form to compact and symmetrical, flat topped, dwarf, and weeping branched. Some varieties grow rapidly, while others take ten years to grow 10 feet. Blue spruce is widely planted outside its optimum growing area. It survives, but may suffer from heat and drought stress. It is often planted as a living Christmas tree.

Mexican Pinyon Pine

Ponderosa Pine

Mexican Pinyon Pine, *Pinus cembroides*
Colorado Pinyon Pine, *Pinus edulis*
Remote Pinyon, *Pinus remota*

NATIVE DISTRIBUTION: higher elevations, 4000–6000 feet, from West Texas to California, north to Wyoming; Mexico.

LANDSCAPE ZONE: 2, 3, 5, 6, 9.

SIZE: 10–25 feet.

LEAVES: evergreen, 1–2-inch needles.

FRUIT: 2-inch cone with edible nuts.

SOIL: variable, well draining.

EXPOSURE: full sun, partial shade.

TEMPERATURE TOLERANCE: cold hardy.

WATER: drought tolerant, 16 inches/year.

PROPAGATION: fresh seeds.

These small-proportioned evergreen conifers add a touch of charm to yards and patios throughout the Southwest and the western half of Texas. Pinyons accent and add year-round greenery to bare walls and corners of buildings and even can be used as large container plants. They provide an attractive focal plant in mixed plantings with other western species, such as Apache plume, woolly butterfly bush, and mountain mahogany. Younger specimens have dense foliage and a pyramid shape, resembling a 10- to 15-foot Christmas tree. Pinyons grow slowly and with age (probably decades) develop an open rounded canopy. Mexican pinyon and Colorado pinyon are both available in the nursery trade, with remote pinyon beginning to make its appearance. Colorado pinyon comes from the highest elevations and is the most cold tolerant. Mexican pinyon is more heat tolerant and survives well as far north as the Rocky Mountains. Both languish in desert conditions, so avoid them in Phoenix or El Paso. Remote pinyon, native to the dry limestone hills of Central Texas, is the most heat and drought tolerant.

Ponderosa Pine, *Pinus ponderosa*

NATIVE DISTRIBUTION: above 3000 feet in mountains from West Texas to California, north into Canada; Mexico.

LANDSCAPE ZONE: 9, 10, limited 2, 3, 5.

SIZE: 60–100 feet.

LEAVES: evergreen, bundles of 2–3 needles, 5–11 inches long.

FRUIT: 3–6-inch cone.

SOIL: adaptable, well draining.

EXPOSURE: full sun, partial shade.

TEMPERATURE TOLERANCE: cold hardy, not heat tolerant.

WATER: drought tolerant, 16–20 inches/year.

PROPAGATION: fresh seeds.

Ponderosa pine has been planted ornamentally for years and is widely available. These pines like the coolness of mountain altitudes. Landscapers have learned that if you live below 7000-foot elevations, don't plant one near pavement or reflected heat, or it will be heat stressed and need year-round supplemental watering. Under the proper conditions, they grow rapidly and develop from a bushy youth into a stately adult with an open spirelike crown. Ponderosa pines are widespread over the western United States with various varieties and races. Try to buy one propagated from local trees so it will be adapted to your area. A ponderosa growing on a hot, dry 4000-foot mountain in Texas has different habitat requirements from one in a moist forest in the high Rockies.

Loblolly Pine

Texas Pistache

Loblolly Pine, *Pinus taeda*

NATIVE DISTRIBUTION: East Texas to Florida, Illinois to New York.

LANDSCAPE ZONE: 7, 8.

SIZE: 50–100 feet.

LEAVES: evergreen bundles of 3 needles, 5–10 inches long.

FRUIT: 3–5-inch cone.

SOIL: sandy, loam, acid, well draining.

EXPOSURE: full sun, partial shade.

TEMPERATURE TOLERANCE: cold hardy.

WATER: moderately drought tolerant, 30 inches/year.

PROPAGATION: fresh seed.

When planted alone in a landscape situation, loblollies develop open crowns and branches that spread low on the trunk. The tall limbless trunks of the forest trees result from lack of light due to crowding. Loblolly makes an attractive evergreen for mass plantings, especially when mixed with yaupon and wax myrtle, evergreen shrubs that naturally occur in pine forests. Loblolly pines grow rapidly, reaching 60 feet in thirty years, so be sure you give them ample space. Though evergreen, pines lose leaves and cones and require as much ground maintenance as a large-leafed deciduous tree. If not raked, the leaves form a dense mat and inhibit the growth of grass. After raking, save the needles – they make excellent acid mulch for gardens and shrubs. Loblollies planted in alkaline soil or with poor drainage grow slowly or suffer from chlorosis. All pines require well-draining sandy, sandy loam, or gravelly soil. If this isn't your yard, don't plant a pine, or it may become a detraction instead of an addition to your landscape. The shortleaf pine, *Pinus echinata*, has similar habitat requirements and landscape applications. Its smaller cones and needles require less raking, which may be a consideration, but it grows more slowly. The longleaf pine, *Pinus palustris*, has elegant 10- to 15-inch needles, but is the slowest growing pine. It spends the first decade or so as a seedling, developing roots, before it starts growing upward.

* * *

Texas Pistache, *Pistacia texana*

NATIVE DISTRIBUTION: limestone canyons in Val Verde and Terrell Counties, Texas; Mexico.

LANDSCAPE ZONE: 1–4, 6.

SIZE: 10–30 feet.

LEAVES: evergreen or persistent.

FRUIT: clusters of small red to black berrylike drupes on female trees, not edible.

SOIL: adaptable, well draining.

EXPOSURE: full sun, partial shade.

TEMPERATURE TOLERANCE: cold hardy to 20 degrees F.

WATER: drought hardy, 12 inches/year.

PROPAGATION: fresh seeds, semi-hardwood cuttings.

If you plant a Texas pistache, you'll have a tree that combines two ornamental features seldom occurring together: evergreen foliage and seasonal color. The new spring foliage is a beautiful red, and if freezing temperatures occur in the winter, the persistent leaves turn a rusty red. In the summer, clusters of red seeds add even more color to your landscape. The plant typically has many branches spreading from the base and forms a large rounded shrub or small tree 15 to 30 feet in height, but you can trim it into a specimen tree, or conversely into a hedge. The small leaflets cast an open shade. Its evergreen leaves and spring color perfectly complement a planting of deciduous shrubs. It adds visual interest to broad open areas, walks, entryways, and patios. Texas pistache does best in dry, alkaline soil, but reportedly grows well as far east as Houston. The related Chinese pistache is often seen in the nursery trade.

79

Texas Ebony

Sycamore

Texas Ebony, Ape's Earring, or Ebano, *Pithecellobium flexicaule*

NATIVE DISTRIBUTION: South Texas; Mexico.

LANDSCAPE ZONE: 1–4.

SIZE: 15–30 feet.

LEAVES: evergreen.

FLOWER: May–August, fragrant, creamy, cylindrical spike; fruit, 4–6-inch woody pods.

SOIL: adaptable, deep, well draining.

EXPOSURE: full sun, partial shade.

TEMPERATURE TOLERANCE: cold hardy to 10 degrees F.

WATER: drought tolerant, 16 inches/year.

PROPAGATION: scarified seed.

You'll find the deep green foliage, zigzag branching, and profuse, fragrant flowers of Texas ebony a delightful addition to your yard or patio planting. The dense evergreen foliage and rounded crown provide year-round shade. You can shear Texas ebony into a dense shrub or hedge. The thick growth of thorny, zigzag branches makes a good security hedge. A hedge planted around the Visitor's Center at Santa Ana National Wildlife Refuge grew 4 feet tall and extremely dense within four years. The bean pods may remain on the tree for over a year. Texas ebony is popular in Phoenix and Tucson and in Texas as far north as Laredo and Corpus Christi. It suffers leaf and twig damage at freezing temperatures and in hard freezes may die back to the ground. The abundant woody pods can cause considerable ground litter.

Sycamore, *Platanus occidentalis*

NATIVE DISTRIBUTION: bottomlands from Central Texas to Florida, north into Canada.

LANDSCAPE ZONE: 4–8.

SIZE: 60–100 feet.

LEAVES: deciduous

FRUIT: 1-inch seed balls.

SOIL: adaptable, deep, moist, well draining.

EXPOSURE: full sun.

TEMPERATURE TOLERANCE: cold hardy

WATER: needs regular moisture.

PROPAGATION: spring-gathered and -planted seeds, cuttings.

The tall, straight trunk, striking white bark, and symmetrical, rounded crown make sycamores elegant shade trees. As the tree matures, the dense canopy of large, deeply lobed leaves will shade your whole yard, so don't plant sun-loving species under one. If you plant a sycamore, buy a good rake. The leaves and strips of bark of a large tree will cover a yard several times over. In the first half of the century, sycamores frequently were planted in yards and along streets, and these graceful trees shade many older neighborhoods. But in the last few decades, developers have favored faster-growing smaller trees that don't live as long and certainly are less majestic. Sycamores normally grow in river bottoms, so unless you have deep, rich, moist soil and get about 30 inches of rain per year, your tree will need deep watering in the summer. In Arizona and New Mexico (Landscape Zones 2, 9), choose the Arizona sycamore, *Platanus wrightii*, which is native to desert and grassland waterways at 2000- to 7000-foot elevations.

Eastern Cottonwood

Quaking Aspen

Eastern Cottonwood, *Populus deltoides*
Arizona Cottonwood, *Populus fremontii*

NATIVE DISTRIBUTION: stream banks, bottomlands; *P. deltoides*: Central Texas to the Atlantic. *P. fremontii*: West Texas to California from sea level to 6500 feet.

LANDSCAPE ZONE: 1–10.

SIZE: 40–90 feet.

LEAVES: deciduous

FRUIT: allergenic pollen on male trees, cottony pods on female trees.

SOIL: deep, moist, well draining.

EXPOSURE: full sun.

TEMPERATURE TOLERANCE: cold hardy.

WATER: needs regular moisture.

PROPAGATION: fresh seeds, semi-hardwood cuttings.

First the good news: cottonwoods grow fast, live long, and have gold foliage in the fall. Now the bad news: they need regular moisture, throw an abundance of cottonlike wind-blown fruit, and have an invasive root system. The water-greedy roots invade sewer pipes, rob water from your lawn, and heave pavement. If you have an average-sized yard, you don't have room for a cottonwood. But if you have acreage or a large back yard and want a large shade tree, this is a good choice. If planted in rich, moist soil, one can grow into an attractive shade tree in four to five years. In Texas, plant eastern cottonwood, *Populus deltoides* var. *deltoides*, as far west as Uvalde. In the Panhandle, choose *P. deltoides* var. *occidentalis*. Arizona cottonwood, *P. fremontii*, grows from West Texas through New Mexico and Arizona and is the species of choice for those areas.

Quaking Aspen, *Populus tremuloides*

NATIVE DISTRIBUTION: above 6000 feet in the Southwest; northern United States; Canada.

LANDSCAPE ZONE: 9, 10.

SIZE: 20–60 feet.

LEAVES: deciduous.

FLOWER: spring, 2-inch catkins; fruit, small, cottony seeds.

SOIL: moist, sandy, well draining.

EXPOSURE: cool, full sun, partial shade.

TEMPERATURE TOLERANCE: cold hardy, but not heat tolerant.

WATER: needs moisture, 20 inches/year.

PROPAGATION: seeds, root cuttings.

Few trees can match the ornate qualities of quaking aspen. With smooth white bark, leaves that whisper with the wind, and brilliant golden fall colors, the aspen is hard to resist. No wonder I've seen it planted, and struggling to survive, in hot, dry yards in Albuquerque. This fast-growing beauty needs moist, cool soil to keep its roots healthy. With a northern exposure and lots of mulch, an aspen might survive at lower elevations, but it would be stressed. If you live in Santa Fe, Prescott, or Flagstaff, go for it, but at lower, hotter elevations, avoid the temptation.

Honey Mesquite

Screwbean Mesquite

Honey Mesquite, *Prosopis glandulosa* var. *glandulosa*

NATIVE DISTRIBUTION: brush lands, prairies, hills, Texas to New Mexico, north to Kansas; Mexico.

LANDSCAPE ZONE: 1–7.

SIZE: 15–30 feet.

LEAVES: deciduous.

FLOWER: May–June; 2-inch fragrant yellow spikes; fruit, 4–8-inch pods.

SOIL: adaptable, deep, well draining.

EXPOSURE: full sun.

TEMPERATURE TOLERANCE: cold and heat tolerant.

WATER: drought tolerant, 8 inches/year.

PROPAGATION: fresh or scarified seeds, root cuttings.

Southwest ranchers might shake their heads in disbelief at the notion of planting thorny mesquites in city yards. Although it is despised on rangeland, mesquite is prized as an arid climate landscape tree. The open crown, airy foliage, and twisted, often multiple, trunks add western charm to your yard or patio. And older trees lose their thorns. The bright green drooping leaves provide light shade, allowing you to plant sun-loving shrubs and wildflowers or a buffalograss lawn. You can water it to speed its growth, but once a mesquite sinks its taproot, it can survive the driest summer. Mesquites are famous for their root system, which might penetrate 150 feet deep looking for water, so don't plant one near a septic system. The Arizona mesquite, *Prosopis juliflora* var. *velutina*, is a smaller, shrubbier tree. NOTE to all nursery owners: Texas has 60 million acres of mesquite-infested rangeland, so please call us before you order mesquites from Argentina and Chile!

Screwbean Mesquite or Tornillo, *Prosopis pubescens*

NATIVE DISTRIBUTION: desert waterways; West Texas to California; Mexico.

LANDSCAPE ZONE: 1–4, 6.

SIZE: 10–20 feet.

LEAVES: deciduous.

FLOWER: spring, creamy 3-inch spikes; fruit, twisted 1–2-inch pods.

SOIL: moist, well draining.

EXPOSURE: full sun.

TEMPERATURE TOLERANCE: probably cold tolerant to 10 degrees F.

WATER: moderately drought tolerant, 16 inches/year or more.

PROPAGATION: fresh or scarified seed, root cuttings.

Don't confuse the screwbean mesquite with its drought-tolerant relative, honey mesquite. Screwbean needs periodic watering in desert climates, so if your yard doesn't get flash floods or isn't near a desert spring, you'll have to use a hose. The creamy flowers and feathery foliage resemble the honey mesquite, but this smaller tree has distinctively twisted bean pods. The flowers and ornate pods will add visual interest to mixed plantings, pools, or courtyards. You can prune it into a single- or multiple-trunk tree or into a shrub.

Laurel Cherry

Mexican Plum

Laurel Cherry, *Prunus caroliniana*

NATIVE DISTRIBUTION: fields, forests, East Texas to North Carolina.

LANDSCAPE ZONE: 2, 6–8.

SIZE: 15–40 feet.

LEAVES: evergreen.

FLOWER: March–April, creamy 1–2-inch clusters; fruit, black, ½-inch drupes, inedible.

SOIL: deep, moist, neutral, well draining.

EXPOSURE: full sun, partial shade.

TEMPERATURE TOLERANCE: cold hardy to 10 degrees F.

WATER: moderately drought tolerant, 32 inches/year.

PROPAGATION: double stratification, cuttings.

With lustrous evergreen foliage, spectacular early-spring flowers, and ornate fruit in the fall, the laurel cherry provides year-round interest for your landscape. From February to April, clusters of tiny white flowers obscure the branch tips, and the ornate but inedible black cherries remain on the tree through the fall. Large trees tend to have a short trunk and a thick, rounded crown, but young trees are densely foliated and shrublike. The glossy evergreen leaves provide deep shade. You can prune laurel cherry into an informal or sheared hedge or shrub, but it's usually more attractive in its natural form. Choose one of the shorter cultivars, such as compacta, if you want a shrub or smaller version of the tree. Plant 2 feet apart for a clipped hedge, and 6 to 8 feet apart for a screen planting. If you live outside its native range, avoid hot, dry, sunny exposures and provide supplemental water in the summer. Chlorosis is a problem in alkaline soils.

Mexican Plum, *Prunus mexicana*

NATIVE DISTRIBUTION: rocky slopes, prairies, bottomlands, from Central to East Texas; Mexico.

LANDSCAPE ZONE: 6–8.

SIZE: 15–25 feet.

LEAVES: deciduous.

FLOWER: March–April, 1 inch, white; fruit, edible 1½-inch, red to purple plums.

SOIL: adaptable, well draining.

EXPOSURE: full sun, partial shade.

TEMPERATURE TOLERANCE: cold hardy.

WATER: moderately drought tolerant, 24 inches/year.

PROPAGATION: double-stratified seed, cuttings.

While the leaves of most deciduous trees are still in bud, the Mexican plum bursts into glorious bloom. Clusters of white blossoms cover the branches like a late snowfall. By mid-summer the reddish purple plums dangle from the tree like Christmas ornaments. Mexican plum grows rapidly and has an irregular spreading crown. It does well either as an understory tree or in a sunny location. Its small size enhances confined areas, such as side yards and corners; however, avoid planting it where the falling fruit would make a mess on walks, patios, or drives. The flamboyant flowers add spring color and in mass plantings complement other early-blooming species, such as redbud and Mexican buckeye. The plums make delicious jelly or jam, but are a bit tart for table use.

Black Cherry

Chokecherry

Black Cherry, *Prunus serotina* subsp. *eximia, serotina, rufula*

NATIVE DISTRIBUTION: *P. serotina* subsp. *serotina*: East Texas, eastern United States, Canada; *P. serotina* subsp. *eximia*: Edwards Plateau of Central Texas; *P. serotina* subsp. *rufula*: above 4500 feet in the Trans-Pecos area of Texas west to Arizona; Mexico.

LANDSCAPE ZONE: 2–4, 6–8.

SIZE: 25–75 feet.

LEAVES: deciduous, yellow in fall.

FLOWER: March–April, white clusters of tiny flowers; fruit, ⅜-inch black drupes.

SOIL: adaptable according to subspecies, well draining.

EXPOSURE: full sun, partial shade.

TEMPERATURE TOLERANCE: cold hardy.

WATER: drought tolerant, 16 inches/year for western subspecies.

PROPAGATION: double-stratified seeds, cuttings.

The black cherry combines three worthy landscape virtues: attractive spring flowers, good shade in the summer, and colorful autumn foliage. In the spring, 4-inch tassels of tiny flowers cover the tree in dense clusters, followed by ⅜-inch red to black fruit. The lustrous dark green summer foliage provides dense shade, and in the fall, the leaves turn brilliant hues of yellow. One of the three subspecies of black cherry will provide a beautiful shade tree in almost any area of the Southwest. The three subspecies of *Prunus serotina* have adapted to vastly different growing conditions, so be sure you choose the one native or best suited to your landscape zone. The eastern Black cherry (subspecies *serotina*) reaches 100 feet tall and ranks as a massive shade tree. It favors moist neutral to acid soils. The 35-foot escarpment black cherry (subspecies *eximia*) grows in limestone soil and is better adapted to drought. The 30-foot southwestern black cherry (subspecies *rufula*) grows in canyons and mountains of the Southwest on alkaline to acid soils and is the most drought tolerant. Its leaves may persist through the winter. All three have a bitter, but edible if cooked, fruit enjoyed more by birds than humans. The seeds and leaves are toxic.

Chokecherry, *Prunus virginiana*

NATIVE DISTRIBUTION: streams, moist woods above 4500 feet, throughout Southwest; California to North Carolina; Canada.

LANDSCAPE ZONE: 5–9, limited 2, 3.

SIZE: shrubby to 30–foot tree.

LEAVES: deciduous.

FLOWER: April–July, 3–6-inch clusters of white flowers; fruit, July–September, red to black ½-inch drupes.

SOIL: adaptable, well draining.

EXPOSURE: full sun, partial shade.

TEMPERATURE TOLERANCE: cold hardy.

WATER: moderately drought tolerant, 16 inches/year.

PROPAGATION: double-stratified seeds, cuttings.

Widely used in cultivation, chokecherry has dark green lustrous leaves, abundant spring flowers, and attractive bundles of red to black fruit that ripen in the fall. You can trim this versatile plant into a shrub or let it grow as a small tree. Use it as an accent for pool patios or small yards and in mass plantings. You can choose dwarf and full-sized varieties, with broad to narrow leaves and black to amber to yellow fruit. Chokecherry thrives in the higher, cooler climates of the Southwest. If you live in dry cities such as Albuquerque or El Paso, it will require regular summer watering, which contradicts the philosophy of using natives adapted to your area.

OAKS

The Southwest is rich in oak species. From mountain peaks to coastal plains, from the humid East Texas piney woods to the arid western deserts, the Southwest hosts more than forty-five species of oaks, with numerous varieties and hybrids. The great ecological diversity within Texas alone harbors 70 percent of the oak species found in the United States.

The Southwest has mammoth oaks with branches reaching more than 130 feet into the sky and dwarf species that seldom exceed waist height. One of the largest, but shortest, oak forests in the United States covers thousands of sandy acres near Monahans in West Texas. This unusual forest comprises Havard shin oaks, which reach only three to four feet at maturity. The American Forestry Association does not even recognize them as trees.

With such a large number and variety of oaks, it is not surprising that botanists disagree about naming the various species. Most people simply designate evergreen oaks as "live oaks" and the deciduous species as generic "oaks." The term "live oak" has even more specific implications and usually refers to the coastal live oak, *Quercus virginiana*, or the similar plateau live oak, *Q. fusiformis*. The confusion is not helped by oak's tendency to hybridize, especially in landscape locations where several species are planted in proximity. Tree propagators gather acorns from street plantings and grow hybrids that may never occur in nature because of natural geographical separation of the species.

Regardless of names and species designations, oaks are among the most valuable landscape trees. They are long-lived, relatively disease-free, and attractively shaped shade trees. The word oak has instant recognition with connotations of quality, beauty, and worth. Streets, subdivisions, and apartment and condominium complexes are named with endless combinations of the word oak. A large oak tree adds thousands of dollars to the value of a house. It is not surprising that oaks are one of the most desirable landscape trees.

If you choose an oak for your yard or commercial landscape, certain considerations besides availability should influence your choice. The first is whether you want a deciduous or evergreen tree. A deciduous tree on the southwest side of your house will shade the roof and windows in the summer, yet let solar heat through in the winter. Year-round shade and green foliage might be preferred for a northern or windowless exposure and for street and park plantings.

The next consideration is the desired size of your tree. Like pajamas, oaks come in three sizes: small, medium, and large. Small oaks grow to 15 feet tall, medium to 30, and large oaks to over 30 feet in height. You can find an oak to fit practically every landscape design.

A third consideration is where you live. An oak species has a definite range of distribution within the Southwest, usually for specific ecological reasons. Even within its range, it usually prefers certain soil types and moisture conditions. For the best results, choose a species from your area that grows in a habitat similar to your yard.

Other considerations may include fall color, leaf size and color, and crown shape of the tree. Texas oak, red oak, shumard oak, white oak, blackjack oak, gambel oak, willow oak, and Chisos red oak have brilliant fall colors. Coastal live oak and plateau live oak develop large horizontal limbs that spread out from the trunk, and other species have varying degrees of upright, rounded crowns.

This book describes twenty-four species of oaks. In general, species were chosen that have the widest geographical distribution and, consequently, the broadest zone of landscape application. Regardless of your landscape requirements, it is safe to say that some oak is adapted to your climate and soil — one that will provide generations of pleasure and low-maintenance beauty for your yard.

Oak Wilt

Just as the fungal Dutch elm disease decimated American elms across the eastern United States, oak wilt is killing thousands of oaks. Its southern limit now extends into Central Texas, with thirty-two counties reporting losses of live oaks and Texas oaks. An infestation of the fungus *Ceratocustis fagacearum* blocks the flow of water and nutrients to the leaves and can kill a mature tree in one to four weeks. Fungal mats grow under the bark of red oaks and attract sap beetles, which enter the tree through a wound and spread the fungus. Interconnecting roots also spread the disease from tree to tree. Scientists, who have studied the disease since the 1940s, had hoped that the hot Texas summers would kill the fungus, but it survives in the cool interior of the trees.

Symptoms

The best diagnostic sign for oak wilt is a mottled yellow, brown, and green appearance of the leaves. As the leaves start to die, they turn brown first along the veins. Whole limbs may suddenly die in the spring, and the tree may drop all of its leaves. Red oaks usually die within a month, but white oaks, including live oaks, may linger on for a year or two.

Treatment

A chemical cure may be possible in the future, but for now the only treatment is prevention and removal of infected trees. In urban areas, trenching to sever the connecting roots stops the spread underground. Foresters recommend a trench at least three feet deep and seventy-five feet around any tree showing the symptoms. Infected trees should be killed with a silvicide and burned to kill the spores. Since the sap beetles must find an injured site to feed and spread the disease, don't prune between February and June, the time when the beetles and fungal growth are most prevalent. Cover any wound or pruned areas, including large surface roots damaged by mowing, with a pruning paint immediately. Beetles feeding on firewood can also spread the disease. Buy only what you need for the winter, and cover any surplus with clear plastic. The plastic heats up the wood and kills the beetles.

White Oak, *Quercus alba*
Southern Red Oak, *Quercus falcata*

NATIVE DISTRIBUTION: moist forests of East Texas, east to Florida, north to Canada.

LANDSCAPE ZONE: 8

SIZE: 50–100 feet.

LEAVES: deciduous with fall colors.

FRUIT: acorns.

SOIL: adaptable, acid, moist, well draining.

EXPOSURE: full sun, partial shade.

TEMPERATURE TOLERANCE: cold hardy.

WATER: moisture loving, 44 inches/year.

PROPAGATION: fresh acorns.

These two handsome oaks develop into tall trees with broad canopies, so plant them only where they have room to fully develop over the years. Their large proportions suit them best for street and park planting or for expansive lawns. They will dominate and entirely shade a small yard. Avoid planting under utility wires, where pruning by utility companies may remove important limbs and mutilate the canopy shape. The red oak grows faster than most oaks, attaining a height of 80 feet, and transplants easily. White oak grows slowly, but reaches 120 feet. It has a long taproot, making it difficult to transplant. As a bonus, white oaks will add a splash of brilliant fall color to your yard.

* * *

Arizona White Oak, *Quercus arizonica*

NATIVE DISTRIBUTION: mountain slopes 4000–6000 feet, West Texas, New Mexico, Arizona; Mexico.

LANDSCAPE ZONE: 2–9.

SIZE: 20–30 feet.

LEAVES: evergreen.

FRUIT: acorn.

SOIL: well draining.

EXPOSURE: full sun, partial shade.

TEMPERATURE TOLERANCE: cold hardy.

White Oak

WATER: drought tolerant, 16 inches/year.

PROPAGATION: fresh acorns.

This oak is one of the dominant trees of the oak-chaparral woodlands that cover the hills and valleys of southeastern Arizona. With an irregular crown and spreading limbs, it is a smaller version of the famous coastal live oak of the southern states. The graceful profile and dull bluish green leaves of this drought- and heat-tolerant tree will add class to any home or commercial landscape.

* * *

Texas Oak or Spanish Oak, *Quercus buckleyi (Q. texana)*
Shumard Oak, *Quercus shumardii*
Chisos Oak, *Quercus gravesii*

NATIVE DISTRIBUTION: *Q. buckleyi*: Central Texas; *Q. gravesii*: 4000-foot mountains of the southern Trans-Pecos area in Texas; *Q. shumardii*: East Texas, east to Florida, north to Ohio.

LANDSCAPE ZONE: 2–8, depending on species.

SIZE: 15–50 feet.

LEAVES: deciduous with brilliant fall colors.

FRUIT: acorn.

SOIL: adaptable, well draining.

EXPOSURE: full sun, partial shade.

TEMPERATURE TOLERANCE: cold hardy.

Texas Oak

WATER: moderate to drought tolerant, depending on species.

PROPAGATION: fresh acorns.

With brilliant scarlet colors in the fall and a dense rounded canopy, these three oaks have similar landscape features and applications, but very different habitat requirements. Shumard oak grows east of Dallas and San Antonio where it gets more than 32 inches of rain per year. Texas oak grows west of Dallas and Austin in an area of 20 to 32 inches per year. Chisos oak grows on mountain slopes in the Trans-Pecos. Texas and Chisos oaks are handsome, moderately fast-growing trees that reach 30 feet in height, with a spreading to rounded crown of about 25 feet. A Texas oak sapling planted at the Austin Garden Center was a useful shade tree within five years and a beautiful specimen within ten years. Shumard oak, which reaches 50 to 100 feet, needs a large yard. All provide excellent deciduous shade, cooling your yard and house in the summer while letting the sun's warmth through in the winter. For the best fall color and the healthiest tree, be sure to plant the species native to your area. Unfortunately, red oaks are susceptible to oak wilt, a fatal malady affecting live and red oaks primarily in central Texas. Like most oak species, red oaks usually host many insect galls, but suffer no damage from the parasites.

Emory Oak

Emory Oak, *Quercus emoryi*

NATIVE DISTRIBUTION: elevations of 3000–8000 feet in West Texas, New Mexico, Arizona; Mexico.

LANDSCAPE ZONE: 2, 3.

SIZE: 20–40 feet.

LEAVES: partially evergreen.

FRUIT: acorn.

SOIL: igneous, acid, well draining.

EXPOSURE: full sun, partial shade.

TEMPERATURE TOLERANCE: cold hardy.

WATER: drought tolerant, 16 inches/year.

PROPAGATION: fresh acorns.

This drought- and heat-tolerant oak is one of the dominant trees of the oak-chaparral woodlands of the mountains of southern Arizona and New Mexico and West Texas. As a medium-sized landscape tree with a rounded crown, it adds the classic charm of an evergreen oak to your yard. Its shiny hollylike leaves complement green foliated shrubs such as three-leaf sumac, sotol, desert willow, and agarita. Emory oak is medium to slow growing and apparently always grows in nature on igneous-derived acid soils.

Gambel Oak

Gray Oak

Silverleaf Oak

Lacey Oak

Gambel Oak, *Quercus gambelii*

NATIVE DISTRIBUTION: mountain slopes at 4500–8000-foot elevations, West Texas to Arizona, Utah, Colorado; Mexico.

LANDSCAPE ZONE: 2, 9, 10.

SIZE: shrubby to 30 feet.

LEAVES: deciduous with fall colors.

FRUIT: acorns.

SOIL: adaptable, well draining.

EXPOSURE: full sun, partial shade.

TEMPERATURE TOLERANCE: cold hardy, subject to heat stress at low elevations.

WATER: drought tolerant, 16 inches/year.

PROPAGATION: fresh acorns.

This adaptable oak will bring fall hues of yellow, orange, and red to your yard or background plantings. You can use it alone as a specimen tree or as an accent for a mixed planting. It grows slowly and develops a rounded crown with a dense canopy of deeply lobed dark green leaves. Don't plant a Gambel oak in a hot location in the lower range of its altitude zone, or it might suffer heat stress and leaf spot diseases.

Gray Oak, *Quercus grisea*

NATIVE DISTRIBUTION: 3400–7800-foot elevations in mountains of West Texas, into Arizona; Mexico.

LANDSCAPE ZONE: 2, 3, 9.

SIZE: 15–25 feet.

LEAVES: deciduous to almost evergreen.

FRUIT: acorns.

SOIL: adaptable, acid or alkaline, well draining.

EXPOSURE: full sun, partial shade.

TEMPERATURE TOLERANCE: cold hardy.

WATER: drought tolerant, 16 inches/year.

PROPAGATION: fresh acorns.

You can add subtle shades of gray-green to your yard with this handsome medium-sized tree. Its neutral gray-colored leaves complement other gray-foliated species such as woolly butterfly bush, cenizo, rabbitbrush, and silver buffaloberry. It has a rounded crown and is suitable for landscapes with limited area. Its drought tolerance and adaptability to both acid and alkaline soils make gray oak a useful landscape tree over a wide range of the southern half of the Southwest.

Silverleaf Oak, *Quercus hypoleucoides*

NATIVE DISTRIBUTION: at 4000–8500-foot elevations in West Texas and southern New Mexico and Arizona; Mexico.

LANDSCAPE ZONE: 2, 3, 9.

SIZE: 15–40 feet.

LEAVES: deciduous to almost evergreen.

FRUIT: acorns.

SOIL: igneous, well draining.

EXPOSURE: full sun, partial shade.

TEMPERATURE TOLERANCE: cold hardy.

WATER: drought tolerant, 16 inches/year.

PROPAGATION: fresh acorns.

With dark green lance-shaped leaves with silver undersides, this medium-sized tree will make a striking specimen tree for your yard. It gives a regal accent to a group planting or to your courtyard. Its narrow crown provides moderate shade. Under harsh environmental conditions in nature, it remains shrubby, so it would probably be suitable for container planting. This attractive tree should become more available in the nursery trade.

Lacey Oak, *Quercus laceyi (Q. glaucoides)*

NATIVE DISTRIBUTION: Central and the Trans-Pecos of Texas; Mexico.

LANDSCAPE ZONE: 3–7.

SIZE: 20–35 feet.

LEAVES: deciduous with some fall color.

FRUIT: acorns.

SOIL: adaptable, well draining.

EXPOSURE: full sun, partial shade.

TEMPERATURE TOLERANCE: cold hardy.

WATER: drought tolerant, 12 inches/year.

PROPAGATION: fresh acorns.

Lacey oak will grace your landscape with different colors each season. It greets the spring with mottled pinks from the emerging leaves, has bluish gray foliage throughout summer, and turns shades of gold in fall. Its erect branches and rounded crown provide moderate shade. Because of its medium size, it fits well into a small yard without dominating smaller trees and shrubs. It complements similar-sized trees such as goldenball lead tree, little walnut, bigtooth maple, and pinyon pine, while its smoky-colored foliage contrasts well with bright green shrubs such as agarita, shrubby boneset, and desert willow.

Laurel Oak

Bur Oak

Blackjack Oak

Laurel Oak, *Quercus laurifolia*

NATIVE DISTRIBUTION: Southeast Texas to Florida, north to Virginia.

LANDSCAPE ZONE: 8.

SIZE: 50–100 feet.

LEAVES: evergreen.

FRUIT: acorns.

SOIL: moist, wet to moderately well draining.

EXPOSURE: full sun, partial shade.

TEMPERATURE TOLERANCE: cold hardy.

WATER: moisture loving, 40 inches/year.

PROPAGATION: fresh acorns.

This large evergreen shade tree has a densely foliated rounded crown that casts deep shade. Its upright profile makes the tree suitable for street and park planting. For home landscaping, use it where a tree of its large proportions will not be overwhelming. Plant only shade- and moisture-tolerant shrubs, such as yaupon, wax myrtle, beautyberry, and elderberry, near the tree. It thrives in the wet, poor-draining clays of Houston and Beaumont. Laurel oaks have a shallow root system, making them easy to transplant.

Bur Oak, *Quercus macrocarpa*

NATIVE DISTRIBUTION: Central Texas east to Florida, north to Canada.

LANDSCAPE ZONE: 4–9.

SIZE: 50–75 feet.

LEAVES: deciduous.

FRUIT: acorns.

SOIL: adaptable, well draining.

EXPOSURE: full sun, partial shade.

TEMPERATURE TOLERANCE: cold hardy.

WATER: drought tolerant, 24 inches/year.

PROPAGATION: fresh acorns.

This fast-growing oak has large, spreading limbs forming a broad, rounded crown, qualities that make it a premier shade tree. Its shiny green 6- to 12-inch lobed leaves with stylish grayish undersides are one of its most attractive features. The ornate acorns reach 2 inches in diameter, with a dense mosslike growth rimming the woody cup. Bur oak is a large-proportioned tree in all respects, so plant it only where it has ample room to develop its full size. For most city lots, one mature tree is all you have room for in either the front or back yard. Plant one 15 to 20 feet away from the southwest side of your house for energy-saving, deciduous shade in the summer and warming sun in the winter. My bur oak has grown 3 feet per year since I planted it five years ago as a seedling. Wildlife, especially squirrels and deer, feast on the acorns.

Blackjack Oak, *Quercus marilandica*
Post Oak, *Quercus stellata*

NATIVE DISTRIBUTION: sandy, gravelly soils, Central Texas, east to Atlantic, north to Kansas, New York.

LANDSCAPE ZONE: 4–8.

SIZE: 30–50 feet.

LEAVES: deciduous.

FRUIT: acorns.

SOIL: acidic sands, clays, loams, well draining.

EXPOSURE: full sun, partial shade.

TEMPERATURE TOLERANCE: cold hardy.

WATER: drought tolerant, 20–24 inches/year.

PROPAGATION: fresh acorns.

These two attractive oaks both have broad, rounded crowns and dark green lustrous leaves that provide deep shade. Plant them where a medium-sized shade tree is desired. They are particularly suitable for areas with sandy soil and should never be planted on blackland prairie of heavy clay soils. The trees have a reputation for slow growth, probably a result of the infertile soil where they naturally grow. In a landscape situation, they should grow as fast as any oak. Their acorns grow to ¾-inch long and are favored by deer, turkeys, and other wildlife.

Chinkapin Oak

Water Oak

Vasey Oak

Chinkapin Oak, *Quercus muehlenbergii*

NATIVE DISTRIBUTION: mountain canyons and uplands of West and Central Texas, east to Florida, north to Wisconsin, Maine; Mexico.

LANDSCAPE ZONE: 2-7,9.

SIZE: 30–60 feet.

LEAVES: deciduous.

FRUIT: acorns.

SOIL: calcareous clay, loam, alkaline, well draining.

EXPOSURE: full sun, partial shade.

TEMPERATURE TOLERANCE: cold hardy.

WATER: drought tolerant, 32 inches/year.

PROPAGATION: fresh acorns.

The shiny green leaves of this oak have ornate wavy margins, creating a very distinctive appearance. Chinkapin oak grows rapidly, lives long, and is relatively free of insects and disease. It develops an upright profile with a narrow crown providing dense shade. If you want a large shade tree for yard, street, or park plantings, and have moist, calcareous soil, this oak is right for you. Wildlife relish the ½- to 1-inch black acorns. My wife made the best waffles I've ever eaten from Chinkapin oak acorns, and it only took her eight hours to shell, leach, bake the acorns, and grind them into flour!

Willow Oak, *Quercus phellos*
Water Oak, *Quercus nigra*

NATIVE DISTRIBUTION: wet forests, East Texas to Florida, north to New Jersey.

LANDSCAPE ZONE: 8.

SIZE: 30–50 feet.

LEAVES: deciduous.

FRUIT: acorns

SOIL: clay, loam, acidic, poor draining.

EXPOSURE: full sun, partial shade.

TEMPERATURE TOLERANCE: cold hardy.

WATER: moisture loving, 40 inches/year.

PROPAGATION: fresh acorns.

If you live on the heavy gumbo clays common around Houston and Beaumont, you're probably familiar with these popular landscape trees. With tall trunks and upward-growing limbs, they are commonly planted in areas where access under the tree is important, such as along streets and in parks. Water oak and willow oak are closely related, and both develop a densely foliated, rounded crown that casts deep summer shade over a wide area. Plant only shade- and moisture-tolerant shrubs, such as yaupon, roughleaf dogwood, and American beautyberry, near them. The slender leaves of willow oak give your yard some yellow color in the fall, while the spoon-shaped leaves of water oak may be almost evergreen. Both grow rapidly and have shallow root systems, making transplanting easy.

* * *

Mexican Blue Oak, *Quercus oblongifolia*

NATIVE DISTRIBUTION: woodlands from 4500–6000-foot elevations, mountains of extreme southern Arizona, New Mexico, and Texas; Mexico.

LANDSCAPE ZONE: 2-7, 9.

SIZE: 25 feet.

LEAVES: evergreen.

FRUIT: acorns.

SOIL: well draining.

EXPOSURE: full sun, partial shade.

TEMPERATURE TOLERANCE: cold hardy.

WATER: drought tolerant, 16 inches/year.

PROPAGATION: fresh acorns.

Though not widely available, this small oak has superb landscaping qualities. Its rounded crown and spreading, contorted branches provide year-round shade for your yard. With distinctive bluish green leaves, this tree complements gray-foliated plants such as rabbitbrush, butterfly bush, and the artemisias. Its neutral color blends well with rock gardens and adobe or masonry walls. As an extra color bonus, the young leaves have a reddish blush in the spring. This species is closely related to gray oak, *Quercus grisea*.

* * *

Vasey Oak, *Quercus pungens* var. *vaseyana*

NATIVE DISTRIBUTION: limestone hills, Central and the Trans-Pecos of Texas; Mexico.

LANDSCAPE ZONE: 1–7.

SIZE: shrubby to 25 feet.

LEAVES: evergreen.

FRUIT: acorns.

SOIL: adaptable, well draining.

EXPOSURE: full sun, partial shade.

TEMPERATURE TOLERANCE: heat and cold tolerant.

WATER: drought tolerant, 16 inches/year.

PROPAGATION: fresh acorns.

Throughout much of its range, Vasey oak forms shrubby thickets, but in the proper habitat it can grow into a handsome tree with a rounded crown. Its tolerance to dry, rocky soil and its small bright green leaves with ornate lobed margins make this oak a perfect choice for much of the Southwest. Its small size adapts it for planting in small yards and courtyards, either as a specimen tree or as a focal point in a mixed planting. In Texas, it might lose its leaves in the winter or suffer from prolonged freezes if planted north of Lubbock.

Shrub Live Oak

Plateau Live Oak

Carolina Buckthorn

Shrub Live Oak, *Quercus turbinella*

NATIVE DISTRIBUTION: dry slopes and mesas at 1800–6000-foot elevations, West Texas to California; Mexico.

LANDSCAPE ZONE: 1–6.

SIZE: shrub to 15 feet.

LEAVES: evergreen.

FRUIT: acorn.

SOIL: adaptable, well draining.

EXPOSURE: full sun, partial shade.

TEMPERATURE TOLERANCE: heat and cold tolerant.

WATER: drought tolerant, 12–25 inches/year.

PROPAGATION: fresh acorns.

As the name of this tree implies, it often appears in nature as a waist- to head-high shrub. In your yard, its small size lets you use it in limited areas, where you can show off its landscape qualities. Its hollylike, bluish gray leaves and densely branched crown make it an excellent specimen plant. In mass plantings, it complements agarita, beargrass, yuccas, and cenizo. It grows slowly, so you don't have to worry about it outgrowing your landscape plan.

Coastal Live Oak, *Quercus virginiana*
Plateau Live Oak, *Quercus fusiformis*

NATIVE DISTRIBUTION: *Q. virginiana*: Southeast Texas to Florida, north to Virginia; *Q. fusiformis*: Central Texas, north into Oklahoma; Mexico.

LANDSCAPE ZONE: 2–8.

SIZE: 30–60 feet.

LEAVES: evergreen.

FRUIT: acorns.

SOIL: moist to well draining, according to species.

EXPOSURE: full sun.

TEMPERATURE TOLERANCE: cold hardy.

WATER: moderate to drought tolerant, depending on species.

PROPAGATION: fresh acorns.

These two live oaks have such similar appearances and landscape applications that I grouped them here, even though they have different growth requirements. The true coastal live oak requires about 40 inches of rain per year and will grow in poor-draining clays. The plateau live oak grows in well-draining limestone soil and survives well with 16 to 32 inches of rain annually. A broad belt of hybrids of the two species extends between the Texas coast and Austin. In southern Arizona, the Heritage variety of *Q. virginiana* is a common yard tree. Live oaks provide deep shade, which inhibits growth of any but the most shade tolerant plants. Both oaks are long-lived and may take ten years to become an effective shade tree of 25 feet, and twenty years to develop their characteristic massive trunk and lower limbs. These trees often host mosses and insect galls, but neither harm the trees. Oak wilt, a fungus spread through the roots and by beetles, has decimated live and red oaks in Central Texas. The only known prevention to date is deep trenching to isolate the roots. Live oaks have a shallow network of surface roots and should never be covered with more than 1 inch of fill dirt.

* * *

Carolina Buckthorn, *Rhamnus caroliniana*

NATIVE DISTRIBUTION: bottomlands, hills, Central Texas east to Florida, north to Missouri.

LANDSCAPE ZONE: 4–8.

SIZE: 12–20 feet.

LEAVES: deciduous with fall colors.

FRUIT: fall, clusters of red to black drupes.

SOIL: adaptable, well to poor draining.

EXPOSURE: full sun, partial shade.

TEMPERATURE TOLERANCE: cold hardy.

WATER: drought tolerant, 16 inches/year.

PROPAGATION: fresh or stratified seeds, cuttings.

As a small tree seldom exceeding 15 feet, Carolina buckthorn makes an ideal specimen plant for a limited area. It fits well in a small front or side yard, and its lustrous leaves will brighten an entrywalk or accent a patio or courtyard. Or you can plant this shade-tolerant tree in mottled sunlight under a larger canopy tree. The distinctive bright green leaves, which have prominent veins, remain on the tree into the winter, then turn yellow before falling. Black berrylike fruits decorate the tree in the autumn and are eaten by wildlife, but are inedible to humans. Despite its common name, Carolina buckthorn has no thorns. In the west, California buckthorn, *Rhamnus californica*, is suitable for Landscape Zone 2. As an evergreen shrub or small tree, it has landscape applications similar to Carolina buckthorn's.

Prairie Flameleaf Sumac

New Mexico Locust

Sabal Palm

Prairie Flameleaf Sumac, *Rhus lanceolata*

NATIVE DISTRIBUTION: calcareous soils, Central Texas, west into New Mexico, north into Oklahoma; Mexico.

LANDSCAPE ZONE: 2, 3, 5–7.

SIZE: 10–30 feet.

LEAVES: deciduous with red fall color.

FLOWER: spring, dense clusters of white blossoms; fruit, hard red drupes in fall.

SOIL: adaptable; well draining.

EXPOSURE: full sun, partial shade.

TEMPERATURE TOLERANCE: cold hardy.

WATER: drought tolerant; 16 inches/year.

PROPAGATION: scarified seeds, semi-hardwood cuttings.

If you want a fast-growing, medium-sized tree that provides spring, summer, and fall color, this may be just the plant for you. In the spring and summer, large bundles of white flowers decorate the plants, followed by attractive grapelike clusters of red seeds in the fall. The leaves turn brilliant hues of red and orange in the autumn. Because of their moderate size, flame leaf sumacs can be used in mass plantings, along sidewalk easements, as border plants for walls and property lines, and in confined areas. You can prune them heavily to get the desired shape. I wanted a thick-branching screen to shade the southwest side of my house and pruned mine back each winter. In three years the multi-trunked plant was taller than my roof and was sending out root suckers 30 feet into my lawn. In East Texas (Landscape Zone 8), shining sumac, *Rhus copallina*, replaces *R. lanceolata*. The fruit has a pleasant tart flavor and makes a refreshing drink when soaked in water. Some people are allergic to the oil in the plant.

* * *

New Mexico Locust, *Robinia neomexicana*

NATIVE DISTRIBUTION: mountain slopes at 4000–8500-foot elevations, West Texas to Arizona, Colorado to Nevada.

LANDSCAPE ZONE: 2, 9.

SIZE: 12–20 feet.

LEAVES: deciduous.

FLOWER: April–August, clusters of delicate rose pealike flowers; fruit, bean pods in fall.

SOIL: adaptable, well drained.

EXPOSURE: full sun, partial shade.

TEMPERATURE TOLERANCE: cold hardy.

WATER: drought tolerant, 12 inches/year.

PROPAGATION: scarified seeds, root cuttings.

If you see a New Mexico, or rose, locust when it's covered with showy pink blossoms in the spring and through the summer, you'll know why it's a popular accent plant in the Southwest. Its small size adapts it to courtyard, patio, and mixed plantings. In the fall, 2- to 4-inch bean pods dangle from the limbs. In the wild this tree spreads aggressively by root suckers and forms thorny thickets. You can prune it in cultivation into a single- or multi-trunked tree and control suckering by mowing or limiting water. You can plant this fast-growing tree for erosion control, as a wind break, or as a screen planting. Once established, it's difficult to eradicate. The black locust, *Robinia pseudo-acacia*, is larger and has showy white flowers, but I don't recommend it as a landscape plant. Its sparse branching, thorns, and open profile make it unattractive and a poor shade tree, and its weedy root suckers make it hard to control.

* * *

Sabal Palm, *Sabal mexicana (S. texana)*

NATIVE DISTRIBUTION: southern tip of Texas; Mexico.

LANDSCAPE ZONE: 1, 4.

SIZE: 20–45 feet.

LEAVES: evergreen.

FRUIT: clusters of red to black drupes.

SOIL: deep, rich, moist, well to poor draining.

EXPOSURE: full sun, partial shade.

TEMPERATURE TOLERANCE: cold hardy north to Austin.

WATER: needs moisture, 24 inches/year.

PROPAGATION: fresh or stratified seeds.

Palm trees add a tropical flavor to a landscape setting, and the native Texas species is as stately and picturesque as any imported ones. Sabal palms grow along the streets of many towns and beautify numerous old homes from South Texas as far north as Austin. The large bright green leaves form a dense rounded crown with a 15-foot spread. Instead of being flat like a fan, the leaves, or fronds, are folded in the center, like a half-closed book, with the central axis greatly curved. The distinctive curved fronds add a graceful touch of elegance to this palm and separate it from other species with flat leaves.

The Sabal palm is the perfect example of a beautiful indigenous tree that for decades has been bypassed in favor of imported palms less suited to Texas climate. The Sabal palm's slow growth and difficulty in transplanting after the trunk reaches 1 foot have limited its availability. Sabals are floodplain palms and, for germination and rapid growth, need moisture and deep, rich soil. One planted at Santa Ana National Wildlife Refuge grew 15 feet tall in twelve years. One of the most widespread palms in the nursery trade, the California fan palm, *Washingtonia filifera*, is native to southern California and Arizona. It is the palm to choose for street and lawn plantings in the desert Southwest (Landscape Zone 1). It grows 40 to 60 feet tall and is cold hardy to 18 degrees F.

Mexican Elder

Western Soapberry

Eve's Necklace

Mexican Elder, *Sambucus mexicana*

NATIVE DISTRIBUTION: drainages in desert chaparral and mountains, 1000–5000-foot elevations, West Texas to California; Mexico.

LANDSCAPE ZONE: 1–4.

SIZE: 10–20 feet.

LEAVES: evergreen, deciduous in drought.

FLOWER: September–June, flat-topped cluster of yellowish white blooms; fruit, bluish black in clusters.

SOIL: adaptable, deep, moist, poor or well draining.

EXPOSURE: full sun, partial shade

TEMPERATURE TOLERANCE: cold hardy.

WATER: drought tolerant, 16 inches/year.

PROPAGATION: scarified, stratified seeds, softwood cuttings.

This plant reverses the seasons and gives character to your landscape in the winter. As cool weather arrives, it develops lush foliage, and it's covered with clusters of creamy flowers into the spring. In a typical Phoenix or El Paso summer, it sheds its leaves. For year-round foliage color, plant it with blue palo verde, Texas ebony, mesquite, and desert willow. This fast-growing plant develops a rounded crown with dense foliage, but you'll have to use your pruning shears to train it into a handsome tree.

In the wild it's often a large-spreading shrub, making it excellent for windbreak or screen plantings. This plant normally grows along desert waterways, so give it a few good drinks during the summer. Supplemental water accelerates the growth of young plants and greatly improves fall foliage. The shrubby elderberries are described in the shrub section.

* * *

Western Soapberry, *Sapindus drummondii (S. saponaria* var. *drummondii)*

NATIVE DISTRIBUTION: western two-thirds of Texas, southern New Mexico, and Arizona, east to Louisiana, north to Kansas; Mexico.

LANDSCAPE ZONE: 2–8.

SIZE: 15–30 feet.

LEAVES: deciduous with fall color.

FLOWER: May–June, showy white panicles; fruit, clusters of amber berries on female trees.

SOIL: widely adaptable, well draining.

EXPOSURE: full sun, partial shade.

TEMPERATURE TOLERANCE: cold hardy.

WATER: drought tolerant, 8–16 inches/year.

PROPAGATION: scarified, stratified seeds.

If you want a plant that has abundant spring flowers and brilliant autumn color and will grow almost anywhere, consider the soapberry. Despite its unglamorous name, it has high landscaping value. In the spring, 5- to 10-inch cascading clusters of cream-colored blossoms decorate the branch tips. The showy flowers contrasted against the light green foliage make a colorful addition to any setting. Fall weather paints the leaves with striking shades of gold and yellow. The amber fruit remains on the tree all winter. Soapberries grow moderately fast, reaching 30 feet in rich soil, with an erect shape and a rounded crown. Its moderate size suits small home lots, side yards, or business fronts. The deciduous foliage provides moderate shade, which becomes denser as the tree increases in size. Put some berries in a jar, mash them slightly, fill with water and shake, and you'll see how the tree got its name. Though toxic, the berries have been used in past times to make soap.

* * *

Eve's Necklace, *Sophora affinis*

NATIVE DISTRIBUTION: limestone hills, Central Texas into Oklahoma, Arkansas, Louisiana.

LANDSCAPE ZONE: 4, 6, 7.

SIZE: 10–20 feet.

LEAVES: deciduous.

FLOWER: April–June, cascades of pink blossoms; fruit, necklacelike black bean pods.

SOIL: adaptable, alkaline, well draining.

EXPOSURE: full sun, partial shade.

TEMPERATURE TOLERANCE: cold hardy.

WATER: drought tolerant, 24 inches/year.

PROPAGATION: scarified seeds.

You'll know spring has arrived when the lustrous green leaves of Eve's necklace burst from bud, soon followed by 6-inch drooping cascades of decorative flowers. The pea-type flowers vary from white to rosy pink and contrast well with the shiny green foliage. As a small tree, it grows fast, develops spreading branches, and provides filtered shade. You can plant it alone to accent an open area or corner, or in a mixed planting. The foliage is particularly compatible with other plants with compound leaves, such as evergreen sumac, Texas mountain laurel, and goldenball leadtree. As a shrub or container plant, it adds spring and summer color to patio and pool decors at the times you use them the most. The plant is named after the black pods, which are so highly constricted between the seeds that they resemble beads on a necklace.

Bald Cypress

Bald Cypress, *Taxodium distichum*

NATIVE DISTRIBUTION: swamps and permanent waterways, Central Texas to Florida, north to Illinois, Delaware.

LANDSCAPE ZONE: 6–8.

SIZE: 50–100 feet.

LEAVES: deciduous with rusty fall color.

FRUIT: round, 1-inch cone.

SOIL: adaptable, moist.

EXPOSURE: full sun, partial sun.

TEMPERATURE TOLERANCE: cold hardy.

WATER: needs regular moisture, 32 inches/year.

PROPAGATION: fresh or stratified seeds with resin removed.

If you want a tree your great-great-great-grandchildren and beyond can enjoy, plant a bald cypress. Specimens seven hundred years old are common. But you don't have to wait that long to enjoy this hardy tree. They're fast growing and have an ornate pyramid shape when young, gradually developing the classic swollen trunk and towering profile. In the autumn, the tiny needlelike leaves will accent your landscape with a rusty brown color before dropping. If you live in the eastern half of Texas and have deep soil, consider this stately tree. The bald cypress grows in various habitats, ranging from standing swamp water

to dry limestone soil along permanent streams, so try to obtain one from your locale. It will probably be better adapted to your environment. The evergreen Montezuma cypress, *Taxodium mucronatum*, barely reaches into South Texas, but has been grown as far north as San Antonio and Houston.

* * *

American Elm, *Ulmus americana*

NATIVE DISTRIBUTION: bottomlands, eastern half of Texas, eastern United States; Canada.

LANDSCAPE ZONE: 6–8.

SIZE: 30–75 feet.

LEAVES: deciduous, some fall color.

FRUIT: small winged seeds in spring.

SOIL: adaptable, deep, rich, well draining.

EXPOSURE: full sun, partial shade.

TEMPERATURE TOLERANCE: cold hardy.

WATER: needs some moisture, 24 inches/year.

PROPAGATION: fresh seeds, softwood cuttings.

I remember growing up in Dallas shaded by towering American elms in my back yard, along the streets, and on the school grounds. The large size and graceful vaselike profile have made this beautiful tree a favorite for centuries. Even in the winter when it has lost all its leaves, its stately profile enlivens a landscape. Dutch elm disease entered the scene in 1930 and left hundreds of thousands of dead elms in its wake as it spread westward. Fortunately, Texans can still enjoy this tree. The malady has little affected Texas trees, though it's a problem in other areas of the Southwest. If you have deep, rich soil and want a large, long-lived, fast-growing shade tree, American elm will fill the bill. But it does have invasive roots that search out sewer lines, and in the spring its pollen may cause hay fever in sensitive individuals.

Cedar Elm

Cedar Elm, *Ulmus crassifolia*

NATIVE DISTRIBUTION: hillsides, woods, Central Texas to Mississippi, Arkansas.

LANDSCAPE ZONE: 4, 6–8.

SIZE: 30–60 feet.

LEAVES: deciduous with some fall color.

FRUIT: small winged seeds in fall.

SOIL: adaptable, well draining.

EXPOSURE: full sun, partial shade.

TEMPERATURE TOLERANCE: cold hardy.

WATER: drought tolerant; 18 inches/year.

PROPAGATION: fresh seeds.

The cedar elm is the most common elm in Texas and one of the most valuable shade trees. With a straight trunk, spreading crown, crooked and often interlacing limbs, and a dense cover of leaves, it will cast cool shade across your yard, patio, or house roof. Cedar elms live long and grow moderately fast. They occur most frequently on limestone-derived caliche, loams, and prairie soils, but are widely adaptable to well-drained soils. This is the elm species to plant in subhumid, semiarid portions of Texas. The fall pollen may cause hay fever for sensitive individuals.

Mexican Buckeye

Farkleberry

Rusty Blackhaw

Mexican Buckeye, *Ungnadia speciosa*

NATIVE DISTRIBUTION: rocky slopes and stream banks, from Dallas west to New Mexico, south into Mexico.

LANDSCAPE ZONE: 2–8.

SIZE: 8–15 feet.

LEAVES: deciduous.

FLOWER: March–April, small pink blossoms; fruit, three-chambered pod with black seeds.

SOIL: adaptable, well drained.

EXPOSURE: full sun, partial shade.

TEMPERATURE TOLERANCE: cold hardy.

WATER: drought tolerant, 16 inches/year.

PROPAGATION: fresh seeds.

You'll know spring has arrived when clusters of small pink flowers decorate the limbs of the Mexican buckeye. The fragrant blossoms appear with the new leaves and accent the barren limbs. Mexican buckeye is a fast-growing large shrub or small tree. You can use it as a specimen plant for small lawns, side yards, and patios or to accent entryways, walks, and drives. Its size and early blooming make it an ideal companion for redbud and Mexican plum in mass or screen plantings. The tree is densely foliated, with shiny dark green leaves, and in the winter, cinnamon-colored, three-lobed seed pods dangle like ornaments from the limbs. Each pod contains three black, round, poisonous seeds. With colorful flowers, lustrous foliage, and ornate seed pods, Mexican buckeye gives your landscape visual interest throughout most of the year.

✳ ✳ ✳

Farkleberry, *Vaccinium arboreum*

NATIVE DISTRIBUTION: moist woods, swamps, East Texas to Florida, north to Missouri, Virginia.

LANDSCAPE ZONE: 7, 8.

SIZE: shrubby to 20 feet.

LEAVES: almost evergreen with red fall color.

FLOWER: spring, small, white, bell shaped; fruit, edible black berries.

SOIL: sandy, moist, acidic, well draining.

EXPOSURE: full sun or shade.

TEMPERATURE TOLERANCE: cold hardy.

WATER: regular moisture, 40 inches/year.

PROPAGATION: stratified seeds, softwood and hardwood cuttings.

If the tiny fragrant flowers and fruit remind you of blueberries, you're right. This large shrub or small tree is a member of the blueberry family, a fact appreciated by the numerous wildlife that feast on the somewhat dry berries in the winter. With persistent leaves, spring flowers, fall color, and winter fruit, farkleberry adds visual interest to your yard throughout the year. It normally grows as a slender tree with crooked, spreading branches, a beautiful shape to accent entryways, courtyards, or a corner. When pruned, it develops dense foliage. You can train it into a low hedge or allow it to grow into a head-high shrub. It is shade tolerant and suitable for planting under trees, in planter boxes, and in group plantings with yaupon, dogwood, beautyberry, and coralberry.

✳ ✳ ✳

Rusty Blackhaw, *Viburnum rufidulum*

NATIVE DISTRIBUTION: Central Texas, east to Florida, north to Virginia.

LANDSCAPE ZONE: 6–8.

SIZE: 10–30 feet.

LEAVES: deciduous with red, yellow fall colors.

FLOWER: March–April, flat-topped clusters of white flowers; fruit, July–October, bluish black drupes.

SOIL: adaptable, well draining.

EXPOSURE: full sun, partial shade.

TEMPERATURE TOLERANCE: cold hardy.

WATER: drought tolerant; 24 inches/year.

PROPAGATION: fresh seeds, semi-hardwood cuttings.

When rusty blackhaw buds out in the spring, it will dazzle your yard with lustrous green leaves and bouquets of creamy white flowers. The tiny flowers cover the tree in flat-topped clusters 6 inches in diameter. By October, the fruit matures into clusters of bluish black drupes, and the foliage turns brilliant hues of reds, oranges, and yellows. You'll want to plant this beautiful tree in a prominent place in your landscape so it can show off its seasonal beauty. In an open setting, it develops a spreading crown with limbs that branch close to the ground. In East Texas, rusty blackhaw is considered a half-evergreen. The fruit is sweet and edible and relished by wildlife.

Shrubs and Small Trees

Black Brush

Century Plant

Black Brush, *Acacia rigidula*

NATIVE DISTRIBUTION: South and the Trans-Pecos of Texas; Mexico.

LANDSCAPE ZONE: 1, 3, 4.

SIZE: 10–15 feet.

LEAVES: deciduous.

FLOWER: April–May, 2-inch fragrant yellow spikes; fruit, 3-inch pods.

SOIL: sandy, limestone, well drained.

EXPOSURE: full sun, partial shade.

TEMPERATURE TOLERANCE: cold hardy to about 20 degrees F.

WATER: drought tolerant; 20 inches/year.

PROPAGATION: fresh seeds.

In the spring, the branches of black brush blaze with golden yellow flowers. As early as February, the twig and branch tips look as though they are painted with fragrant blossoms. This multistemmed shrub can have a 20-foot spread — large enough to make a showy specimen or background plant. Its numerous thorny branches form impenetrable thickets in South Texas. You can prune it into a dense hedge, and with its needlelike thorns and stiff branches, it makes an effective physical barrier. Black brush adds a gorgeous splash of color to a mixed planting.

* * *

Century Plant or Agave, *Agave* species

NATIVE DISTRIBUTION: deserts, mountain slopes to 8000 feet in the Southwest; Mexico.

LANDSCAPE ZONE: 1–10.

SIZE: 2–6 feet in diameter.

LEAVES: evergreen, swordlike with vicious thorns.

FLOWER: June–August, yellow clusters on 6–15-foot stalk.

SOIL: adaptable, well draining.

EXPOSURE: full sun.

TEMPERATURE TOLERANCE: heat tolerant, cold hardy.

WATER: drought tolerant, 8 inches/year.

PROPAGATION: fresh seeds, root suckers.

These classical plants of the Southwest add a distinctive desert flavor to your landscape. The perfectly symmetrical rosette of grayish green leaves creates a natural focal point for cactus gardens or a commanding accent for a corner planting. The long, stiff, viciously armed leaves have needlelike thorns at the tips and catclaw teeth along the edges. For this reason, avoid planting them along walks or entryways where human contact, especially by children, is probable.

Agaves come in all sizes, so be sure to choose one compatible with your landscape. *Agave americana* is the largest species, with leaves up to 6 feet long. Several horticultural varieties exist, including ones with yellow- and white-striped leaves. The leaf blades of *A. havardiana*, *A. palmeri*, and *A. parryi* reach 2 feet in length. *Agave toumeyana*, *A. schottii*, and *A. neomexicana* have 1-foot leaves. *Agave parviflora* is the smallest, forming a rosette about 6 inches in diameter. Agaves grow rapidly for eight to twenty years and then send up a tall flowering stalk. The plant dies after flowering, but by then is usually surrounded by many suckers.

Bee Brush or White Brush, *Aloysia gratissima*

NATIVE DISTRIBUTION: rocky soils at 1000–5000-foot elevations, Central Texas west to California; Mexico.

LANDSCAPE ZONE: 1–4, 6–8.

SIZE: 3-10 feet.

LEAVES: deciduous.

FLOWER: March–November, spikes of fragrant white flowers.

SOIL: adaptable, limestone soil, poor or well draining.

EXPOSURE: full sun, partial shade.

TEMPERATURE TOLERANCE: cold hardy.

WATER: drought tolerant.

PROPAGATION: fresh seeds, softwood cuttings.

The fragrant flowers of bee brush will perfume your yard throughout the spring and fall following heavy rains. The small white flowers with their distinct vanilla aroma densely cover erect spikes on the branch tips. You can use this slender, intricately branched plant as a background along a wall or fence or in a mass planting, or prune it into an upright profile. Its small leaves contribute to mixed plantings of black brush, brasil, and three-leaf sumac. It makes a good deciduous companion for evergreens such as Apache plume, mountain mahogany, and desert yaupon. You may have to prune it back heavily every few years to keep it dense and encourage flowering. In Arizona and New Mexico (Landscape Zones 1, 2), a closely related species, *Aloysia wrightii*, overlaps *A. gratissima* and has the same habitat and landscape features.

✳ ✳ ✳

False Indigo, *Amorpha fruticosa*

NATIVE DISTRIBUTION: woods and stream banks to 6000 feet, Texas to California, north to Wyoming; eastern United States.

LANDSCAPE ZONE: 2–9.

SIZE: 4-10 feet.

Bee Brush

LEAVES: deciduous.

FLOWER: May–June, purple spike.

SOIL: adaptable, well draining.

EXPOSURE: full sun, partial shade.

TEMPERATURE TOLERANCE: cold hardy.

WATER: drought tolerant.

PROPAGATION: scarified seeds, softwood and hardwood cuttings.

The distinctive 6-inch spikes of yellow-tipped deep purple flowers make false indigo an attractive addition to your landscape. The yellow stamens extend just beyond the purple petals, providing a dramatic contrast of colors. You can prune this plant into a multi-stemmed specimen or a clumped shrub. Its attractive foliage and flowers add interest to background plantings along a fence or wall, to entry gardens, or to mixed groupings. The bright green leaves and purple flowers make a striking companion with other small-leafed species such as agarita, catclaw mimosa, desert sumac, and daleas. This widespread plant has many varieties including a white-flowering form, one with crispy-looking leaves, one with variegated leaves, and a dwarf form that is not cold hardy.

False Indigo

Flame Anisacanthus, *Anisacanthus quadrifidus* var. *wrightii*
Desert Honeysuckle, *Anisacanthus thurberi*

NATIVE DISTRIBUTION: *A. quadrifidus*: limestone hills of Central Texas; Mexico; *A. thurberi*: southern Arizona, New Mexico, West Texas at 2000–5000-foot elevations; Mexico.

LANDSCAPE ZONE: 1–4, 6, 7.

SIZE: 3–5 feet.

LEAVES: deciduous.

FLOWER: April–November, orange, tube shaped.

SOIL: adaptable, well draining.

EXPOSURE: full sun, partial shade.

TEMPERATURE TOLERANCE: heat tolerant, cold hardy.

WATER: drought tolerant, 12–16 inches/year.

PROPAGATION: fresh seeds, cuttings.

The orange to red tubular flowers of flame anisacanthus and its western counterpart, desert honeysuckle, will add brilliant color to your yard from June through December. It seems like the hotter and drier it gets, the more these heat- and drought-tolerant shrubs bloom. They have irregular branches with narrow olive green leaves. Cutting the plant back every two to three years rejuvenates flower and foliage growth. These colorful shrubs

Flame Anisacanthus

make striking specimen plants if planted alone, and I've seen them used as low informal hedges. Although densely foliated, they don't shear well into a shaped hedge. Their small size suits them for borders along walks, for patio plants, or for plantings in front of windows. The honeysucklelike flowers attract hummingbirds throughout the summer.

Sand Sagebrush

Big Sagebrush

Desert Broom

Sand Sagebrush, *Artemisia filifolia*

NATIVE DISTRIBUTION: desert grasslands, 2500–7000 feet, West Texas to Arizona; Mexico.

LANDSCAPE ZONE: 2, 3, 9.

SIZE: 2–4 feet.

LEAVES: evergreen, threadlike.

FLOWER: allergenic fall pollen.

SOIL: sandy, gypsum, calcareous, well draining.

EXPOSURE: full sun, partial shade.

TEMPERATURE TOLERANCE: cold hardy.

WATER: drought tolerant, 8 inches/year.

PROPAGATION: seed.

This plant thrives in sandy locations that would stifle most other plants. Its silky, fine-textured leaves add a bluish green accent to group plantings or rock gardens. You can use it as a border planting along a fence, wall, or drive. It will eventually occupy a 4-by-4-foot area, but may need cutting back to maintain dense foliage. Most people, except those sensitive to the allergenic pollen common to all artemisias, consider the minute fall flowers insignificant.

Big Sagebrush, *Artemisia tridentata*

NATIVE DISTRIBUTION: deserts to timberline in arid soils of the western half of United States; Canada, Mexico.

LANDSCAPE ZONE: 1, 2, 9.

SIZE: 3–8 feet.

LEAVES: evergreen.

FLOWER: allergenic fall pollen.

SOIL: adaptable, well draining.

EXPOSURE: full sun.

TEMPERATURE TOLERANCE: cold hardy.

WATER: drought tolerant, 10 inches/year.

PROPAGATION: seeds.

Though big sagebrush is probably the most common range plant in the Great Plains, it deserves a place in our city landscapes. Its aromatic leaves produce the refreshing desert aroma that fills the air after a thunderstorm. In your yard, the small three-lobed grayish green leaves will contrast pinyons and junipers and complement Apache plume and desert sumac. Big sagebrush grows rapidly if water is available. Occasionally, you may have to cut it back to maintain dense branching and foliage. As with all artemisias, its pollen may cause allergenic reactions in sensitive people.

Desert Broom, *Baccharis sarothroides*

NATIVE DISTRIBUTION: sandy hillsides, bottomlands, 1000–5500 feet, southwestern New Mexico to southern California; Mexico.

LANDSCAPE ZONE: 1–3, 6.

SIZE: 3–9 feet tall.

LEAVES: evergreen.

FLOWERS: fall–winter, heads of small white flowers; fruit, white seed heads on female plants.

SOIL: sandy, rocky, well draining.

EXPOSURE: full sun, partial shade.

TEMPERATURE TOLERANCE: cold hardy.

WATER: drought tolerant.

PROPAGATION: seeds.

Plant this large, bushy evergreen to screen a fence or to provide a privacy hedge, background, or windbreak. Its dense array of slender branches creates a thick, rounded profile. In the fall, white flower heads cover the branch tips as though the plant had been dusted with snow. Choose a male plant and avoid the copious amounts of messy seeds produced by the females. The bright green leaves contrast well with gray-foliated plants such as woolly butterfly bush, rabbitbrush, the sages, and cenizo.

Anacacho

Agarita

Scarlet Bouvardia

Anacacho Orchid Tree, *Bauhinia congesta*

NATIVE DISTRIBUTION: limestone hills in Kinney County, Texas; Mexico.

LANDSCAPE ZONE: 4, 6, 7.

SIZE: 6–12 feet.

LEAVES: deciduous.

FLOWER: March–May, clusters of white blossoms; fruit, 3-inch bean pods.

SOIL: alkaline, well draining.

EXPOSURE: full sun, partial shade.

TEMPERATURE TOLERANCE: heat tolerant, cold hardy.

WATER: drought tolerant, 18 inches/year.

PROPAGATION: fresh seed.

In early April soon after the leaves bud out, clusters of delicate 1-inch white flowers cover each slender branch of this unusual shrub. The olive green leaves of this densely foliated plant are ornately split into two leaflets. You can train your Anacacho orchid tree into a multi-stemmed shrub or a small tree. It grows rapidly from seed and flowers the second year. Use it as a colorful accent plant for a small open area, courtyard, corner plot, or mixed planting. As a container plant, it adds visual interest to patios and poolsides. Though limited in natural range to the Anacacho Mountains in Texas, this rare plant has been planted widely from Houston westward. In Austin, you

can see it on the north side of the State Capitol, a shady location, and in full sun on the University of Texas campus. It's tender farther north, but reportedly has survived in Dallas in protected locations with a sunny southern exposure.

* * *

Agarita, *Berberis trifoliolata*
Red Barberry, *Berberis haematocarpa*

NATIVE DISTRIBUTION: *B. trifoliolata*: from the South Texas coast to southern Arizona; Mexico. *B. haematocarpa*: West Texas to central Arizona.

LANDSCAPE ZONE: 1–7.

SIZE: 3–6 feet.

LEAVES: evergreen, hollylike.

FLOWER: February–April, clusters of small yellow blooms; fruit, May–August, edible red berries.

SOIL: adaptable, alkaline, well drained.

EXPOSURE: full sun, partial shade.

TEMPERATURE TOLERANCE: heat tolerant, cold hardy.

WATER: drought tolerant, 16 inches/year.

PROPAGATION: stratified seed.

In late winter and early spring, clusters of lemon yellow flowers accent the spiny, hollylike leaves of agarita and red barberry;

and by May, bright red berries cover the shrubs. Their ornamental evergreen leaves, fragrant flowers, and abundant red berries make them premier landscape shrubs for most of the Southwest. These low-maintenance shrubs make attractive specimen plants, hedges, and borders along walkways and drives. Their light green prickly leaves naturally complement silver-leafed shrubs such as cenizo and woolly butterfly bush and spiny plants such as yucca and agave. The ornate leaves of agarita have three lobes joined at a point, while those of red barberry have five to nine leaflets along a central rib. A variety of agarita has gray leaves. The closely related Texas barberry, *Berberis swaseyi*, from Central Texas, has leaves that turn red and yellow in the fall. In Landscape Zones 9 and 10, plant Fremont barberry, *Berberis fremontii*. The tart fruit of these species makes a delicious jelly.

* * *

Scarlet Bouvardia, *Bouvardia ternifolia*

NATIVE DISTRIBUTION: mountain canyons at 3000–7500-foot elevations, West Texas to Arizona; Mexico.

LANDSCAPE ZONE: 2–4, 6.

SIZE: 1–3 feet.

LEAVES: deciduous.

FLOWER: spring–fall; clusters of 1-inch red,

tube-shaped blooms.

SOIL: adaptable, well drained.

EXPOSURE: full sun, partial shade.

TEMPERATURE TOLERANCE: moderately cold hardy.

WATER: drought tolerant, 16 inches/year.

PROPAGATION: seed, softwood cuttings.

Throughout the summer and fall, bundles of slender scarlet flowers crown the branch tips of this delightful shrub. Its small size and brilliant flowers adapt it to a host of applications. You can beautify your patio, pool, and entryway gardens, or plant it in a container so you can bring it inside during hard freezes. Use it as a colorful foreground shrub for terraced, corner, and mixed plantings. Bouvardia is a compatible companion for *Dalea, Salvia, Lantana,* and *Parthenium* species. Smooth bouvardia, *Bouvardia glaberrima*, grows to 9000-foot elevations and is suitable in Flagstaff and moderate elevations of Landscape Zone 9.

Woolly Butterfly Bush

Fairy Duster

American Beautyberry

Woolly Butterfly Bush, *Buddleja marrubiifolia*

NATIVE DISTRIBUTION: desert mountains, the southern Trans-Pecos in Texas; Mexico.

LANDSCAPE ZONE: 1–4, 6.

SIZE: 2–4 feet.

LEAVES: almost evergreen.

FLOWER: spring–fall, ½-inch round head with tiny orange flowers.

SOIL: limestone, well drained.

EXPOSURE: full sun.

TEMPERATURE TOLERANCE: heat tolerant, cold tolerant to at least 15 degrees F.

WATER: drought tolerant, 12 inches/year.

PROPAGATION: seeds, softwood and hardwood cuttings.

Gumball-sized clusters of red to orange flowers decorate this delightful shrub throughout the summer, and the gray velvet-covered leaves last into the winter. Its ornamental leaves and flowers add variety to any landscape design. You can use this densely branched shrub for border plantings, landscape islands, pool and patio designs, and container pots. Its commanding appearance makes it an appropriate focal plant for a mixed planting of small shrubs or for a foreground accent when planted with larger species. The ashen foliage and the bright flowers create a striking contrast, especially when mixed with green-foliated species such as brasil, guayacan, creosote bush, and Texas mountain laurel.

* * *

Fairy Duster, *Calliandra eriophylla*

NATIVE DISTRIBUTION: limestone hills, dry plains, South Texas, southern New Mexico, Arizona; Mexico.

LANDSCAPE ZONE: 1–4.

SIZE: 3–4 feet.

LEAVES: semievergreen.

FLOWERS: October–April; clusters of pink heads with 1-inch tassellike stamens.

SOIL: adaptable, well draining.

EXPOSURE: full sun, partial shade.

TEMPERATURE TOLERANCE: heat tolerant, cold hardy to 20 degrees F.

WATER: drought tolerant, 12 inches per year.

PROPAGATION: seeds.

This small shrub brings color to a mixed planting in the early spring, when rose to pink tassels cover the slender limbs. With extra water, it might carry its unusual flowers into the summer, then get ready for another burst of blooms in the fall and winter. Use fairy duster as a low border, for foundation plantings, or in mass plantings. Its flowers really draw attention to a patio or courtyard garden.

The dainty blooms complement its lacy leaflets, and the grayish green color of the foliage contrasts well with creosote bush, green cloud cenizo, autumn sage, and the daleas. The similar species, *Calliandra conferta*, is sometimes lumped with this species.

* * *

American Beautyberry, *Callicarpa americana*

NATIVE DISTRIBUTION: along streams and rich woods, Central Texas east to Florida, north to Virginia; Mexico, Caribbean.

LANDSCAPE ZONE: 4, 6–8.

SIZE: 3–6 feet.

LEAVES: deciduous.

FRUIT: late summer–fall, clusters of purple berrylike drupes.

SOIL: adaptable, moist to well draining.

EXPOSURE: partial shade, full sun.

TEMPERATURE TOLERANCE: cold hardy.

WATER: requires moisture, 32 inches/year.

PROPAGATION: fresh seeds, softwood and hardwood cuttings.

The genus name of this shrub tells it all: *calli* means "beauty" in Greek, and *carpa* "fruit." American beautyberry lives up to its name. From fall until long after they lose their leaves, the arching limbs droop with tight clusters of shiny purple fruit scattered along the branches at each leaf node. You can plant this shrub as a background or specimen plant in either well-draining or low areas and under trees that cast moderate shade. It's particularly attractive in mixed plantings with species with similar-sized leaves, such as roughleaf dogwood, button bush, and Turk's cap. The colorful berries will add autumn interest to plantings of the evergreen wax myrtle, yaupon, and American holly. You can cut it back severely every winter to encourage dense branching and fruiting. A white-fruiting variety, *lactea*, is available. Birds and other animals enjoy the fleshy fruit.

Button Bush

Winterfat

Button Bush, *Cephalanthus occidentalis*

NATIVE DISTRIBUTION: moist soil along streams throughout United States; Canada, Mexico, West Indies, Asia.

LANDSCAPE ZONE: throughout in moist habitats.

SIZE: 6–12 feet.

LEAVES: deciduous.

FLOWER: June–August, 1-inch head of white flowers; fruit, clusters of brown nutlets.

SOIL: adaptable, moist.

EXPOSURE: full sun, partial shade.

TEMPERATURE TOLERANCE: cold hardy.

WATER: requires moist soil.

PROPAGATION: fresh seeds, softwood, semihardwood, and hardwood cuttings.

Plant button bush in poorly draining areas, around ponds, or in low places where water stands after a rain. It takes lots of water to thrive. This fast-growing shrub has dense foliage and globe-shaped clusters of white flowers. The golfball-sized flower heads resemble round pincushions. As a shrub that easily grows head high or taller, it's suitable for mass plantings along fencerows and property lines, as a background plant, or in landscape islands occupying large areas. Its summer flowers and dark green deciduous leaves make it a good companion for wax myrtle, American beautyberry, and coral honeysuckle. Birds eagerly devour the fall nutlets.

Winterfat, *Ceratoides lanata (Eurotia lanata)*

NATIVE DISTRIBUTION: dry soils of deserts and mountains 2000 to 7000 feet in elevation, West Texas to California, north to Canada.

LANDSCAPE ZONE: 2, 3, 5, 9.

SIZE: 1–3 feet tall.

LEAVES: evergreen.

FRUIT: fall–winter, showy cottony seed heads along stems of female plants.

SOIL: adaptable, alkaline, well draining.

EXPOSURE: full sun.

TEMPERATURE TOLERANCE: heat tolerant, cold hardy.

WATER: drought tolerant, 8 inches/year.

PROPAGATION: stratified seeds, softwood cuttings.

Numerous erect slender branches grow from a woody base of this ornate addition to your landscape garden. Woolly hairs densely cover the narrow bluish green leaves that crowd the stems, and from September through December, plumes of fluffy white seeds cover the female plants. They remind me of miniature sticks of cotton candy, especially when they glow in the afternoon sun. You can use this fast-growing plant as a color accent for evergreen species such as starleaf Mexican orange, agarita, Mormon tea, and jojoba. Its spreading root system and low profile make it a good groundcover for hot, arid locations. You'll probably need to trim it back before it begins its spring growth, to keep it thick. Winterfat requires climates with cold nights to thrive, which limits its use in much of Texas.

Silverleaf Mountain Mahogany

Fernbush

Starleaf Mexican Orange

Silverleaf Mountain Mahogany, *Cercocarpus montanus* var. *argenteus*

NATIVE DISTRIBUTION: rocky canyons and dry mountain slopes at 3500–9000 feet, Central Texas to Arizona, north to Wyoming; Mexico.

LANDSCAPE ZONE: 2, 3, 5, 6, 9, 10.

SIZE: 5–15 feet.

LEAVES: almost evergreen.

FRUIT: fall, 2-inch feathery tail on seed.

SOIL: adaptable, well draining.

EXPOSURE: full sun.

TEMPERATURE TOLERANCE: heat tolerant, cold hardy.

WATER: drought tolerant, 12 inches/year.

PROPAGATION: scarified, stratified seeds, softwood cuttings.

If you want a densely foliated almost evergreen shrub with an interesting fall display, plant a mountain mahogany. Just when many plants are fading, this shrub is coming into its most beautiful season. As the seeds begin to mature, they develop a twisted feathery tail, and by September they almost obscure the leaves. You can shape it into a compact shrub or hedge suitable for screen, border, or foundation plantings. When planted alone, mountain mahogany attractively accents an open area. Given time and proper pruning, this slow-growing plant will become a small tree.

Another species with exceptional landscape value is curl-leaf mountain mahogany, *Cercocarpus ledifolius*, which has evergreen leaves with white undersides.

* * *

Fernbush, *Chamaebatiaria millefolium*

NATIVE DISTRIBUTION: 4000–7000-foot elevations, New Mexico and Arizona north to Wyoming.

LANDSCAPE ZONE: 2, 9.

SIZE: 3–6 feet.

LEAVES: mostly evergreen.

FLOWER: summer–fall, clusters of ½-inch creamy flowers.

SOIL: adaptable, well draining.

EXPOSURE: full sun, partial shade.

TEMPERATURE TOLERANCE: cold hardy.

WATER: drought tolerant, 15 inches/year.

PROPAGATION: stratified seeds.

At first glance, you might think this densely foliated shrub is some kind of fern. Its leaves look like tiny fronds, but the woody branches and dense spikes of small white flowers will change your mind. The unusual leaves and profuse flowers add a midsummer attraction to your landscape at a time when the accent of a blooming shrub is most welcome. Fernbush is large and dense enough to use for screen, background, and border plantings or as a specimen plant. In a mixed planting, the texture of its leaves complement golden current, big leaf sage, mountain mahogany, and cliffrose, plants that share its habitat requirements. Extra water helps it develop dense foliage. Fernbush is abundant and commonly planted on the South Rim of the Grand Canyon.

* * *

Starleaf Mexican Orange, *Choisya dumosa*

NATIVE DISTRIBUTION: sandy and rocky slopes of desert grasslands and oak woodlands at 4000–7000-foot elevations; West Texas to Southeast Arizona; Mexico.

LANDSCAPE ZONE: 2, 3, 6.

SIZE: 2–4 feet.

LEAVES: evergreen.

FLOWER: spring–fall, 1-inch cluster of white flowers.

SOIL: adaptable, limestone, igneous, well draining.

EXPOSURE: full sun, partial shade.

TEMPERATURE TOLERANCE: heat and cold tolerant.

WATER: drought tolerant, 16 inches/year.

PROPAGATION: fresh-seed stratified, hardwood and semihardwood cuttings.

I predict that someday this member of the citrus family will be as popular in Southwest landscapes as cenizo and century plants. It has a compact form, evergreen highly aromatic leaves, and showy flowers from April through September, a combination that provides year-round interest for your yard. You can use this low-growing, intricately branched plant to accent rock gardens and group plantings, as a border plant along drives and walks, and in a container for patios and poolsides. The plant normally grows 2 to 3 feet in height, which makes it ideal for providing a shrubby groundcover or for stabilizing a rocky slope. With its low, rounded profile, starleaf Mexican orange attractively complements mixed plantings of larger shrubs and adds winter color when used with deciduous species. The olive green leaves provide color variety when planted with gray-leafed species such as cenizo, winterfat, woolly butterfly bush, or sages. This plant of many uses absolutely requires well-draining soil.

Damianita

Damianita, *Chrysactinia mexicana*

NATIVE DISTRIBUTION: limestone hills from Central Texas through New Mexico; Mexico.

LANDSCAPE ZONE: 1–4, 6.

SIZE: 1–2 feet.

LEAVES: evergreen.

FLOWER: April–September, profuse yellow flowers.

SOIL: sand, loam, limestone, alkaline, well draining.

EXPOSURE: full sun.

TEMPERATURE TOLERANCE: moderately cold hardy.

WATER: drought tolerant, 12 inches/year.

PROPAGATION: fall-sown or stratified seeds, hardwood and semihardwood cuttings.

Any plant that can bloom profusely during the heat of summer in arid West Texas is a favorite of mine. From spring through September, showy lemon yellow flowers completely cover this compact rounded shrub. Damianita forms dense clumps usually 1 to 2 feet in height and several feet in width. The spherical shape and mass of golden blooms make it an outstanding choice as a border plant along walks, for patio and pool gardens, or as a foreground accent plant. In mass plantings it stabilizes and provides brilliant color to dry, rocky slopes. And the highly aromatic

Rabbitbrush

leaves add an extra zest to your yard. With a long flowering season, this perennial evergreen contributes color to your landscape throughout the year.

✳ ✳ ✳

Rabbitbrush or Chamisa, *Chryso-thamnus nauseosus*

NATIVE DISTRIBUTION: dry soils, mesas, plains at 2000–8000-foot elevations, West Texas to California, north to Canada; Mexico.

LANDSCAPE ZONE: 2, 5, 9.

SIZE: 2–5 feet.

LEAVES: partially evergreen.

FLOWER: August–September, heads of showy yellow flowers.

SOIL: adaptable, alkaline, well draining.

EXPOSURE: full sun, partial shade.

TEMPERATURE TOLERANCE: cold hardy, requires cool summers.

WATER: drought tolerant, 8 inches/year.

PROPAGATION: fresh seeds, hardwood cuttings.

With bluish green leaves, woolly white stems, and fall yellow flowers, rabbitbrush accents your landscape throughout the year. The slender, erect stems grow from a woody base and are densely covered with the narrow ashen leaves. You can plant it in mass as an

Roughleaf Dogwood

unsheared hedge along fences or drives. With mixed species, it provides a striking contrast with evergreens like agarita, starleaf Mexican orange, and pinyon pine. For a bouquet of fall colors, plant it with red yucca, autumn sage, and feather dalea. You may have to prune this fast-growing plant back in the winter to keep it full and to encourage blooming.

✳ ✳ ✳

Roughleaf Dogwood, *Cornus drummondii*

NATIVE DISTRIBUTION: along streams and in moist woods from Central Texas to Florida, north to Virginia.

LANDSCAPE ZONE: 7, 8.

SIZE: 8–15 feet.

LEAVES: deciduous.

FLOWER: May–August, 2–3-inch flat-topped clusters of white flowers; fruit, white drupes.

SOIL: moist, rich clay, loam, alkaline.

EXPOSURE: full sun, partial shade.

TEMPERATURE TOLERANCE: cold hardy.

WATER: needs moisture, 32 inches/year.

PROPAGATION: scarified, stratified seeds, softwood or semihardwood cuttings in summer, hardwood in winter.

This robust spreading shrub with shiny green leaves and showy clusters of white flowers makes an attractive background, screen, or row planting. Abundant clusters of snow-white flowers highlight the lustrous foliage in the spring, followed by bunches of ¼-inch white drupes in the summer and fall. Though deciduous and barren in the winter, it adds showy spring flowers to a mixture of evergreens, such as wax myrtle, American holly, or yaupon. It grows rapidly, reaching 10 feet in about two years, and spreads by root shoots. You may have to prune it severely to maintain a desired size and dense foliage. Since it requires a moist soil or climate, use it in the eastern half of Texas or at sites with deep, moist soil in Central Texas.

Cliffrose

Feather Dalea

Cliffrose, *Cowania mexicana*

NATIVE DISTRIBUTION: dry slopes and mesas at 3000–8000-foot elevations, New Mexico to California, north to Colorado, Nevada; Mexico.

LANDSCAPE ZONE: 1–3, 9, 10.

SIZE: 4–15 feet.

LEAVES: evergreen.

FLOWER: April–July, 1 inch, creamy; fruit, seeds with feathery tails.

SOIL: limestone soils, well draining.

EXPOSURE: full sun, partial shade.

TEMPERATURE TOLERANCE: heat tolerant, cold hardy.

WATER: drought tolerant, 12 inches/year.

PROPAGATION: stratified seeds.

From spring through summer, cliffrose is a mass of fragrant snowy flowers. The roselike, 1-inch blooms crowd the branches and accent the dark green foliage. When the flowers go to seed, feathery plumes cover the shrub. The evergreen foliage, showy flowers, and ornamental seeds make cliffrose a year-round attraction in your landscape. Use it as a screen or in a mixed planting, or plant it alone to accent the corner of your yard, a pool, or patio. You can prune this intricately branched, densely foliated plant into formal or informal designs, but I like its natural gnarled shape best. It's a slow grower, but can develop into a picturesque small tree with brown shredding bark. Its summer flowers and small leaves make it an attractive companion plant for fernbush, golden current, three-leaf sumac, and scarlet bouvardia. Heath cliffrose, *Cowania ericaefolia*, grows in the mountains of West Texas and should do well in landscape settings over much of the western half of Texas.

Feather Dalea, *Dalea formosa*
Black Dalea, *Dalea frutescens*

NATIVE DISTRIBUTION: dry soils, 2000–6500-foot elevations, Central Texas west to Arizona; Mexico.

LANDSCAPE ZONE: 1–7.

SIZE: 2–3 feet.

LEAVES: deciduous.

FLOWER: *D. formosa*: April–October, small purple, pealike bloom; fruit, seeds with feathery tails. *D. frutescens*: blooms July–October.

SOIL: adaptable, well draining.

EXPOSURE: full sun.

TEMPERATURE TOLERANCE: heat tolerant, cold hardy to midteens.

WATER: drought tolerant, 8 inches/year.

PROPAGATION: fresh seeds, semi-hardwood cuttings.

Feather dalea, or purple dalea as it is sometimes called, is true to its species name, *formosa*, which means "beautiful." Richly colored blossoms and feathery flower cups combine to make it make one of the most valuable ornamental shrubs of the Southwest. From March to June and often again in September, masses of the small blooms completely cover the shrub. The deep purple blossom has a yellow throat surrounded by feathery plumes. Tiny grayish green leaves punctuate the attractive flowers. This shrub has rigid zigzag branches and a naturally rounded shape. Black dalea is similar in shape, flower, and landscape application, but lacks the ornate feather plumes. The leaflets are slightly larger and a bright green. You can use these daleas as low border shrubs or as foreground accents in a mixed planting. Or you can plant them in mass for a groundcover with a dramatic splash of color. They grow moderately fast. Occasional pruning keeps them dense and compact.

Broom Dalea

Sotol

Joint Fir

Broom Dalea, *Dalea scoparia (Psorothamnus scoparia)*

NATIVE DISTRIBUTION: deep sand of Rio Grande drainage, West Texas to New Mexico, Arizona; Mexico.

LANDSCAPE ZONE: 2, 3

SIZE: 2–4 feet high and wide.

LEAVES: minute.

FLOWER: August–September, clusters of purple ½-inch blooms.

SOIL: sand, well draining.

EXPOSURE: full sun.

TEMPERATURE TOLERANCE: heat tolerant, cold hardy.

WATER: drought tolerant, 8 inches/year.

PROPAGATION: fresh seeds.

This low-growing, mounding shrub makes up for its almost nonexistent leaves with profuse flowering. The small, intensely purple blooms cover the dense array of gray branches in August and September. Use this colorful plant as a groundcover to beautify sandy waste areas. For a real splash of color, combine it with desert marigold, penstemons, giant four-o'clock, and scarlet gilia. It is particularly useful in El Paso and Albuquerque. Occasional deep watering will encourage profuse flowering.

Sotol, *Dasylirion* species

NATIVE DISTRIBUTION: South and Central Texas, upper desert grasslands at 3000–5000-foot elevations from West Texas to Arizona; Mexico.

LANDSCAPE ZONE: 1–4, 6, 7.

SIZE: 2–4 feet tall, 3–6 feet wide.

LEAVES: evergreen, narrow, 3–4 feet long with spines on margin.

FLOWER: May–July, creamy spike on 10–16-foot stalk; fruit, reddish seed heads.

SOIL: sandy, rocky, well draining.

EXPOSURE: full sun, partial shade.

TEMPERATURE TOLERANCE: heat tolerant, cold hardy.

WATER: drought tolerant, 8 inches/year.

PROPAGATION: fresh seeds.

Sotols give your home or commercial landscape a distinctive Southwest flavor. Their rounded profile provides a pleasing complement and natural focal point for rock gardens and mixed plantings of cacti, century plants, and yuccas. The symmetry of the tall flower stalk growing from the spherical rosette adds balance to any garden or group planting. Their low stature makes them ideal in front of windows and other places where you don't want a visual barrier. Since sotols are adapted to arid, marginal conditions, you can use them to beautify a rocky slope or other areas where a low-maintenance plant is required. The plant sends up its tall flowering stalk from May through July, and the rusty seed head retains its ornamental appearance through the fall. Because of the thorny leaves, plant sotols only in areas where no human contact is anticipated.

* * *

Joint Fir or Mormon Tea, *Ephedra* species

NATIVE DISTRIBUTION: sandy, rocky soils, Central Texas to California; Mexico.

LANDSCAPE ZONE: 1–6, 9.

SIZE: 2–5 feet.

LEAVES: minuscule, scalelike.

SOIL: sandy, rocky, well draining.

EXPOSURE: full sun, partial shade.

TEMPERATURE TOLERANCE: heat tolerant, cold hardy.

WATER: drought tolerant, 8 inches/year.

PROPAGATION: fresh or stratified seeds.

The smooth green to yellowish pencillike stems of these densely branching plants provide eye-catching interest in your rock garden or mixed planting. In the absence of leaves, the broomlike stems carry on photosynthesis and give the plant its green color. You may not be able to find one commercially, but if you have one growing naturally in your yard, plan your landscape design around it. You can complement it with beargrass, sotol, cacti, ocotillo, and yucca.

Larchleaf Goldenweed

Shrubby Boneset

Kidneywood

Larchleaf Goldenweed, *Ericameria laricifolia*

NATIVE DISTRIBUTION: desert mountains and grasslands, 3000–6000 feet, West Texas to Arizona; Mexico.

LANDSCAPE ZONE: 2, 3, 5, 6.

SIZE: 2–3 feet tall.

LEAVES: evergreen.

FLOWER: September–November, heads of small yellow flowers.

SOIL: limestone, well draining.

EXPOSURE: full sun.

TEMPERATURE TOLERANCE: cold hardy.

WATER: drought tolerant, 8 inches/year.

PROPAGATION: seeds.

The compact shape, dense branching, and attractive fall flowers make this little-known plant a perfect landscape choice. An array of bright yellow flowers crowns the stiff, erect branches from September through November. Its lemon flowers and dark green leaves make an attractive border for your walk or drive or a foreground accent in a mixed planting. For year-round color, plant it with spring-blooming Texas mountain laurel, black brush, agarita, and Anacacho orchid tree. The aromatic leaves give the plant another name, turpentine bush. An occasional trim will keep the foliage dense.

Shrubby Boneset, *Eupatorium havanense*

NATIVE DISTRIBUTION: limestone hills, Central and West Texas; Mexico.

LANDSCAPE ZONE: 2–4, 6.

SIZE: 2–6 feet.

LEAVES: deciduous.

FLOWER: October–November, clusters of small white blooms.

SOIL: adaptable, well draining.

EXPOSURE: full sun, partial shade.

TEMPERATURE TOLERANCE: cold hardy.

WATER: drought tolerant, 24 inches/year.

PROPAGATION: fresh seeds, softwood and semihardwood cuttings.

With beautiful masses of white flowers, shrubby boneset brightens your yard throughout the fall. The dense clusters of tiny flowers accent the lustrous green foliage. You can trim the plant into a small shrub or allow it to develop into a large plant up to 6 feet in height. Its naturally rounded shape and dense, dark green leaves suit it for corner plantings, landscape islands in broad open areas, and mass plantings along fences and property lines. When interplanted with evergreens, this deciduous shrub contributes flowering beauty until late in the year. After it loses it leaves, the adjacent evergreen species provide foliage color until spring. A hedge of mixed species has more visual interest than traditional single-species hedges and foundation plantings. Severe pruning in the winter keeps the plant bushy and encourages flowering. Wright boneset, *Eupatorium wrightii*, a similar species native to West Texas, grows to 2 feet and has smaller flower heads and leaves.

❋ ❋ ❋

Kidneywood, *Eysenhardtia texana*

NATIVE DISTRIBUTION: limestone hills, Central and West Texas; Mexico.

LANDSCAPE ZONE: 2–4, 6.

SIZE: 4–8 feet.

LEAVES: deciduous.

FLOWER: May–October, especially after rain, spikes of tiny white flowers.

SOIL: limestone, well draining.

EXPOSURE: full sun, partial shade.

TEMPERATURE TOLERANCE: heat tolerant, cold hardy.

WATER: drought tolerant, 16 inches/year.

PROPAGATION: fresh seeds, softwood and semihardwood cuttings.

You can train this intricately branching shrub with fragrant flowers and tiny leaves into an attractive shrub or informal hedge. Pruning encourages dense branching and flowering, but don't try to shear it into a hedge. Though not compact or densely foliated, it has a graceful, airy appearance. Use it as a background plant or in a group planting. Its abundant flowers add beauty to rocky slopes and other marginal areas difficult to landscape. It grows moderately fast and is planted along sidewalks at the San Antonio Zoo. A western species, *Eysenhardtia polystachya*, has similar landscape applications. The rare *Eysenhardtia spinosa* from West Texas reaches 3 feet in height and has blue flowers. It would make an attractive groundcover.

Apache Plume

Cliff Fendlerbush

Ocotillo

Apache Plume, *Fallugia paradoxa*

NATIVE DISTRIBUTION: upper desert rocky soils, 3000–8000-foot elevations from Central Texas to California; Mexico.

LANDSCAPE ZONE: 2–6, 9, 10.

SIZE: 2–8 feet.

LEAVES: usually evergreen.

FLOWER: May–September, 1-inch roselike white bloom; fruit, tassellike seed head.

SOIL: adaptable, well draining.

EXPOSURE: full sun, partial shade.

TEMPERATURE TOLERANCE: heat tolerant, cold hardy.

WATER: drought tolerant, 8 inches/year.

PROPAGATION: fresh seeds, layering, root suckers.

With snow-white flowers, feathery seed tassels, semievergreen foliage, and a well-rounded shape, Apache plume has a lot to contribute to your landscape. The fragrant flowers bloom continually until October, and the pink feathery plumes almost obscure the shrub through the winter, making it attractive most of the year. The seed heads resemble miniature feather dusters and reminded early settlers of the headdress worn by the Apaches. This ornamental plant can be a specimen plant, or can add color to a mass planting. It forms dense clumps, making it suitable for hedges, screens, and background plantings. This rapid-

growing plant flowers the first or second year from seed. Do your pruning in the winter, since it flowers on new spring growth. An occasional deep watering in the summer encourages flowering.

* * *

Cliff Fendlerbush, *Fendlera rupicola*

NATIVE DISTRIBUTION: rocky slopes and canyons from Central Texas to Arizona at 3000–7000-foot elevations; Mexico.

LANDSCAPE ZONE: 2, 3, 5, 6, 9.

SIZE: 4–6 feet.

LEAVES: deciduous.

FLOWER: May–June, ¾-inch white flowers.

SOIL: adaptable, well draining.

EXPOSURE: full sun, partial shade.

TEMPERATURE TOLERANCE: cold hardy.

WATER: drought tolerant, 12 inches/year.

PROPAGATION: fresh seeds, softwood cuttings.

In the spring, this intricately branched shrub will dazzle your yard with showy masses of snow-white flowers. The fragrant blossoms have four delicate, pink-tinged petals and profusely cover the branch tips. You can use it as a specimen shrub or in background or mixed planting. Moderate pruning keeps it

from getting too rangy. The specific name *rupicola* means "rock loving," so be sure you plant it in loose, well-draining soil. The variety *falcata* has larger flowers, up to 1½ inch across.

* * *

Ocotillo, *Fouquieria splendens*

NATIVE DISTRIBUTION: deserts, West Texas to California; Mexico.

LANDSCAPE ZONE: 1–3, 6.

SIZE: 6–15 feet.

LEAVES: briefly after rain.

FLOWER: March–June, clusters of red flowers.

SOIL: sandy, rocky, well draining.

EXPOSURE: full sun.

TEMPERATURE TOLERANCE: cold hardy to about 10 degrees F.

WATER: drought tolerant, 8 inches/year.

PROPAGATION: fresh seeds, cuttings.

Ocotillo is one of the strangest plants of the arid West, and one that has been used in Southwest landscapes for centuries. Numerous thorn-covered wandlike branches sprout from a short stem or root crown. Most of the year, the branches are barren, but after a rain, tiny green leaves sprout and temporarily cover the plant. In the spring, clusters of scarlet bell-shaped flowers crown each waving branch tip. The intense contrast between the spiny branches and the brilliant flowers adds flair to your landscape design. The airy structure of the plant accents without dominating a group planting, making it a good balance in a rock garden. Interestingly, one of its earliest landscape uses was as a living fence. When planted in a trench and woven together with wire, the thorny branches sprout and grow into a fence impenetrable to predators and humans alike. In humid climates, ocotillo is prone to rot and seldom flowers.

Silktassel

Guayacan

Red Yucca

Silktassel, *Garrya ovata (G. lindheimeri)*

NATIVE DISTRIBUTION: mountains and canyons, Central Texas to New Mexico; Mexico.

LANDSCAPE ZONE: 2, 3, 6, 9.

SIZE: 6–15 feet.

LEAVES: evergreen.

FRUIT: ¼-inch purple drupe on female plants.

SOIL: adaptable, well draining.

EXPOSURE: full sun, shade.

TEMPERATURE TOLERANCE: heat tolerant, cold hardy.

WATER: drought tolerant, 12 inches/year.

PROPAGATION: scarified, stratified seeds, semihardwood cuttings.

You couldn't ask for much more in a landscape plant. Silktassel is evergreen, fast growing, densely foliated, and drought and shade tolerant. The only thing lacking here is showy flowers and fruit, but I guess you can't have everything. When used alone as a specimen plant, silktassel develops a full, symmetrical shape, growing as large as 10 to 15 feet. The lustrous green leaves contribute year-round color to a mixed planting with deciduous species. It makes an ideal visual screen or privacy hedge, or you can prune it into a medium-sized foundation or boundary hedge.

A 6-inch seedling in my yard grew into a 10-foot bushy shrub in four years. Wright silktassel, *Garrya wrightii*, a smaller version that reaches 6 feet, grows from extreme West Texas to Arizona. It is reported to do poorly in alkaline soil.

* * *

Guayacan, *Guaiacum angustifolium (Porlieria angustifolia)*

NATIVE DISTRIBUTION: Central, South, and West Texas; Mexico.

LANDSCAPE ZONE: 2–4, 6.

SIZE: 6–12 feet.

LEAVES: evergreen.

FLOWER/FRUIT: March–September, ½-inch purple flower; scarlet seeds.

SOIL: adaptable, well drained.

EXPOSURE: full sun, partial shade.

TEMPERATURE TOLERANCE: heat and cold tolerant.

WATER: drought tolerant, 12 inches/year.

PROPAGATION: seeds.

With colorful foliage, flowers, and seeds, guayacan gives your landscape beauty throughout the year. After spring and summer rains, small but fragrant flowers crowd among the tiny bright green leaves, and in the fall, shiny red seeds accent the foliage. It's a delightful specimen plant for your entryway, patio, or poolside. You can enjoy the natural look of the crooked branches or prune them into a somewhat compact plant, but it's not densely foliated enough to form a classic hedge. With an upright shape and stout limbs, it can be espaliered to decorate a wall or fence. The numerous flowers provide a good source of food for honeybees. During the heat of the day, the leaflets fold up to conserve water. It's cold hardy, but will freeze to the ground in severe winters and sprout from the base the following spring.

* * *

Red Yucca, *Hesperaloe parviflora*

NATIVE DISTRIBUTION: limestone hills of Central Texas; Mexico.

LANDSCAPE ZONE: 1–7.

SIZE: 2–4 feet across.

LEAVES: evergreen, swordlike.

FLOWER: March–September, spike of 1-inch pink to red flowers on 4–8-foot stalk.

SOIL: adaptable, well draining.

EXPOSURE: full sun, partial shade.

TEMPERATURE TOLERANCE: heat tolerant, cold hardy.

WATER: drought tolerant, 16 inches/year.

PROPAGATION: seeds.

The small size, symmetrical cluster of leaves, and graceful arching flower stalk give this yuccalike plant an artistic, picturesque shape. It's the perfect accent for your rock or cactus garden, and it provides a natural focal point for small landscape gardens in your yard, on the patio, or at poolside. But that's not all: this versatile plant can surround a tree or lamp post, or serve as a groundcover or a container plant. The abundant coral flowers decorate nodding stalks and provide color until the first freeze. Unlike true yuccas, the long, stiff leaves of red yucca are thornless, making it safe to use as a border plant along walks and drives.

Deciduous Yaupon

Yaupon Holly

Texas Lantana

Deciduous Yaupon or Possum Haw, *Ilex decidua*

NATIVE DISTRIBUTION: woods and along streams, Central Texas to Florida, north to Illinois.

LANDSCAPE ZONE: 4–8.

SIZE: shrub to 15 feet.

LEAVES: deciduous.

FRUIT: winter, ¼-inch red drupe on female trees.

SOIL: adaptable, poor to well draining.

EXPOSURE: full sun, partial shade, shade.

TEMPERATURE TOLERANCE: cold hardy.

WATER: moderately drought tolerant, 24 inches/year.

PROPAGATION: fresh or scarified, stratified seeds, semihardwood cuttings.

Deciduous yaupon will paint your winter landscape with a brilliant splash of color. When it loses its leaves, bright red berries decorate the barren limbs like Christmas ornaments. It's an ideal accent for a mixed planting of evergreen and deciduous plants, or specimen for a small area. It has leaves and fruit similar to yaupon holly's, but this compact shrub develops an open-branching shape with spreading limbs. It's most gorgeous when trained into a large shrub or small tree. As with all hollies, only female plants produce fruit, so a male must be nearby. Birds and wildlife, including opossums, eat the fruit; hence the common name, possum haw. The berries are poisonous to humans.

* * *

Yaupon Holly, *Ilex vomitoria*

NATIVE DISTRIBUTION: limestone hills, piney woods, Central Texas to Florida.

LANDSCAPE ZONE: 4–8.

SIZE: shrub to 15 feet.

LEAVES: evergreen.

FRUIT: fall, ¼-inch shiny red drupe on female trees.

SOIL: adaptable, poor to well draining.

EXPOSURE: full sun, partial shade, shade.

TEMPERATURE TOLERANCE: cold hardy.

WATER: moderately drought tolerant, 24 inches/year.

PROPAGATION: fresh or scarified, stratified seeds, semihardwood cuttings.

Yaupon has a treasure chest of landscape qualities and applications. It has glossy evergreen leaves, dense branching and foliage, and bright red berries through the winter. It shears well into a thick formal hedge or into imaginative shapes, or you can train it into a picturesque multi-trunked tree. In addition to these premier qualities, it grows in almost any soil, well draining or not, in full sun or the shade of a tall tree. No wonder my family's nursery shipped them out by the truckload. A 3-foot dwarf form, "nana," makes a good groundcover when planted on 3-foot centers. Yellow-berry forms also exist. You'll need male plants nearby for the females to produce the ornamental fruit. Since the plant is so widespread, try to obtain one from your area that is adapted to your particular soil and moisture conditions. The berries are poisonous to humans.

* * *

Texas Lantana, *Lantana horrida*

NATIVE DISTRIBUTION: sandy, rocky soils, Texas; naturalized from Mississippi to California; Mexico.

LANDSCAPE ZONE: 1–8.

SIZE: 2–6 feet.

LEAVES: deciduous.

FLOWER: spring–winter, 1-inch head of orange and red flowers; fruit, black drupes, poisonous to humans.

SOIL: adaptable, well draining.

EXPOSURE: full sun, partial shade.

TEMPERATURE TOLERANCE: heat tolerant, cold hardy.

WATER: drought tolerant, 12 inches/year.

PROPAGATION: fresh seeds, softwood and semihardwood cuttings.

The multicolored flowers of this fast-growing shrub provide brilliant colors for your yard from the heat of summer to the first frost. Each flower head is a miniature bouquet of tiny yellow blossoms surrounded by bright orange blooms. Lantanas grow into a sprawling shrub up to 6 feet, but typically are 2 to 3 feet tall. As a low shrub, they are suitable for groundcovers, slope and curb plantings, or terraced landscapes. You can use them as colorful surround plants for trees and posts, in a mixed planting, or as a container plant pruned into a poodle shape or other imaginative form. In rich soil, you'll have to cut them back severely every winter or they will take over your yard. Numerous horticultural varieties of lantana occur in the nursery trade, including the similar nonnative *Lantana camera* and many dwarf and trailing forms.

Creosote Bush

Cenizo

Creosote Bush, *Larrea tridentata*

NATIVE DISTRIBUTION: deserts from West Texas to California, north to Utah; Mexico.

LANDSCAPE ZONE: 1–4, 6.

SIZE: 3–6 feet.

LEAVES: evergreen.

FLOWER: spring–winter, yellow, ½ inch; fruit, a fuzzy capsule.

SOIL: adaptable, well draining.

EXPOSURE: full sun.

TEMPERATURE TOLERANCE: heat and cold hardy.

WATER: drought tolerant, 4 inches/year.

PROPAGATION: seeds.

Creosote bush grows in the hottest, driest deserts in the Southwest. When given the advantages of a landscape setting, it develops into a beautiful specimen plant with dense foliage and a naturally rounded profile. Lemon yellow flowers or fuzzy seeds accent the deep green leaves throughout most of the year. You can shear this evergreen into a formal shape or a border hedge. In desert gardens or mixed plantings, it complements guayacan, cenizo, ocotillo, woolly butterfly bush, and Apache plume. Creosote bush adds a Southwest flavor to an open area when planted in an informal grouping or as a screen. And when mass planted, they add more than looks to your yard. After a rain, they will perfume the air with that distinctive desert aroma. Extra water in the summer speeds up growth, but over-watering kills.

Cenizo or Texas Ranger, *Leucophyllum frutescens, Leucophyllum candidum*

NATIVE DISTRIBUTION: limestone hills, South and West Texas; Mexico.

LANDSCAPE ZONE: 1–7.

SIZE: 4–8 feet.

LEAVES: evergreen.

FLOWER: anytime, especially after rain, 1 inch, purple, pink, or white.

SOIL: adaptable, well draining.

EXPOSURE: full sun, partial shade.

TEMPERATURE TOLERANCE: heat tolerant, cold hardy to 5 degrees F.

WATER: drought tolerant, 8 inches/year.

PROPAGATION: seeds, cuttings.

Rarely does a plant have as many premier landscape qualities as cenizo. It has striking evergreen (ever-gray) foliage, spectacular flowers, and a long blooming season; it is rapid growing with dense foliage and the ability to survive harsh conditions. These shrubs have an erect, rounded shape ideal for mass or mixed plantings, or you can shear them into a more formal shrub or hedge. If they get too rangy looking, cut them back severely every few years to keep the foliage dense. You can choose between several outstanding varieties of *Leucophyllum* species. Green cloud and green leaf are vigorous growers with green foliage. If you want a 3-foot dwarf variety, choose silver cloud, rain cloud, thunder cloud, compacta, or white cloud (white flowers).

White Honeysuckle

White Honeysuckle, *Lonicera albiflora*

NATIVE DISTRIBUTION: rocky, sandy soils, Oklahoma, Texas, New Mexico, Arizona; Mexico.

LANDSCAPE ZONE: 2–9.

SIZE: 4–6 feet.

LEAVES: nearly evergreen.

FLOWER: March–May, cluster of creamy tube-shaped flowers; fruit, orange to red berries in fall.

SOIL: adaptable, well draining.

EXPOSURE: shade, partial shade.

TEMPERATURE TOLERANCE: heat tolerant, cold hardy.

WATER: drought tolerant, 16 inches/year.

PROPAGATION: fresh or stratified seeds, softwood or semihardwood cuttings.

Creamy funnel-shaped flowers cover this bushy evergreen shrub in the early spring, and colorful red berries in the fall. The flower clusters and scarlet fruit nestle tightly against paired olive green leaves. Its twining, arching branches and rounded shape make it suitable for foundation plantings, informal hedges, and mass plantings. The shrub grows thick enough for background plantings and barrier hedges, or you can trim it into a densely foliated small shrub. And you have the luxury of planting it in shady locations. You'll probably have to prune it yearly, with severe pruning every few years to keep the foliage dense.

* * *

Wolfberry or Desert Thorn, *Lycium pallidum*

NATIVE DISTRIBUTION: creosote bush deserts and dry mountain slopes at 3000–7000-foot elevations, West Texas to California; Mexico.

LANDSCAPE ZONE: 1–6.

SIZE: 3–5 feet.

LEAVES: deciduous during droughts.

FLOWER: April–May, ¼ inch, funnel shaped, purple; fruit, ⅜-inch red juicy berry.

SOIL: adaptable, well draining.

EXPOSURE: full sun, partial shade.

TEMPERATURE TOLERANCE: heat tolerant, cold hardy.

WATER: drought tolerant, 8 inches/year.

PROPAGATION: fresh seeds, semi-hardwood cuttings.

This thorny, densely branched shrub often forms thickets in the wild. In your yard, its small flowers, red berries, bluish white leaves, and arching limbs will add a distinctive flavor to your desert garden or mixed planting. This hardy, symmetrically shaped shrub maintains

Wolfberry

Turk's Cap

lush foliage when given ample water; otherwise, it responds to drought by dropping its leaves. About a dozen species of *Lycium* grow in the Southwest deserts, but this is the most widespread. Carolina wolfberry, *Lycium carolinianum*, is an attractive small shrub or groundcover for Landscape Zone 4.

* * *

Turk's Cap or Wax Mallow, *Malvaviscus drummondii (M. arboreus* var. *drummondii)*

NATIVE DISTRIBUTION: rocky, sandy soils from Central and South Texas to Florida; Mexico.

LANDSCAPE ZONE: 4–8.

SIZE: 2–6 feet.

LEAVES: evergreen until freeze.

FLOWER: spring–fall, 1-inch red partially closed flowers; fruit, ¾-inch mealy red fruit.

SOIL: adaptable, moist, well draining.

EXPOSURE: full sun, partial shade, shade.

TEMPERATURE TOLERANCE: freezes to ground, root hardy.

WATER: moderately drought tolerant, 16 inches/year.

PROPAGATION: fresh seeds, softwood cuttings.

From spring through fall, scarlet flowers punctuate the heavily textured dark green leaves of Turk's cap. The unusual 1-inch blossoms, which have long protruding stamens, never quite open. Hummingbirds flock to the flowers, and wildlife relish the small applelike fruit. You can use this bushy shrub as a colorful background plant against a fence or wall, as a pole surround, or as an understory plant for shady areas. Give it plenty of room to spread; it can rapidly take over a 6-foot area. In South Texas, it may reach 8–10 feet in height, but in most of its range the plant is a 3–4-foot shrub. Freezes kill it back to the ground; otherwise, you may have to prune it severely every year or so to maintain its compact shape.

Fragrant Mimosa

Wax Myrtle

Fragrant Mimosa, *Mimosa borealis*

NATIVE DISTRIBUTION: limestone hills, Central Texas to New Mexico, Oklahoma; Mexico.

LANDSCAPE ZONE: 1–6.

SIZE: 2–3 feet.

LEAVES: deciduous.

FLOWER: April–July, fragrant pink puffball; fruit, 1–2-inch bean pod.

SOIL: adaptable, limestone, well draining.

EXPOSURE: full sun, partial shade.

TEMPERATURE TOLERANCE: heat tolerant, cold hardy.

WATER: drought tolerant, 8 inches/year

PROPAGATION: scarified seeds, semi-hardwood cuttings.

At first, you may think that only a diabolic landscaper would suggest a plant armed with such vicious catclaw thorns. But when this compact, rounded shrub blooms, you'll change your mind. Pink puffball flower heads blanket the plant and perfume the air. Use it to accent rock or cactus gardens or under an open-canopy tree like mesquite, retama, or palo verde. Periodic trimming maintains dense branching and encourages flowering. Two other widespread species have similar habitat requirements and landscape applications: catclaw mimosa, *Mimosa biuncifera*, and velvet pod mimosa, *M. dysocarpa*, which has larger flower heads.

Wax Myrtle, *Myrica cerifera*

NATIVE DISTRIBUTION: moist woods, East Texas to Florida, North to New Jersey.

LANDSCAPE ZONE: 7, 8, coastal 4.

SIZE: shrubby to 12 feet.

LEAVES: evergreen, aromatic.

FRUIT: fall, dry nutlet.

SOIL: adaptable, moist, acid, well to poor draining.

EXPOSURE: partial shade, full sun.

TEMPERATURE TOLERANCE: cold hardy.

WATER: moderately drought tolerant, 24 inches/year.

PROPAGATION: stratified seeds, softwood and semihardwood cuttings.

The shiny yellowish green foliage and a large, rounded shape will make this evergreen shrub one of your favorite plants. You can use it for screen and background plantings or for foundation, boundary, privacy, or barrier hedges. Or you can train it into a small multi-trunked tree to accent an empty corner. Since it's an understory plant in the woods, you can use it in shady locations. Plant this rapid-growing shrub where it has ample room to spread, unless you plan on regular pruning. Wax myrtle has highly scented leaves, and the hard, waxy fruit once was prized for its bayberry scent. In Beaumont, we called it "fleabush" and threw branches under the house where the dogs slept. But it gained respectability when landscapers discovered it, and our nursery began shipping it by the truckloads.

Another versatile shrub is dwarf wax myrtle, *Myrica pusilla*. In nature, it rarely reaches 6 feet in height, and often is smaller in cultivation. It spreads by underground stems and makes a great groundcover when planted on 2-foot centers. Use it wherever you need a small evergreen. It grows in the same range as its larger relative. Birds eagerly eat the fruit of both species.

Beargrass

Guayule

Rose Pavonia

Beargrass or Sacahuista, *Nolina* species

NATIVE DISTRIBUTION: slopes, ravines, open areas, Central Texas to California: Mexico.

LANDSCAPE ZONE: 1–6.

SIZE: 2–4 feet high and wide.

LEAVES: evergreen.

FLOWER: March–July, on 1–6-foot stalk, depending on species.

SOIL: sandy, rocky, loam, well draining.

EXPOSURE: full sun, partial shade.

TEMPERATURE TOLERANCE: heat tolerant, cold hardy.

WATER: drought tolerant, 8 inches/year.

PROPAGATION: seeds, plant division.

A nolina looks like a rounded clump of thick-bladed grass, until it sends up its yuccalike flower stalk. The flower stalks range from 1 to 6 feet according to species, but all have clusters of creamy white flowers. The symmetrical profile and arching, spreading leaves make nolina an ideal focal plant for a cactus garden or grouping of desert plants. Its wiry grasslike leaves complement thick-bladed plants like yuccas and agaves. You can plant them on 3- to 4-foot centers for a groundcover or a stabilizer for rocky slopes. Nolina is particularly attractive in a planter or along a ledge with its long leaves dangling over the edge.

Of the many species in the Southwest, *Nolina texana* and *N. microcarpa* are the most widespread. Their compact size adapts them well to most landscape settings. *Nolina erumpens* and *N. bigelovii*, which develop short trunks, can spread to 6 to 8 feet wide.

* * *

Guayule, *Parthenium argentatum*

NATIVE DISTRIBUTION: Chihuahuan Desert, the Trans-Pecos area of Texas into Mexico.

LANDSCAPE ZONE: 1–6.

SIZE: 1–2 feet.

LEAVES: evergreen.

FLOWER: spring–fall, clusters of yellowish flowers on 6-inch stem.

SOIL: sand, gravel, caliche, igneous, well draining.

EXPOSURE: sun.

TEMPERATURE TOLERANCE: heat tolerant, cold hardy.

WATER: drought tolerant, 8 inches/year.

PROPAGATION: scarified, stratified seeds.

With ornate silvery leaves and a compact profile, this small rounded shrub looks beautiful in the foreground of a group planting, as a groundcover for slopes or rocky areas, or as a border along a walk or garden. It will bloom all summer if you give it extra water. Its neutral color contrasts well with starleaf Mexican orange, damianita, and other green-leafed species. You'll want to trim out the dead flower stems to keep the plant neat looking and to prune the bush back every few years to keep it dense. The closely related plant, mariola, *Parthenium incanum*, grows from West Texas to Arizona and has similar landscape applications. It has smaller leaves and is not as densely foliated.

* * *

Rose Pavonia or Rose Mallow, *Pavonia lasiopetala*

NATIVE DISTRIBUTION: woods and rocky slopes, Central, West Texas into Mexico.

LANDSCAPE ZONE: 3, 4, 6–8.

SIZE: 2–4 feet.

LEAVES: deciduous.

FLOWER: spring–fall, 2 inch, pink.

SOIL: adaptable, well draining.

EXPOSURE: full sun, partial shade, shade.

TEMPERATURE TOLERANCE: root hardy, will freeze to the ground.

WATER: drought tolerant, 18 inches/year.

PROPAGATION: fresh seeds, softwood cuttings.

This bushy open-branched shrub will decorate your yard with showy pink flowers from spring until the first freeze. The brilliant petals open widely to reveal a long stamen column with yellow filaments. The plant grows 4 feet tall with slender, spreading branches and broad dark green leaves. It's often not densely branching or foliated, but it provides a colorful accent. Its beautiful flowers add a delicate touch to courtyard, pool, and patio landscapes. Its foliage, size, and habitat are compatible with silktassel, agarita, and black dalea, and its flowers provide a color complement to the larger Texas mountain laurel, evergreen sumac, and Texas persimmon. You'll probably want to prune it back to the ground every year to keep it bushy. Though only living a few years, it reseeds itself readily.

Shrubby Cinquefoil

Smooth Sumac

Shrubby Cinquefoil, *Potentilla fruticosa*

NATIVE DISTRIBUTION: mountain grasslands, forests at 6000–10,000-foot elevations, New Mexico to California, north to Alaska, east to New Jersey; Canada.

LANDSCAPE ZONE: 2, 9.

SIZE: 2–3 feet.

LEAVES: usually evergreen.

FLOWER: June–September, 1 inch, yellow, roselike.

SOIL: adaptable, moist, well draining.

EXPOSURE: full sun, partial shade, shade.

TEMPERATURE TOLERANCE: cold hardy.

WATER: moderately drought tolerant, 20 inches/year.

PROPAGATION: seeds.

This delightful little shrub graces your landscape with bright yellow flowers from summer through fall. The five-petaled, roselike blossoms decorate the leafy stems like drops of golden paint. The five-fingered leaves crowd the intricately branching limbs to create a densely foliated shrub. The long blooming season, showy flowers, and attractive foliage make this plant a good choice for almost any landscape design. But it likes cool climates; it's stressed in Albuquerque's heat and reportedly tends to die out and suffer from spider mites. This plant is popular around the world, with numerous varieties available, including small and large heights, various tints of leaves, and red, orange, white, and shades of yellow flower colors.

* * *

Smooth Sumac, *Rhus glabra*

NATIVE DISTRIBUTION: dry hills from Arizona east to the Atlantic; Mexico.

LANDSCAPE ZONE: 2, 4–9.

SIZE: 3–10 feet.

LEAVES: deciduous with red fall color.

FLOWER: May–August, large cluster of white flowers; fruit, winter, clusters of hard red drupes.

SOIL: adaptable, well draining.

EXPOSURE: full sun, partial shade.

TEMPERATURE TOLERANCE: cold hardy.

WATER: drought tolerant, 16 inches/year.

PROPAGATION: scarified, stratified seeds, semihardwood cuttings.

In the spring, large bundles of white flowers decorate this shrubby sumac, followed by attractive grapelike clusters of red seeds. This species has the longest, most ornamental leaves of the sumacs. Come autumn, the dark green leaves turn brilliant hues of red and orange. This fast-growing plant spreads by root suckers and will form a thicket if naturalized in an unmowed area. Because of its moderate size, it's good for background, screen, and border plantings or as an attractive specimen plant. Or you can train it into a small tree. Wildlife eat the seeds, which can be made into a tart lemonade-type drink. Some people are allergic to the oil on the fruit and leaves. Several varieties are recognized, including one with yellow fruit and a dwarf form.

* * *

Little-leaf Sumac or Desert Sumac, *Rhus microphylla*

NATIVE DISTRIBUTION: dry hill and plains at altitudes of 1000–6400 feet, West Texas to southern Arizona; Mexico.

LANDSCAPE ZONE: 2–6

SIZE: 4–10 feet.

LEAVES: deciduous.

FLOWER: spring, small white flowers; fruit, summer, hard red drupes.

SOIL: adaptable, well draining.

Little-leaf Sumac

EXPOSURE: full sun, partial shade.

TEMPERATURE TOLERANCE: heat tolerant, cold hardy.

WATER: drought tolerant, 12 inches/year.

PROPAGATION: scarified, stratified seeds, cuttings.

The thick foliage and intricate branching of this shrub make it ideal for foundation, border, and privacy hedges. You can shear it into a thick low hedge or groundcover or a head-high hedge forming a visual barrier or plant it alone. If you use it as a hedge, you may want to mix it with evergreens since it's deciduous. The tiny compound leaves give little-leaf sumac its common and specific name. Spherical clusters of minute white flowers emerge in the spring before the leaves, and the decorative red fruit provides abundant ornamental color throughout the summer. Birds and other wildlife relish the fruit. Attractive specimens of this plant grow at Indian Lodge in Davis Mountains State Park, where it is used both as a sheared privacy hedge and as a shrubby groundcover.

Three-leaf Sumac

Evergreen Sumac

Golden Current

Three-leaf Sumac or Aromatic Sumac, *Rhus trilobata* (including *R. aromatica*)

NATIVE DISTRIBUTION: throughout Texas; chaparral, pinyon-juniper woodlands to 8000-foot elevations in New Mexico and Arizona; throughout United States into Canada, Mexico.

LANDSCAPE ZONE: 2–9.

SIZE: 2–6 feet.

LEAVES: deciduous with red and orange fall color.

FLOWER: March–June, clusters of yellowish flowers before leaves; fruit, hard red drupes.

SOIL: adaptable, well draining.

EXPOSURE: full sun, partial shade.

TEMPERATURE TOLERANCE: cold hardy.

WATER: drought tolerant, 10 inches/year.

PROPAGATION: scarified, stratified seeds, cuttings.

You can prune this small shrub into a moderately compact rounded form for background or specimen plantings. It grows fast, and the three dark green leaflets give your yard a delightful display of red and orange hues in the autumn. The foliage provides a striking contrast with gray-leafed species both in the summer and fall. Clusters of red fruit decorate the shrub in the summer, until the birds and other wildlife gobble them up. You also can plant this thicket-forming sumac in mass for groundcover and erosion control. A prostrate cultivar exists that forms a rounded mound up to 6 feet wide and 18 inches high. Crushed leaves have a tart scent described as sweet by some and skunklike by others.

* * *

Evergreen Sumac, *Rhus virens* (includes *R. choriophylla*)

NATIVE DISTRIBUTION: rocky hills of Central Texas, west through southern New Mexico and Arizona; Mexico.

LANDSCAPE ZONE: 1–4, 6–8.

SIZE: 4–10 feet.

LEAVES: evergreen, colorful after freezes.

FLOWER: August–October, clusters of small white flowers; fruit, hard red drupes.

SOIL: adaptable, well draining.

EXPOSURE: full sun, partial shade.

TEMPERATURE TOLERANCE: cold hardy to about 10 degrees F.

WATER: drought tolerant, 12 inches/year.

PROPAGATION: fresh scarified seeds.

If you have well-draining soil and need a moderate-sized evergreen, this is the plant for you. It's naturally bushy and needs little pruning to grow into a beautiful specimen. Or you can use it in a screen or background planting or as a border hedge. However you use it, you, the birds, and the bees will enjoy the late-summer flowers and ornate red fruit. The deep green glossy leaves provide year-round color and contrast well with cenizo and other gray-foliated plants. If you live in Phoenix, this sumac will appreciate a little extra summer water. The similar evergreen, sugarbush, *Rhus ovata*, native to the 4000- to 7000-foot chaparral belt in Arizona, has comparable habitat requirements and landscape applications.

* * *

Golden Current, *Ribes aureum*

NATIVE DISTRIBUTION: moist canyons, hillsides in 3500–8000-foot mountains, West Texas to California, north into Canada.

LANDSCAPE ZONE: 2, 9, 10.

SIZE: 3–6 feet tall.

LEAVES: deciduous with red fall colors.

FLOWER: March–June, clusters of 2-inch golden flowers; fruit, ¼-inch berry maturing reddish black by late summer.

SOIL: adaptable, well draining.

EXPOSURE: full sun, partial shade.

TEMPERATURE TOLERANCE: cold hardy.

WATER: moderately drought tolerant, 16 inches/year.

PROPAGATION: stratified seeds, dormant hardwood cuttings.

When golden clusters of trumpet-shaped, spicy-scented flowers turn this plant into a mound of color in the spring, you'll know how it got its name. The dense covering of small maplelike leaves, colorful summer fruit, and brilliant autumn shades of burgundy, red, and yellow make this a premier plant for your landscape. Use it for mass plantings or hedges or as a component in a mixed planting. Its habitat requirements complement fernbush, cliffrose, mountain mahogany, shrubby cinquefoil, and pinyon pine. You can prune it lightly to make it more dense, or shear it to the size you desire. At low elevations it needs regular deep watering in the summer. Wildlife devour the sweet fruit, which is tasty raw or made into jelly.

Palmetto

Autumn Sage

Mountain Sage

Palmetto, *Sabal minor*

NATIVE DISTRIBUTION: streambanks, moist woods, swamps, Central Texas to Florida, north to Arkansas, North Carolina.

LANDSCAPE ZONE: 4, 7, 8.

SIZE: 3–8 feet.

LEAVES: evergreen.

FLOWER: spring, small white flowers on 2–8-foot stalk; fruit, cluster of ¼-inch black drupes.

SOIL: adaptable, moist, poor draining.

EXPOSURE: shade, partial shade, full sun.

TEMPERATURE TOLERANCE: cold hardy.

WATER: needs moisture, 35 inches/year.

PROPAGATION: stratified seeds.

You don't have to live in a swamp to plant this trunkless palm, but it would help. Palmetto grows abundantly in the wet woodlands around Houston and Beaumont, but it also occurs in moist limestone soil along a few creeks in Central Texas. If not planted in moist soil, it will need plenty of water to become established (several years) and to help it get through dry summers. If your yard can support a palmetto, the plant will add a tropical flavor with its cluster of bright green fan-shaped leaves. The leaves, which may reach 5 feet in diameter, sprout from an underground stem in a vaselike profile. Use

them as specimen or background plants or in patio or poolside landscape gardens.

* * *

Autumn Sage or Cherry Sage, *Salvia greggii*

NATIVE DISTRIBUTION: rocky canyons of Central, South, West Texas; Mexico.

LANDSCAPE ZONE: 1–4, 6–8.

SIZE: 1–3 feet.

LEAVES: nearly evergreen.

FLOWER: spring–winter, clustered 1-inch red, purple, pink, or white flowers.

SOIL: adaptable, well draining.

EXPOSURE: full sun, partial shade.

TEMPERATURE TOLERANCE: cold hardy to 16 degrees F.

WATER: drought tolerant, 12 inches/year.

PROPAGATION: spring-planted seeds, softwood and semihardwood tip cuttings.

Rosy red tube-shaped blooms cover this plant from June through November. The profusion of brilliant flowers provides a striking contrast against the bright green aromatic leaves. You can use this densely foliated, low-growing shrub as a natural or shaped border hedge to add color to walks, drives, walls, and foundations. When planted in mass or as a ground-cover, it spreads a spectacular blanket of col-

or across your yard. It makes a colorful companion to daleas, rose pavonia, anisacanthus, and agarita. The colorful 1-inch flowers bloom profusely after rains or when water is available. You can choose varieties with red, pink, purple, and white blossoms. Keep your salvia densely foliated by trimming before spring growth, with severe pruning every few years. The plants lose their leaves in freezing weather. In Texas, it does well in landscapes as far north as Lubbock and Wichita Falls.

* * *

Mountain Sage or Royal Sage, *Salvia regla*

NATIVE DISTRIBUTION: wooded canyons 4500–7000-foot elevations in the Chisos Mountains, West Texas; Mexico.

LANDSCAPE ZONE: 1–4, 6–8.

SIZE: 2–6 feet.

LEAVES: deciduous.

FLOWER: spring–fall, 1 inch, red.

SOIL: adaptable, well draining.

EXPOSURE: partial shade.

TEMPERATURE TOLERANCE: Mount Emory cultivar root hardy to 0 degrees F.

WATER: drought tolerant, 12 inches/year.

PROPAGATION: spring planted seeds, softwood and semihardwood tip cuttings.

If you want a plant that adds spectacular fall color to your yard, plant a mountain sage. The scarlet tube-shaped flowers covering this rounded shrub will draw the attention of your friends — and every hummingbird in the neighborhood. Use it in mass and mixed plantings, for pool or patio beds, or as a large container plant. It adds seasonal color when planted with spring-flowering species or will complement other fall-blooming shrubs and wildflowers. Trim it back before spring growth to keep it bushy and to encourage flowering. This Mexican plant isn't naturally cold hardy, so look for the cultivar Mount Emory, which survives winters north to Dallas.

115

Elderberry

Desert Yaupon

Shrubby Senna

Elderberry, *Sambucus canadensis*

NATIVE DISTRIBUTION: streams and swamps, Central Texas east to Florida, north to Canada.

LANDSCAPE ZONE: 4–8.

SIZE: 6–12 feet tall.

LEAVES: deciduous.

FLOWER: May–July, 10-inch flattened clusters of white flowers; fruit, black berrylike drupes.

SOIL: deep loam, moist, pH 4–8.5.

EXPOSURE: full sun, partial shade.

TEMPERATURE TOLERANCE: cold hardy.

WATER: needs moisture.

PROPAGATION: scarified, stratified seeds, softwood and semihardwood cuttings.

With bright green leaves, showy symmetrical flower heads, and ornate clusters of black fruit, elderberry adds color to your landscape for much of the year. You can plant this many-branched, multistemmed shrub alone as a specimen, but only where you want a dominant shrub. Its large size and spreading shape make it suitable for background and mass plantings along fences, walls, or property lines. In mixed plantings, it is compatible in size and habitat with rusty blackhaw, roughleaf dogwood, and button bush. You can select among varieties with black, red, or green fruit

and golden, grayish green, or dissected leaves. In Landscape Zones 2, 3, and 9, plant the western species, blue elderberry, *Sambucus caerulea*, which tends to be evergreen. It grows in moist soils at 5000- to 10,000-foot elevations from the chaparral belt to spruce-fir forests. Numerous birds and mammals eat the berries, which are popularly used for jelly, pies, and wine. Raw berries are slightly toxic.

✳ ✳ ✳

Desert Yaupon, *Schaefferia cuneifolia*

NATIVE DISTRIBUTION: rocky slopes in South and West Texas; Mexico.

LANDSCAPE ZONE: 1–4, 6.

SIZE: 2–8 feet.

LEAVES: evergreen.

FRUIT: summer–fall, shiny red ¼-inch drupe on females.

SOIL: adaptable, well draining.

EXPOSURE: full sun, partial shade.

TEMPERATURE TOLERANCE: dies back in severe winters.

WATER: drought tolerant, 12 inches/year.

PROPAGATION: fresh seeds, root sprouts.

With evergreen foliage, scarlet berries, and dense foliage, desert yaupon rates a high score for landscape versatility. It seems destined to become as popular in the West as its namesake,

yaupon holly, is in the East. Unlike the unrelated holly, desert yaupon is adapted to hot, arid climates. You can use this shrub as an attractive sheared hedge for foundations, borders, or fences. Its dense foliage provides visual privacy, and the stiff branches make an effective barrier hedge. When planted alone, the shrub, with its naturally spreading shape, will accent entry walks and patio and pool decors. You'll need male plants nearby for the females to produce the ornate berries. Like its holly look-alike, it grows slowly, which currently limits its availability in the nursery trade. It freezes to the ground in severe winters, but sprouts from the base the following spring.

✳ ✳ ✳

Shrubby Senna, *Senna wislizenii* (*Cassia wislizenii*)

NATIVE DISTRIBUTION: dry hills 3000–5000 feet, the southern Trans-Pecos of Texas to southeastern Arizona; Mexico.

LANDSCAPE ZONE: 1–4, 6.

SIZE: 4–9 feet.

LEAVES: deciduous.

FLOWER: May–September; 4-inch clusters of yellow pealike blooms; fruit, 3–6-inch bean pods.

SOIL: adaptable, limestone, igneous, well draining.

EXPOSURE: full sun, partial shade.

TEMPERATURE TOLERANCE: heat tolerant, moderately cold hardy.

WATER: drought tolerant; 12 inches/year.

PROPAGATION: fresh seed, semihardwood cuttings.

The masses of showy bright yellow flowers contrasted against the dark green leaves, and a long blooming season, make this a colorful choice for hot, arid landscapes. You know it's hardy because it's native to Presidio, Douglas, and Bisbee, cities known for blazing summers. Its rigid, spreading limbs, dense branching, and moderate size make it a good background or specimen shrub, or you can group it with a mixed planting of compatible species, such as jojoba, Apache plume, ocotillo, yellow trumpet flower, or catclaw acacia.

Silver Buffaloberry

Silver Buffaloberry, *Shepherdia argentia*

NATIVE DISTRIBUTION: along streams 3000–7500-foot elevations in pinyon belt, New Mexico to California, north to Canada.

LANDSCAPE ZONE: 2, 9.

SIZE: 6–10 feet.

LEAVES: deciduous.

FRUIT: summer, ¼-inch edible red to yellow drupes on females.

SOIL: adaptable, well draining.

EXPOSURE: full sun, partial shade.

TEMPERATURE TOLERANCE: cold hardy.

WATER: drought tolerant, 12 inches/year.

PROPAGATION: fresh or stratified seeds.

The ornate 2-inch silver leaves give this thorny shrub both its name and its landscape value. It makes a beautiful gray background plant and, since it forms thickets in the wild, is great for mass plantings and erosion control. You can plant them close together and trim them into a hedge, or put one in a mixed planting to contrast the green foliage of pinyons, mountain mahogany, cliffrose, and shrubby cinquefoil. You'll need both male and female plants to get the colorful summer fruit. Wildlife enjoy the berries, which make a tart jelly. You can use this plant as a native substitute for the all too common Russian olive. The roundleaf

Jojoba

buffaloberry, *Shepherdia rotundifolia,* a compact 3-foot shrub occurring at 5000- to 8000-foot elevations, also has excellent landscaping qualities.

* * *

Jojoba, *Simmondsia chinensis*

NATIVE DISTRIBUTION: rocky, chaparral-covered slopes and foothills at 1500–5000-foot elevations, southwestern Arizona to California; Mexico.

LANDSCAPE ZONE: 1.

SIZE: 3–6 feet.

LEAVES: evergreen.

FRUIT: summer, 1-inch, acornlike nuts on females.

SOIL: sandy, rocky, well draining.

EXPOSURE: full sun.

TEMPERATURE TOLERANCE: heat tolerant, cold hardy to 20 degrees F.

WATER: drought tolerant, 10 inches/year.

PROPAGATION: spring-planted seeds.

The 2-inch grayish green leathery leaves cover this rounded shrub all the way to the ground, making it an ideal hedge. Plant them 2 feet apart for a clipped hedge resembling boxwood, or 4 feet apart for a background or screen planting. With a symmetrical shape and ornate paired leaves, jojoba provides year-round foliage color as a specimen or a member

of a mixed planting. You'll need both male and female plants to produce the fruit, which has become commercially important because of its high oil content. These plants grow slowly, but require no maintenance or extra water. Frost kills the seedlings of these low-desert plants. Even El Paso gets too cold for them.

* * *

Texas Mountain Laurel or Mescal Bean, *Sophora secundiflora*

NATIVE DISTRIBUTION: limestone hills to 5000 feet, Central and South Texas west into New Mexico; Mexico.

LANDSCAPE ZONE: 1–4, 6.

SIZE: shrubby to 15 feet.

LEAVES: evergreen.

FLOWER: spring, cascades of fragrant purple flowers; fruit, woody pods with red poisonous seeds.

SOIL: adaptable, alkaline, well draining.

EXPOSURE: full sun, partial shade.

TEMPERATURE TOLERANCE: cold

Texas Mountain Laurel

hardy to 15 degrees F.

WATER: drought tolerant, 14 inches/year.

PROPAGATION: scarified seeds.

Many landscapers consider this plant one of the ten best ornamental shrubs in the nation. In March and April, showers of vibrant purple flowers cover the plant and perfume the air with the scent of grape Kool-Aid. Its compact, upright shape and the striking contrast between the deep purple flowers and shiny green leaves make it eye-catching as either a specimen or a component of a mixed planting. It colorfully accents a patio or pool decor, whether in a small landscape garden or a large planter. You can prune, but not shear, it into an informal foundation, border, or privacy hedge. Since it's an understory tree in nature, it will grow in filtered shade, though not as fast. Extra water speeds its growth, while cool summers impede it. Even small plants bloom, but a late March or April freeze will nip the flowers. With time, mountain laurel develops into an ornate small tree. The seeds are deadly, but fortunately, the hard seed coat usually prevents children from chewing them.

Coralberry

Yellow Trumpet Flower

Coralberry or Indian Current, *Symphoricarpos orbiculatus*

NATIVE DISTRIBUTION: moist woods, streams, East Texas to Florida, north through Oklahoma to South Dakota, New York.

LANDSCAPE ZONE: 2, 4–9.

SIZE: 2–4 feet.

LEAVES: persistent to deciduous.

FRUIT: fall, dense clusters of red ¼-inch drupes.

SOIL: adaptable, acid to slightly alkaline, well draining.

EXPOSURE: partial shade.

TEMPERATURE TOLERANCE: cold hardy.

WATER: drought tolerant, 20 inches/year.

PROPAGATION: firm wood cuttings of new growth.

The gracefully arching branches of this low-growing plant add a woodsy charm to your yard when clustered under a tree or grouped with a mixed planting. From September or October until late winter, profuse clusters of red berries decorate the shrub. This fast-growing thicket-forming plant spreads by stolons, which makes it ideal for a ground-cover or erosion control. Or you can use it to border a landscape garden. If it gets too rangy, prune it back severely in the winter to encourage dense growth and flowering. Several varieties exist, including forms with white fruit and yellow variegated leaves. Other species with similar landscape characteristics include western snowberry, *Symphoricarpos occidentalis*, mountain snowberry, *S. oreophilus*, and fragrant snowberry, *S. longiflorus*. These have white fruit. Select the species best adapted to your habitat.

Yellow Trumpet Flower or Yellow Bells, *Tecoma stans* var. *angustata*

NATIVE DISTRIBUTION: desert grasslands, oak woodlands, 2000–5500 feet, West Texas through southern New Mexico and Arizona; Florida; Mexico through South America.

LANDSCAPE ZONE: 2–4, 6.

SIZE: 3–8 feet.

LEAVES: deciduous.

FLOWER: April–November, clusters of 4-inch yellow flowers; fruit, 6-inch capsules.

SOIL: caliche, loam, sand, well draining.

EXPOSURE: full sun.

TEMPERATURE TOLERANCE: heat tolerant, limb damage at 28 degrees, freezes to ground at 20 degrees F.

WATER: drought tolerant, 12 inches/year.

PROPAGATION: fresh seeds, semi-hardwood cuttings.

True to its name, this shrub has gorgeous trumpet- or bell-shaped flowers, making it one of the most beautiful landscaping plants in the Southwest. The clusters, each with five or more lemon yellow flowers, cover the ends of the branches. With profuse blooms and a long flowering season, it makes a colorful mass, screen, or background planting. It's a colorful companion to evergreens such as desert yaupon, Texas mountain laurel, Arizona rosewood, and jojoba. Trumpet flower freezes to the ground in mild winters, but recovers rapidly to form a 4- to 5-foot shrub. Plant it in a large pot to complement your patio or poolside. Smaller specimens are rounded, but tend to become upright as they grow larger. You'll need to remove dead branches before spring growth begins.

Arizona Rosewood

Skeleton Leaf Goldeneye

Arizona Rosewood, *Vauquclinia californica*

NATIVE DISTRIBUTION: desert grasslands and chaparral-oak woodlands at 2500–5000-foot elevations in mountains of southern New Mexico and Arizona, into California; Mexico.

LANDSCAPE ZONE: 1–7.

SIZE: 6–15 feet.

LEAVES: evergreen.

FLOWER: June–August, 3-inch clusters of white flowers.

SOIL: adaptable, alkaline, well draining.

EXPOSURE: full sun, partial shade.

TEMPERATURE TOLERANCE: cold hardy.

WATER: drought tolerant, 12 inches/year.

PROPAGATION: fresh seeds, softwood and semihardwood cuttings.

This member of the rose family has an erect profile, dense evergreen foliage, and slender dark green leaves that cover the plant to the ground. Planted alone, it makes a large specimen shrub suitable for corner or background plantings. It's large enough to provide a visual screen when planted in mass. You can trim it into a shaped shrub, but it loses its character. Its slender, serrated leaves and abundant flower clusters give an ornamental accent to entrywalks, patios, and poolside gardens. In mass plantings, the lustrous green color and narrow width of the leaves naturally complement desert willow and yellow trumpet. It's compatible in appearance and habitat with Texas pistache, Eve's necklace, pinyon pine, palo verde, and Gregg ash. Like many species adapted to drought and poor soil, this plant grows slowly, but it speeds up once its root system becomes established if given extra water. The Chisos rosewood, *Vauquelinia angustifolia*, from the Chisos Mountains in Texas, has the same landscape requirements and applications.

Skeleton Leaf Goldeneye, *Viguiera stenoloba*

NATIVE DISTRIBUTION: sandy, limestone soils of South, Central, West Texas, southern New Mexico; Mexico.

LANDSCAPE ZONE: 1–4, 6.

SIZE: 2–4 feet.

LEAVES: persistent to evergreen.

FLOWER: June–October, 1–2-inch yellow daisylike flowers.

SOIL: adaptable, well draining.

EXPOSURE: full sun, partial shade.

TEMPERATURE TOLERANCE: heat tolerant, moderately cold hardy.

WATER: drought tolerant, 12 inches/year.

PROPAGATION: fresh seeds, softwood tip cuttings.

From summer into the fall, golden flowers blanket this low-growing, rounded perennial. The profusion of lemon yellow blooms provides a pleasing contrast with the bright green threadlike foliage. This bushy wildflower makes a colorful addition to perennial flower gardens and slope plantings throughout most of the year. You can use it as a border plant or a foreground accent in landscape islands. To keep it compact and neat appearing, remove the 8-inch flower stalks after flowering and periodically cut it back. It's grown north to Midland, Texas, so it's probably cold hardy to about 10 degrees F.

119

Small Soapweed Yucca

Banana Yucca

Beaked Yucca

Trecul Yucca

Shrubby Yuccas

Small Soapweed Yucca, *Yucca angustifolia (Y. glauca)*
Arkansas Yucca, *Yucca arkansana*
Banana Yucca, *Yucca baccata*
Louisiana Yucca, *Yucca louisianensis*
Pale-leaf Yucca, *Yucca pallida*
Twisted-leaf Yucca, *Yucca rupicola*

NATIVE DISTRIBUTION: throughout Southwest.

LANDSCAPE ZONE: 1–10.

SIZE: 1–3 feet tall.

LEAVES: evergreen, swordlike.

FLOWER: spring–summer, large cluster of white flowers on tall stalk; fruit, leathery capsule 1–4 inches long.

SOIL: variable, well draining.

EXPOSURE: full sun.

TEMPERATURE TOLERANCE: cold hardy.

WATER: drought tolerant.

PROPAGATION: fresh seeds.

Small, shrubby yuccas will give your landscape that characteristic Southwestern flavor. Their size adapts them to limited areas, such as patio and pool gardens or corner plantings. The bladelike leaves add variety to a cactus or rock garden. Small yuccas make ideal accent plants and, when they send up their stalk

of flowers, become the center of attention. Like their larger counterparts, these yuccas have needle-tipped leaves, so don't plant them near play or walk areas. All of the small yuccas in the Southwest have great landscape merit.

The small soapweed yucca grows in grassy plains from the Texas Panhandle through northern New Mexico and Arizona and north into Wyoming. The Arkansas yucca occurs from Central Texas north into Arkansas and Oklahoma and does well on limestone, gravelly, or prairie soil. Banana yucca is abundant in deserts and mountains from West Texas to Arizona. The Louisiana yucca grows in the sandy soils east of Dallas to Texarkana and Houston and into Louisiana. Pale leaf yucca is a plant of the blackland prairies from Dallas to Austin. Twisted-leaf Yucca grows in the rocky, limestone soil of Central Texas.

Tree Yuccas

Joshua Tree, *Yucca brevifolia*
Soaptree Yucca, *Yucca elata*
Faxon Yucca, *Yucca faxoniana (Y. carnerosana)*
Beaked Yucca, *Yucca rostrata (Y. thompsoniana)*
Trecul Yucca, *Yucca treculeana*
Torrey Yucca, *Yucca torreyi*

NATIVE DISTRIBUTION: coastal Texas to California.

LANDSCAPE ZONE: dry, arid climates across Southwest.

SIZE: 3–20 feet tall.

LEAVES: evergreen, swordlike.

FLOWER/FRUIT: spring–summer, large cluster of white flowers on tall stalk; leathery capsule 1–4 inches long.

SOIL: variable, well draining.

EXPOSURE: full sun.

TEMPERATURE TOLERANCE: cold hardy.

WATER: drought tolerant.

PROPAGATION: fresh seeds.

With their large multiple branches and tall flower stalks, tree yuccas will gracefully dominate almost any landscape design. So if you plant one in your cactus garden, make it the center of interest. Several planted together create a picturesque setting. Because

of their stiff, needle-tipped leaves, don't plant yuccas near walks and play areas. Tree yuccas grow moderately fast, but may take decades to develop their characteristic trunk. The beaked yucca is probably the most ornamental because of its dense spherical shape, and the Joshua tree the most unusual because of its size and branching. Soaptree yucca is the state flower of New Mexico. All are gorgeous when in bloom and make dramatic additions to any landscape. Most tree yuccas are dug from the wild, which unfortunately has decimated some native populations. All have the same general habitat requirements and landscape applications.

APPENDIX 1: COLORSCAPING WITH FLOWERING TREES, SHRUBS, & VINES

(Note: numbers refer to landscape zones.)

TREES

Acacia greggii—Gregg acacia, 1–7, April–October
Acacia smallii—Huisache, 1–4, 6, February–April
Acacia wrightii—Wright acacia, 1–7, March–May
Arbutus texensis—Madrone, 2, 3, 5, 6, February–March

Cercidium floridum—Blue palo verde, 1, 2, April–July
Cercis canadensis—Redbud, 1–9, March–May
Chilopsis linearis—Desert willow, 1–7, May–June
Chionanthus virginicus—Fringe tree, 7, 8, March–June
Cordia boissieri—Wild olive, 2–4, April–June
Cornus florida—Flowering dogwood, 7–10, March–June

Ehretia anacua—Anacua, 4, March–April

Fraxinus cuspidata—Fragrant ash, 2–7, 9, April–May

Gleditsia triacanthos—Honey locust, 1–9, May–June

Leucaena retusa—Goldenball leadtree, 2–4, 6, 7, April–October

Magnolia grandiflora—Southern magnolia, 7, 8, April–August

Parkinsonia aculeata—Retama, 1–4, 6, 7, March–October
Pithecellobium flexicaule—Ebony, 1–4, May–August
Prosopis glandulosa—Honey mesquite, 1–7, May–August
Prosopis pubescens—Screwbean mesquite, 1–4, 6, May–August
Prunus caroliniana—Laurel cherry, 2, 6–8, March–April
Prunus mexicana—Mexican plum, 6–8, March–April
Prunus serotina—Black cherry, 2–4, 6–8, March–June
Prunus virginiana—Chokecherry, 5–9, April–July

Rhus copallina—Shining sumac, 8, June–August
Rhus lanceolata—Prairie flame leaf sumac, 2, 3, 5–7, June–August
Robinia neomexicana—Rose locust, 2, 9, April–August

Sambucus mexicana—Mexican elder, 1–4, September–June
Sapindus saponaria—Soapberry, 2–8, May–June
Sophora affinis—Eve's necklace, 4, 6, 7, April–June

Ungnadia speciosa—Mexican buckeye, 2–8, March–April

Viburnum rifidulum—Rusty blackhaw, 6–8, March–April

SHRUBS

Acacia rigidula—Black brush, 1, 3, 4, April–May
Agave species—Agave, 1–10, June–August
Aloysia gratissima—Bee brush, 1–4, 6–8, March–November
Aloysia wrightii—Bee brush, 1–4, April–May
Amorpha fruticosa—False indigo, 2–9, May–June
Anisacanthus quadrifidus var. *wrightii*—Flame anisacanthus, 1–4, 6, 7, April–November
Anisacanthus thurberi—Desert honeysuckle, 1–3, April–November

Bauhinia congesta—Anacacho orchid tree, 4, 6, 7, March, May
Berberis fremontii—Fremont barberry, 9, 10, May–July
Berberis haemetocarpa—Red barberry, 1–7, February–April
Berberis repens—Creeping barberry, 5, 9, 10, March–April
Berberis swaseyi—Texas barberry, 1–7, April–May
Berberis trifoliolata—Agarita, 1–7, February–April
Bouvardia ternifolia—Scarlet bouvardia, 2–4, 6, April–October
Buddleja marrubiifolia—Woolly butterfly bush, 1–4, April–September

Calliandra eriophylla—Fairy duster, 1–4, October–April
Cephalanthus occidentalis—Button bush, 1–10, June–August
Chamaebatiaria millefolium—Fernbush, 2, 9, July–September
Choisya dumosa—Starleaf Mexican orange, 2, 3, 6, June–October
Chrysactinia mexicana—Damianita, 1–4, 6, April–September
Chrysothamnus nauseosus—Rabbitbrush, 2, 5, 9, August–December
Cornus drummondii—Roughleaf dogwood, 7, 8, May–August
Cowania mexicana—Cliffrose, 1–3, 9, 10, April–July

Dalea formosa—Feather dalea, 1–7, April–October
Dalea frutescens—Black dalea, 1–7, July–October
Dalea greggii—Gregg dalea, 1–7, March–September
Dalea scoparia—Broom dalea, 2, 3, August–September
Dasylirion species—Sotol, 1–4, 6, 7, May–July

Ericameria laricifolia—Larchleaf goldenweed, 2, 3, 5, 6, September–November
Eupatorium havanense—Shrubby boneset, 2–4, 6, October–November
Eupatorium wrightii—Wright boneset, 1–4, September–October
Eysenhardtia species—Kidneywood, 2–4, 6, May–October

Fallugia paradoxa—Apache plume, 2–6, 9, 10, May–September
Fendlera rupicola—Cliff fendlerbush, 2, 3, 5, 6, 9, May, June
Fouquieria splendens—Ocotillo, 1–3, 6, March–June

Guaiacum angustifolium—Guayacan, 2–4, 6, March– September

Hesperaloe parviflora—Red yucca, 1–7, March–September

Lantana horrida—Texas lantana, 1–8, May–October
Larrea tridentata—Creosote bush, 1–4, 6, February–October
Leucophyllum candidum—Cenizo, 1–7, throughout after rain
Leucophyllum frutescens—Cenizo, 1–7, throughout after rain
Lonicera albiflora—White honeysuckle, 2–9, March–May

Malvaviscus drummondii—Turk's cap, 4–8, April–October
Mimosa species—Catclaw mimosa, 1–6, April–July

Nolina species—Beargrass, 1–6, March–July

Parthenium argentatum—Guayule, 1–6, April–October
Parthenium incanum—Mariola, 1–6, July–October
Pavonia lasiopetala—Rose pavonia, 3, 4, 6–8, April–November
Potentilla fruticosa—Shrubby cinquefoil, 2, 3, June–September

Rhus choriophylla—Evergreen sumac, 1–3, July–August
Rhus glabra—Smooth sumac, 2, 4, 9, May
Rhus trilobata—Three-leaf sumac, 2–9, March–June
Rhus virens—Evergreen sumac, 1–4, 6–8, August–October
Ribes aureum—Golden current, 2, 9, 10, March–June

Salvia greggii—Autumn sage, 1–4, 6–8, April–November
Salvia regla—Mountain sage, 1–4, 6–8, September–November
Sambucus caerulea—Blue elderberry, 2, 3, 9, April–June
Sambucus canadensis—Elderberry, 4–8, May–June
Senna wislizenii—Shrubby senna, 1–4, 6, May–September
Sophora secundiflora—Texas mountain laurel, 1–4, 6, March–April

Tecoma stans—Yellow trumpet flower, 2–4, 6, April–November

Vauquelinia angustifolia—Chisos rosewood, 1–7, June–August
Vauquelinia californica—Arizona rosewood, 1–7, June–August
Viguiera stenoloba—Skeleton leaf goldeneye, 1–4, 6, June–October

Yucca species—Yucca, 1–10, March–June

VINES

Bignonia capreolata—Cross vine, 2, 4–10, March–May

Campsis radicans—Trumpet creeper, 2, 4–10, May–October
Clematis crispa—Curly clematis, 7, 8, April–August
Clematis ligusticifolia—Western virgin's bower, 2, 9, 10, May–September
Clematis pitcheri—Leather flower, 5–9, April–September
Clematis texensis—Scarlet clematis, 2, 4, 6, 7, March–July

Gelsemium sempervirens—Carolina jessamine, 1–8, February–April

Lonicera sempervirens—Coral honeysuckle, 2, 4–10, March–September

Maurandya antirrhiniflora—Snapdragon vine, 1–10, February–October

Passiflora incarnata—Passion flower, 1–10, April–August

APPENDIX 2: PLANTS WITH EVERGREEN, SEMI-EVERGREEN, OR PERSISTENT LEAVES

TREES

Arbutus texensis—Texas madrone

Condalia hookeri—Brasil
Cordia boissieri—Wild olive
Cupressus arizonica—Arizona cypress

Ehretia anacua—Anacua

Ilex opaca—American holly

Juniperus deppeana—Alligator juniper
Juniperus scopulorum—Rocky Mountain juniper
Juniperus virginiana—Eastern red cedar

Magnolia grandiflora—Southern magnolia

Persea borbonia—Redbay
Picea pungens glauca—Blue spruce
Pinus cembroides—Mexican pinyon pine
Pinus echinata—Shortleaf pine
Pinus edulis—Colorado pinyon pine
Pinus palustris—Longleaf pine
Pinus ponderosa—Ponderosa pine
Pinus remota—Remote pinyon
Pinus taeda—Loblolly pine
Pistacia texana—Texas pistache
Pithecellobium flexicaule—Ebony
Prunus caroliniana—Laurel cherry

Quercus arizonica—Arizona oak
Quercus emoryi—Emory oak
Quercus fusiformis—Plateau live oak
Quercus grisea—Gray oak
Quercus hypoleucoides—Silverleaf oak
Quercus laurifolia—Laurel oak
Quercus oblongifolia—Mexican blue oak
Quercus pungens var. *vaseyana*—Vasey oak
Quercus turbinella—Shrub live oak
Quercus virginiana—Coastal live oak

Sabal mexicana—Sabal palm
Sambucus mexicana—Mexican elderberry

Washingtonia filifera—California fan palm

SHRUBS

Agave species—Century plants
Artemisia filifolia—Sand sage
Artemisia tridentata—Big leaf sage

Baccharis sarothroides—Desert broom
Berberis fremontii—Fremont barberry
Berberis haemetocarpa—Red barberry
Berberis swaseyi—Texas barberry
Berberis trifoliolata—Agarita
Buddleja marrubiifolia—Woolly butterfly bush

Calliandra eriophylla—Fairy duster
Ceratoides lanata—Winterfat
Cercocarpus montanus—Mountain mahogany
Chamaebatiaria millefolium—Fernbush
Choisya dumosa—Starleaf Mexican orange
Chrysactinia mexicana—Damianita
Chrysothamnus nauseosus—Rabbitbrush
Cowania mexicana—Cliffrose

Dasylirion species—Sotol

Ephedra species—Joint fir
Ericameria laricifolia—Larchleaf goldenweed

Fallugia paradoxa—Apache plume
Fraxinus greggii—Gregg ash

Garrya ovata—Silktassel
Garrya wrightii—Wright silktassel
Guaiacum angustifolium—Guayacan

Hesperaloe parviflora—Red yucca

Ilex vomitoria—Yaupon holly

Larrea tridentata—Creosote bush
Leucophyllum candidum—Cenizo
Leucophyllum frutescens—Cenizo
Lonicera albiflora—White honeysuckle
Lycium pallidum—Wolfberry

Myrica cerifera—Wax myrtle
Myrica pusilla—Dwarf wax myrtle

Nolina species—Nolina

Parthenium argentatum—Guayule
Parthenium incanum—Mariola
Potentilla fruticosa—Shrubby cinquefoil

Rhus choriophylla—Evergreen sumac
Rhus ovata—Sugar bush
Rhus virens—Evergreen sumac

Sabal minor—Palmetto
Salvia greggii—Autumn sage
Sambucus caerulea—Blueberry elder
Schaefferia cuneifolia—Desert yaupon
Simmondsia chinensis—Jojoba
Sophora secundiflora—Texas mountain laurel
Symphoricarpos orbiculatus—Coralberry

Vaccinium arboreum—Farkleberry
Vauquelinia californica—Arizona rosewood
Vauquelinia angustifolia—Chisos rosewood
Viguiera stenoloba—Skeleton leaf goldeneye

Yucca species—Yucca

VINES

Bignonia capreolata—Cross vine

Gelsemium sempervirens—Carolina jessamine

Lonicera sempervirens—Coral honeysuckle

GROUNDCOVERS

Artemisia ludoviciana—White sage

Berberis repens—Creeping barberry

Marsilea macrocarpa—Water clover

Phyla species—Frogfruit

Sedum species—Stonecrop

BIBLIOGRAPHY

Abbott, Carroll. 1979. *How To Know and Grow Texas Wildflowers*. Kerrville, Texas: Green Horizons Press.

Agave Magazine. March 1987. Phoenix: Desert Botonical Garden.

Ajilvsgi, G. 1984. *Wildflowers of Texas*. Bryan, Texas: Shearer Publishing.

Arizona Native Plant Society. 1989. *Desert Shrubs*.

Arizona Native Plant Society. 1988. *Desert Trees*.

Arnberger, Leslie. 1974. *Flowers of the Southwest Mountains*. Globe, Arizona: Southwest Parks and Monuments Association.

Benson, Lyman. 1969. *The Cacti of Arizona*. Tucson: The University of Arizona Press.

Benson, Lyman, and Robert Darrow. 1981. *Trees and Shrubs of the Southwest Deserts*. Tucson: The University of Arizona Press.

Bowers, Janice Emily. 1989. *100 Desert Wildflowers of the Southwest*. Globe, Arizona: Southwest Parks and Monuments Association.

Bowers, Janice Emily. 1987. *100 Roadside Wildflowers of the Southwest*. Globe, Arizona: Southwest Parks and Monuments Association.

Cooperative Extension Service, Circular 513. 1984. Native Plants for New Mexico Landscapes. Albuquerque: New Mexico State University.

Correll, D. S., and M. C. Johnston. 1970. *Manual of Vascular Plants of Texas*. Renner, Texas: Texas Research Foundation.

Cox, Paul, and Patty Leslie. 1988. *Texas Trees*. San Antonio: Corona Publishing Co.

Desert Botanical Garden Staff. 1988. *Arizona Highways Presents Desert Wildflowers*. Phoenix: Arizona Highways.

Dodge, Nat. 1967. *100 Roadside Wildflowers of the Southwest Uplands*. Globe, Arizona: Southwest Parks and Monuments Association.

Dodge, Nat. 1976. *Flowers of the Southwest Deserts*. Globe, Arizona: Southwest Parks and Monuments Association.

Duffield, Mary Rose, and Warren D. Jones. *Plants for Dry Climates*. Tucson: HP Books.

Elmore, Francis. 1976. *Shrubs and Trees of the Southwest Uplands*. Globe, Arizona: Southwest Parks and Monuments Association.

Enquist, Marshall. 1987. *Wildflowers of the Texas Hill Country*. Austin: Lone Star Botanical.

Gentry, Howard Scott. 1982. *Agaves of Continental North America*. Tuscon: The University of Arizona Press.

Gould, F. W. 1975. *Texas Plants, A Checklist and Ecological Summary*. Texas A&M Exp. Sta. Misc. Pub. 585/Revised.

Grant, Karen, and Verne Grant. 1968. *Hummingbirds and Their Flowers*. New York: Columbia University Press.

Johnson, Eric, and David Harbison. 1985. *Landscaping to Save Water in the Desert*. Rancho Mirage, California: E&P Products.

Kearney, Thomas, and Robert Peeples. 1964. *Arizona Flora*. Berkeley and Los Angeles: The University of California.

Lynch, D. 1981. *Native and Naturalized Woody Plants of Austin and the Hill Country*. Austin: Saint Edwards University.

Mahler, William. 1988. *Shinners' Manual of the North Central Texas Flora*. Dallas: Southern Methodist University Herbarium.

Martin, William, and Charles Hutchins. 1988. *Fall Wildflowers of New Mexico*. Albuquerque: The University of New Mexico Press.

Martin, William, and Charles Hutchins. 1986. *Summer Wildflowers of New Mexico*. Albuquerque: The University of New Mexico Press.

Martin, William, and Charles Hutchins. 1984. *Spring Wildflowers of New Mexico*. Albuquerque: The University of New Mexico Press.

Martino, Steve, and Vernon Swaback. 1986. *Desert Excellence, A Guide to Natural Landscapes*. Phoenix: Bellamah Community Development.

Miller, George. 1988. *A Field Guide to Wildlife of Texas and the Southwest*. Austin: Texas Monthly Press.

Moffat, Ann, and Mark Schiler. 1981. *Landscape Design That Saves Energy*. New York: William Morrow and Co., Inc.

Natural Vegetation Committee, Arizona Chapter, Soil Conservation Society. 1973. *Landscaping with Native Arizona Plants*. Tucson: The University of Arizona Press.

Nelson, Ruth. 1976. *Plants of Zion National Park*. Springdale, Utah: Zion Natural History Association.

Nokes, Jill. 1986. *How to Grow Native Plants of Texas and the Southwest*. Austin: Texas Monthly Press.

Patraw, Pauline. 1977. *Flowers of the Southwest Mesas*. Globe, Arizona: Southwest Parks and Monuments Association.

Phillips, Arthur III. 1979. *Grand Canyon Wildflowers*. Grand Canyon, Arizona: Grand Canyon Natural History Association.

Phillips Judith. 1987. *Southwestern Landscaping with Native Plants*. Sante Fe: Museum of New Mexico Press.

Powell, Michael. 1988. *Trees and Shrubs of the Trans-Pecos Texas*. Big Bend National Park, Texas: Big Bend Natural History Association.

Simpson, Benny. 1988. *A Field Guide to Texas Trees*. Austin: Texas Monthly Press.

Sunset Book Editors. 1988. *Sunset Western Garden Book*. Menlo Park, California: Lane Publishing Co.

Tull, Delena. 1987. *A Practical Guide to Edible and Useful Plants*. Austin: Texas Monthly Press.

Turner, B. L. 1959. *The Legumes of Texas*. Austin: The University of Texas Press.

Vines, R. A. 1984. *Trees of Central Texas*. Austin: The University of Texas Press.

Vines, R. A. 1977. *Trees of East Texas*. Austin: The University of Texas Press.

Vines, R. A. 1960. *Trees, Shrubs, and Woody Vines of the Southwest*. Austin: The University of Texas Press.

Warnock, B. H. 1970. *Wildflowers of the Big Bend Country, Texas*. Alpine, Texas: Sul Ross University.

Warnock, B. H. 1974. *Wildflowers of the Guadalupe Mountains and the Sand Dune Country, Texas*. Alpine, Texas: Sul Ross University.

Wauer, R. H. 1973. *Naturalist's Big Bend*. Santa Fe: Peregrine Productions.

Wasowski, Sally. 1988. *Native Texas Plants*. Austin: Texas Monthly Press.

Weniger, D. 1985. *Cacti of Texas and Neighboring States*. Austin: The University of Texas Press.

Wooton, E. O., and Paul Standley. 1915. *Flora of New Mexico*. New York: Weldon & Wesley, Ltd., Stechert-Hafner Service Agency, Inc.

INDEX

Note: * indicates scientific name no longer used.

125